War and Power

ABOUT THE AUTHOR

Phillips Payson O'Brien is Professor of Strategic Studies at St Andrews. He is the author of *The Strategists*, *How the War Was Won* and *The Second Most Powerful Man in the World*. He has written for the *Atlantic*, the *Spectator* and *Foreign Affairs*, and has a combined following of almost 300,000 on Twitter and Substack.

War and Power

PHILLIPS PAYSON O'BRIEN

PENGUIN
VIKING

VIKING

UK | USA | Canada | Ireland | Australia
India | New Zealand | South Africa

Viking is part of the Penguin Random House group of companies
whose addresses can be found at global.penguinrandomhouse.com.

Penguin Random House UK,
One Embassy Gardens, 8 Viaduct Gardens, London SW11 7BW

penguin.co.uk

Penguin
Random House
UK

First published 2025

001

Set in 12/14.75pt Bembo Book MT Pro
by Six Red Marbles UK, Thetford, Norfolk
Printed and bound in India by Manipal Technologies Limited

The authorized representative in the EEA is Penguin Random House Ireland,
Morrison Chambers, 32 Nassau Street, Dublin D02 YH68

A CIP catalogue record for this book is available from the British Library

HARDBACK ISBN: 978-0-241-74403-1
TRADE PAPERBACK ISBN: 978-0-241-74418-5

Penguin Random House is committed to a sustainable future
for our business, our readers and our planet. This book is made from
Forest Stewardship Council® certified paper.

To the people of Ukraine.
You have had to endure the worst depredations of war because
of a basic inability in others to understand power

Contents

Introduction: The Failure

'I need ammunition, not a ride.'[1] When Volodymyr Zelensky reportedly said this on 25 February 2022, he was speaking with a US government official who was offering to have the Ukrainian president spirited out of his country. While most people have focused on Zelensky's bravery and defiance in the face of the full-scale Russian invasion,* what has been missed is that Zelensky was also offering a stunning rebuke to the US government's vision of war and power. That the offer of a US emergency evacuation was being made to Zelensky speaks volumes about how the US government understood the power balance between Ukraine and Russia, and how the US believed a conventional war between the two was bound to play out. On the other hand, faced with the reality of the Russian Army attacking all around the Ukrainian border, Zelensky was convinced Ukraine could fight – and fight well.

In the US government's mind, Russia was and had been for many years a great power with a modernized and technologically advanced military that was a peer or 'near peer' to America's own.[2] Ukraine, in comparison, was a much weaker state – riddled by corruption and a divided identity – which would be able to offer only limited resistance to mighty Russia. As such, the result of a war, to the US government, seemed certain. In a matter of days, the Ukrainian capital, Kyiv, would be enveloped and Ukrainian conventional resistance devastated, if not completely ended.[3] If Zelensky were not evacuated immediately, the US government judged, he would be imminently overrun by the fast-moving, awesomely powerful Russian military.

This is no overstatement. In closed-door briefings to Congress in early February 2022, the Chairman of the Joint Chiefs of Staff, General Mark Milley, made deeply pessimistic claims about the ability

---

* From now on, the Russian full-scale invasion of 24 February 2022 will be referred to for the sake of clarity as the Russian invasion. This is no way detracts from the fact that the original Russian invasion of Ukraine was in 2014.

of Ukraine to resist a Russian attack. The senior military adviser to the President of the United States, with the resources of the Pentagon at his fingertips, Milley asserted that if the Russians launched an invasion, Kyiv could fall in only seventy-two hours.[4] With more than 100,000 Russian troops massed on the border of Ukraine, Milley judged that the Russians had the firepower and military capabilities to undertake modern 'combined arms' warfare against their Ukrainian target.[5] Indeed, the Russian advantage was considered so great that, even though it was the Russians that would be doing the attacking, Milley estimated that Ukraine would suffer almost four times as many battle deaths. He stated that, should a major Russian invasion occur, the Ukrainians would suffer 15,000 battle deaths in comparison to a Russian total of 4,000.[6] In short, Ukraine would be overwhelmed.

This view was also shared widely in the analytic community that was advising the US government. It's worth stepping back here and pondering the importance of these views of Russia's military strength and the war it would be able to wage. For years it was argued by the supposedly most knowledgeable experts on the Russian state and military that Russia was a 'great power' with battle-tested and devastating forces. As Samuel Charap, one of the leading analysts of the Russian military for the Rand Corporation — arguably the US government's most important strategic studies think tank — described the situation, Russia was so strong that the west should not even bother to arm Ukraine:

> Russia has the ability to carry out a large-scale joint offensive operation involving tens of thousands of personnel, thousands of armored vehicles, and hundreds of combat aircraft. It would likely begin with devastating air and missile strikes from land, air, and naval forces, striking deep into Ukraine to attack headquarters, airfields, and logistics points. Ukrainian forces would begin the conflict nearly surrounded from the very start, with Russian forces arrayed along the eastern border, naval and amphibious forces threatening from the Black Sea in the south, and the potential (increasingly real) for additional Russian forces to deploy into Belarus and threaten from the north, where the border is less than 65 miles from Kyiv itself.[7]

As Charap and his co-author argued, US weapons could 'do nothing' to change the basic flaws in the Ukrainian military, nor did they represent a threat large enough to deter Russia. As such, it would be best to leave Ukraine to accept its doomed fate and throw itself on the mercy of Putin's Russia. This was no one-off. It was a vision of Russian power and Ukrainian weakness that had been used for years to argue against providing Ukraine with modern weaponry – on the assumption that Ukrainian conventional resistance against the great power of Russia and its military was doomed.[8]

In speaking this way, Charap and others were parroting (without properly interrogating) the great power paradigm that has been in wide-scale operation since the nineteenth century.[9] Even more unfortunately, Charap and other analysts who believed Russia would conquer Ukraine easily argued publicly for strict limitations on weapons to be sent to Ukraine.[10] It was part and parcel of why Ukraine was so short of advanced weapons when the Russians invaded, and has arguably resulted in the limitation of what Ukraine has been sent since. This has led to the unnecessary deaths of tens of thousands of Ukrainians (and Russians), and shaped a war that could have been over far more quickly. It should have been the nail in the coffin of a concept that never made much sense to begin with. Sadly, the idea of great powers, probably because of its deceptive ease, has lived on. But we need to drop the whole phrase entirely – before it gets even more people needlessly killed in wars that cannot be won by non-existent 'great' powers.

The Dangers of Great Power Thinking

The notion of there being great powers residing in some upper tier of puissance, lording it over normal states, is usually first seen as emerging out of the post-Napoleonic European world – the time period that this book will cover.* It is the German historian Leopold von Ranke who is said to have first coined the phrase in print, in 1833.[11] To him a great power was one that could 'maintain itself against all others, even when they are united'.[12] Right away a problem should have been seen in this

---

* Though there will be reference to occasional events from Napoleon's time and earlier, the core of this book will run from the origins of World War I in the late nineteenth century to today.

analysis – by Ranke's standard there had not been a real great power, at least in Europe and arguably around the world, for millennia. Certainly Napoleon's brief period of European continental domination – which lasted from approximately 1804, when he had himself crowned Emperor of France, until his 1812 invasion of Russia – showed that even France at its high point could not stand against all others. For all the success of French armies, Napoleon was incapable of competing with Britain on a global stage – if anything, he was losing power and territory around the world while he ruled much of Europe.

It should be noted that the same year he became emperor, 1804, Napoleon was forced to sell the vast Louisiana Territory to the United States – losing France the bulk of its overseas empire. A year later, Napoleon's fleet would be decimated by the Royal Navy at the Battle of Trafalgar, destroying France as a credible global maritime power and allowing Britain to extend its own overseas empire. In other words, Napoleon's ability to stand 'against all others' applied only to land armies and only to the continent of Europe. It might have seemed that Napoleon was supremely powerful to a land-based, Eurocentric scholar such as Ranke (who was born in Saxony and spent most of his career in Berlin), but that was more about his individual perception than anything else.

Sadly, in the almost two centuries since Ranke coined this inadequate phrase, things have got even worse. Indeed, the threshold for being a 'great power' has been regularly redefined, muddied and even lowered, to such a degree that by 2022 an economically weak and politically corrupt system* such as Vladimir Putin's Russia was widely hailed as one. The foundational problem of the great power paradigm was and remains the fact that the criteria for membership in the great power club are unclear. Even the phrase 'great power' has meant vastly different things depending on when and where it is used – which means ultimately it has meant everything and nothing.

---

* The word 'system' appears regularly in this book. For clarity's sake, when you see 'system' on its own, it is normally referring to a weapons system and can cover anything from the most advanced missiles such as the Patriot anti-air system to small arms. When weapons systems or logistics systems, etc., are operated together, that will be referred to as a 'complex operation'. Other uses of the word 'system' will have a prefix such as 'political' or 'economic' to specify what is being referred to.

In the mid-nineteenth century, there was some discussion of the great powers who were and supposedly would go on to dominate the globe. A number of nineteenth-century geopolitical thinkers, including Alexis de Tocqueville and Charles Brandon Boynton, believed that the fate of the world was to be decided by the USA and Russia (in the case of the former) or those two plus the British and French (according to the latter).[13] In the run-up to World War I, Europe was often said to be divided between its five 'great powers', all empires, who supposedly dominated its fate. They were Britain, Germany, France, Russia and Austria-Hungary.[14] Yet, none of them, except for possibly Britain, would have been able to stand against all the others. Austria-Hungary, for instance, with its relatively undeveloped economy, inefficient political system, and society that was divided into many groups with different identities, was even incapable of functioning as an independent power.

World War I also showed that no power could really stand alone in Europe, but that all powers had strengths and weaknesses that made comparison all but impossible – and it was their differences that mattered more than anything else. At the top of the power table were Britain and Germany, the two largest economies in Europe, who produced the largest amount of war materiel and headed their different alliances. Both had to provide massive assistance to their allies in terms of finance and war materiel (France, Russia and later Italy in the case of Britain; and Austria-Hungary and the Ottoman Empire in the case of Germany). However, the military power the British and Germans generated was very different, and this meant that comparing them was highly subjective. While both created large armies and navies, the British remained dominant at sea, winning a long maritime struggle with the Germans, while the German Army remained the most powerful on the continent – able to hold the Allies at bay until being overwhelmed in 1918.

Of course, by the end of the war neither of the most powerful states in Europe was the most powerful state in the world. Between 1914 and 1918 the United States had interjected itself into the equation, and with an economy that towered over that of any European state (or indeed combination of European states) and no immediate military threat on its own borders, the US represented a different class of power. For the rest of the twentieth century and the first two decades of the twenty-first it maintained a position *almost* as a Rankean great power. Even then, as the US would show repeatedly, being able to 'stand alone' against any combination of possible enemies was very different from being able to impose yourself on them – or even win wars against much smaller powers.

However, the limits that even the US would show have made little difference in the great power discussion. Often, great powers are grouped together based on their supposed military success. Writing at the end of the interwar period, E. H. Carr – the British historian, diplomat and leading international relations theorist – claimed that a state's 'recognition as a Great Power is normally the reward of fighting a successful large-scale war'. He then mentioned Germany in the Franco-Prussian War and Japan after the Russo-Japanese War, which should set alarm bells ringing.[15] Both were limited, state-on-state wars, confined in their geographic location and very short in duration. If that was the great power threshold, it would hardly be an exclusive club, and it would be very different from one composed only of powers able to stand against all others.

The results of World War II only reinforced the idea that the great power paradigm was meaningless. Both Germany and Britain had maintained their positions as the economic leaders of Europe and their relative military strengths, which meant that neither was able to existentially threaten the other (Germany dominated the European landmass from 1940, but the British were able to secure command of the sea and air in the North Atlantic). Moreover, in Asia, Japan showed just how ephemeral great power status really was. At first, it had seemed a real force, capable of conquering much of China and the South Pacific – and then winning a series of naval engagements against the United States and the British Empire. However, once the US fully mobilized its economic and technological resources, Japan was shown to be completely out of its depth and was ground down to impotence by the US, using only about half of its resources. The USSR, on the other hand, while a significant power (though its relative strength has been greatly overstated), had to receive massive amounts of aid during the war.[16] Indeed, I believe that the extreme overrating of the USSR's contribution to the defeat of Nazi Germany (the Soviet Union both engaged and destroyed much less of German production than people realized) gave false impetus to the great power idea – which contributed to the extreme overrating of Russian power before 24 February 2022. The USSR never possessed the full range of power that the US did, but instead of understanding that, people seemed obsessed with the scale of casualties that the Soviets suffered and created an idea of Soviet power, which was often directly referenced as a reason why Russia was a great power.[17]

The reality was that the US, which was a power still in its own league when World War II started, only grew in relative strength during the conflict. Possessor of approximately half the world's production by 1945 (with so much money it really did not know what to do with it), and also with the most powerful armed forces in the world and the only working atomic bomb, the US had reached a global power status that was arguably unmatched in human history. Yet, even then, at the height of its power, with the world seemingly at its feet, the ability of the US to achieve clearly stated goals at the end of the war, in countries that it thought were of vital interest, such as China, was shown to be shockingly weaker than expected. So, there was certainly no one standard of great power in World War II that might help us understand the power relationship between the states involved, and nor could the greatest of the so-called great powers in many centuries – the United States – achieve many of its goals.

The fact that the great power paradigm was basically useless between 1914 and 1945 did not stop the phrase from exploding in usage after World War II. Arguably the greatest push behind this was the growth of 'realist' thinking on international relations, which grew in the interwar years and then spread widely afterwards. Realism itself mutated into different forms, including structural realism, neo-realism, defensive realism and offensive realism. Regardless of the type of realist someone might claim to be, all realists believed that power relationships defined the international system. That being said, realists of all stripes tended to be either extraordinarily broad in their understanding of power or far too fixated on military variables – such as Carr. The best example of the former is Hans Morgenthau, one of the 'founding fathers' of realism – or what is sometimes called 'classical realism'.[18]

Morgenthau argued that every state's national interest drives it on a similar course to maximize its power in relation to others. He contrasted his supposedly hard-headed vision of power with, for instance, lawyers who want to see state actions through a prism of legality or ethicists who want to use moral tests.[19] This might have seemed tough and honest, but then Morgenthau made classical realism impossible to actually use by saying that power is made up of almost every variable imaginable (with one glaring oversight). For Morgenthau, national power was affected by geography, access to natural resources, industrial capacity, and military preparedness. Of course, 'military preparedness' itself is a broad term, and Morgenthau considered technological sophistication, leadership quality and the size of a state's armed forces as matters of importance. However, this was just the start. He also argued that population size, national character (defined quite broadly), national morale, the quality of a state's diplomacy and the quality of its government needed to be considered when discussing how powerful a nation was.[20] It's hard to think of a factor that Morgenthau overlooked – except for a vitally important one, the policy choices of individual leaders, which realists tended to maddeningly, and erroneously, downgrade from then on.

Morgenthau's realist notion of power is both determinative and includes so many categories as to be meaningless as a tool of comparison. As a test, try to compare two states using all of Morgenthau's categories and then make a useful judgement of the balance between them. I've tried it a few times, and have never made it work. However, the basic impracticality of Morgenthau's great power understanding did not stop realists, and later neorealists, from making sweeping claims that they understood how power works. In practice, however, the normal realist tendency was to err towards a simplistic understanding of power, saying relatively little beyond that it had something to do with military power.[21]

The offensive realists – such as John Mearsheimer, who played a major role in the academic, and public, discussion of Russian and Ukrainian power before 24 February 2022 – have often fallen back on this. In his book *The Tragedy of Great Power Politics*, Mearsheimer gives a non-quantifiable, military-based definition of what makes for a great power: 'To qualify as a great power, a state must have sufficient military assets to put up a serious fight in an all-out conventional war against the most powerful state in the world.'[22] I defy anyone to define 'serious fight' in a sensible way, and 'all-out conventional war' seems to be a deliberately obscure tautology.

That such a vague formulation could be accepted by offensive realists should call into question their whole idea of what makes a great power. Still, in the run-up to the Russian invasion, Mearsheimer – along with Stephen Walt and others – proceeded to blithely label Russia as a great power and Ukraine as not. This reveals one of the general weaknesses in realist thought, and one that is a major problem for offensive realists in particular: even though they have a very weak definition of 'great power', they have turned the phrase into a self-fulfilling prophecy. It did not matter that there was no commonly accepted notion of a great power; as long as Russia was labelled one and Ukraine was not, that gave the former's claims of interest the greater legitimacy. Basically, in the great power world, the great powers are subjects, and the lesser powers are objects with which the great powers can toy. As Stephen Walt said in a piece in *Foreign Policy*, released only a month before the invasion, lesser power Ukraine was an object of great power Russia's interest – with all that entailed. 'Unpleasant as it may be, the United States and its allies need to recognize that Ukraine's geopolitical alignment is a vital interest for Russia – one it is willing to use force to defend – and this is not because Putin happens to be a ruthless autocrat with a nostalgic fondness for the old Soviet past. Great powers are never indifferent to the geostrategic forces arrayed on their borders.'[23]

It's fascinating that, after a century of seeing supposedly smaller powers getting their way against supposedly great ones, an international relations scholar would speak in such a way. Great powers have regularly had countries on their borders redefine their alignments and even flout the greater power's apparent dominance. From Ireland breaking away from the United Kingdom, to Vietnam regularly defying China (and even besting China in a war in 1979), to Mexico openly flouting US desires at times, these less powerful neighbour states have shown that they are far more than subjects of interest.

And this indicates maybe the greatest problem with the realist conception of power. If you build a supposedly hard-headed school around the overriding importance of power, particularly military power, then it is a major drawback if you don't understand war and power. The fact that realists see both as an immutable phenomenon, regardless of regime or leader, reveals one of the flaws in their outlook. They discount the roles of regimes and leaders in determining how military power is both assembled and used. As Mearsheimer has said, echoing Walt's claim about Putin's supposedly minor role in the decision to invade Ukraine, realism 'is a theory that basically says states care about the balance of power above all else. States want to make sure that they have as much power relative to other great powers as possible. It's a theory that pays little attention to individuals and pays little attention to domestic politics.'[24]

In fact, the opposite is true – leadership and political structure play a massive role in how power is accumulated in peace and employed in war. Over the last two centuries it certainly has mattered who has ruled a country, and within what political or governmental system that person has operated. No German leader *had* to invade Poland in 1939, but Adolf Hitler did (over the doubts of other senior Nazi leaders). On the other hand, Franklin Roosevelt had a very keen interest in having US power interjected forcefully into Europe to stop Hitler, particularly after the German Army conquered France in May–June 1940. However, even then, the very popular American president had to manoeuvre within a political system that constrained his wishes. Roosevelt had to wait until Japan attacked Pearl Harbor and Hitler declared war on the US before he was allowed to go to full-scale war against the Nazis.

It's arguably impossible to look at any of the larger powers in the two world wars and not see that it was a combination of the personalities of the different leaders and how each was moderated (or not) by the political system in which they operated that determined when each nation not only entered each war, but also on which side.* Italy, which had been allied with Germany and Austria-Hungary when World War I started, left that alliance and joined the Allies a few months later, when the two leading Italian politicians of the day – the prime minister Antonio Salandra and foreign minister Sidney Sonnino, operating with almost no oversight – engaged with horse trading between the

---

* This is the subject of my book: *The Strategists: Churchill, Stalin, Roosevelt, Mussolini and Hitler – How War Made Them and How They Made War*. All five of the famous grand strategists had very personal experiences of war early in their lives, primarily in the years 1914–21. These experiences helped shape their individual strategic outlooks, which strongly influenced their policy choices in World War II.

British and Germans about what each would promise Italy. In Japan in 1941, on the other hand, the civilian leadership had been so emasculated by a political system that allowed them no control over the Japanese armed forces that, even though many were sceptical, they gave up and followed the military as the latter pushed the country into war by, foolishly, attacking the United States.

Certainly, it did matter that Vladimir Putin was a dictator/autocrat who had constructed a political system that fed him the information he wanted to hear which confirmed his prejudices towards Ukraine and suppressed any doubts about his decision to invade. On 22 February 2022, in a very public moment broadcast on Russian (and later global) television, Putin humiliated supposedly very senior and powerful members of his state who had doubts about the invasion of Ukraine that he was about to unleash.[25] He was determined to have his invasion.

Not surprisingly, considering how much realists and others have misunderstood power, they, like General Milley, misunderstood how the Russian invasion of Ukraine would proceed. Take, for instance, Michael Kofman, one of the most well-known analysts of the Russian military, who spent the years before 2022 arguing constantly that Russia was a great power that represented a direct military challenge to the US.[26] Just before Putin launched the invasion, Kofman prophesied that it would be an overwhelming and amazingly fast operation, which would see Russia seize more than two-thirds of Ukraine and end the war in just a few 'weeks'.[27] And Kofman's prediction of Russian conventional victory in only weeks seemed remarkably slow in comparison to some other analysts. Rob Lee, a senior analyst of the Russian military at the Foreign Policy Research Institute, stated to the *New York Times* that Russia would achieve victory in such a short time period that it would make the Russian military one of the greatest forces in world history. He claimed just before the invasion that the Russian military could 'devastate the Ukrainian military in the east really quickly, within the first 30–40 minutes', and also stated confidently that if the Russians committed their conventional forces, they could win the war in just a few days.[28]

While these errors of war understanding were particularly egregious, there have been other mistakes in the past. This idea of the short, clinical and decisive war is one of the enduring myths of strategic studies, even though it has been shown to be regularly false. For the past 200 years, states have often gone to war with confident predictions that the war will be decided quickly in decisive battle – or in one common phrase, that it will be over by Christmas. When World War I started, many on both sides believed that Europe was in for a short war, and that the opening engagements would determine the outcome. At one point Germany was said to have gone to war in August 1914 governed by a 'short-war illusion' and that any conflict would be over by Christmas.[29] Even those who challenge that notion argue that German generals who believed the war would be longer, still held that it would last between six months and two years.[30] Today in the US, the push to believe in the short-war idea remains strong – and is arguably a major flaw as the US approaches the idea of war in the Indo-Pacific region.[31]

One of the reasons for such a flawed understanding of war is the focus on wars being decided by decisive battles or large military engagements. This 'battle' idea of war is widespread, though repeatedly shown to be deficient. Both world wars were in their early stages dominated by this notion. In August 1914, when the alliances went to war, the different states enacted plans that they had previously worked out and which would, they thought, result in a military victory that would win the war. The Germans had their well-known Schlieffen Plan, which involved concentrating almost all their force against the French to try to knock France out of the war quickly, before turning to confront Russia. In exchange, the French had their also well-known Plan XVII, which involved attacks directly over the French border into Alsace and Lorraine. The Russians, meanwhile, started assembling their large armed forces under Mobilization Plan 19, to invade eastern Germany. Each one of these plans failed.

A different kind of decisive battle idea appeared early in World War II. Adolf Hitler certainly thought he had won a decisive battle when the German Army conquered France in only two months, in May–June 1940. He started pushing to redesign Berlin as a gaudier, grotesque imperial capital, and believed that he had determined the course of European history for generations. However, by the end of 1941, the Germans found themselves confronted by an alliance that dwarfed them economically, and soon militarily. Just over three years after that, Hitler's empire would be a few blasted streets in central Berlin, and his only option was to put a bullet either through his temple or up through his mouth – depending on the telling.

This idea that military engagement is what decides war would bedevil far greater powers than Nazi Germany. In the 1960s, the supposed superpower United States found itself at war with a relatively tiny North Vietnam, an economically undeveloped, much smaller power by any metric. Yet the insertion of US ground forces, beginning in the 1960s, began a process of more and more troops appearing, always with the premise that the next increase of military force would allow the United States to win the war. Eventually the US deployed more than half a million troops and some of the most advanced military equipment in the world, and yet it made no difference – the US still lost. It won every battle but lost the war.

The US in Vietnam might be the best example, but it is certainly not the only one, that illustrates how you need to look far deeper at the process of war beyond war-gaming what happens when armies meet in the field. Though the US almost always prevailed when its military forces engaged the North Vietnamese in battle, after more than a decade of commitment the US lost the war. This was down to a combination of military variables, including morale and commitment, and larger leadership and societal factors that shaped the American political response.

The pre-24 February 2022 analysis of a possible Russian invasion of Ukraine reads eerily like the precisely written war plans of 1914. The Russian Army was supposed to work efficiently and methodically through phases of war, from an initial and devastating air-power and precision strike phase, to a fast-moving and overwhelming ground attack led by armoured columns with plentiful artillery, to a mopping-up phase when the Russians were to destroy Ukrainian conventional resistance. Everything was supposed to run like clockwork, with the Ukrainians having limited ability to alter their own fate.

In such a clinical view of war, there is little time to discuss the huge problems that normally arise once war breaks out. These can be divided into what might be called 'the systemic' and 'the human'. The human concerns how individuals are prepared (and prepare themselves) for war. This can involve how well trained they are to undertake the operations that will be expected of them. Often, whether it be the Russian Army before the invasion of Ukraine or the Italian Army before World War II, the performance of soldiers in set-piece manoeuvres – even choreographed parades – has been considered indicative of their ability to execute in war. The same goes for morale.

The systemic involves the complex operations needed for a military to be effective. In the case of modern war, arguably the most important are air power (for which in Ukraine it was assumed that the Russians could easily undertake complex operations) and logistics (which was almost entirely ignored). Such assumptions were quite common in the past, but it is interesting to see how they were even more exaggerated when it came to Russia and Ukraine. Going into World War II, for instance, it was widely assumed that modern strategic air power (bombers) would be able to get through to destroy vital targets of the enemy – be they whole cities or specific factories. The 'bomber will always get through' maxim (first uttered by the UK prime minister Stanley Baldwin in 1932) was widely shared and repeated in different forms by people as different as Walt Disney and Benito Mussolini.[32] However, as the war showed, running an efficient strategic bombing campaign was perhaps the most difficult complex operation of the war. It took until 1944 before the western Allies were able to bomb Germany and have the strategic effect desired – and by that point it was the most complex and expensive campaign that the Allies were waging anywhere in the globe.[33] The situation for logistics is the opposite. Hardly mentioned in detail before the Russian invasion of Ukraine, logistics have often been ignored in the study of war, because of the obsession with battle. It might be that the study of production and deployment has less appeal in general to notions of combat and life-and-death human struggle, but regardless it is a major oversight in how we generally understand war and prepare for future conflicts.

This idea of war developing efficiently as planned was one of the most frustrating things about the pre-24 February 2022 analysis. War almost always leads to breakdowns and failures, and ends up going down unexpected (and far longer and bloodier) roads. When in January 2022 I argued against abandoning Ukraine to its supposed fate, I said that Russia was not a great power and should not be deferred to, but also that if Putin were foolish enough to undertake a full-scale invasion, it would more than likely be a disaster for Russia:

> If we have relearned any lesson over the last two decades it is that military operations are expensive, usually counterproductive, and with the

constant possibility of going disastrously wrong for the richest and most advanced economies – let alone weak ones. Certainly Russian military deployments over the last 20 years, from Georgia to Syria, have revealed significant shortcomings. If Russia were actually stupid enough to attack Ukraine, it would tax their military in a way not seen since the Cold War ended.[34]

Wars go off the rails because they are extremely complex and difficult interactions that end up taxing militaries, economies, governments and societies, from the beginnings of the productive process all the way to the battlefields. They are not decided on the battlefield; rather, the battlefield reveals the state of the powers involved. The cause and effect that people normally assume between battles and wars needs to be reversed. Battles don't cause the war to end a certain way; they reveal how a war is developing.

Understanding War and Power

Understanding war and power in such a way that the catastrophic errors made before and since the Russian invasion of Ukraine are not repeated is not just an analytic matter. Overhanging everything in the world today is the possibility that the two most powerful nations (along with their allies) are confronting the very real possibility of war. The United States and China, easily the two largest economies in the world with the two most powerful militaries, stand poised and armed in the western Pacific. The result of a war between them would be a catastrophe far greater than the one we have seen in Ukraine.

This book has been written with the possibility of such a war very much in mind. What it aims to do is provide a methodology of sorts, or an analytical framework, through which to understand war and power. This methodology will not produce one answer, such as *the United States is definitely more powerful*, or *China will definitely win a long war*. Instead, what it will provide is a way of judging how the power of these countries can be compared, and what questions will be important if they ever do go to war.

The first five chapters address what needs to be considered when assessing the power of a state – which boils down to the foundation of power and how that foundation is shaped. For a state to have power, it must have economic/technological strength. It needs not only to make 'stuff', but also to make the most complex and advanced stuff in large amounts. It must also have the economic capacity to maintain and recreate a significant mass of this stuff, and the ability to finance all of this efficiently. You cannot fake economic/technological capabilities, nor make them up quickly on the spot. Normally the greatest disaster that can befall a state is to take on a strategic burden that its economic/technological base cannot sustain.

However, just being economically and technologically powerful is not enough, as post-1945 Japan and Germany can attest. Here we get into the shaping variables. First, the political leadership of a state has an enormous influence on how economic/technological power can be used (or abused). One of the great fallacies of international relations is that there is some abstractly understood national interest to which all leaderships aspire. It is more accurate to say that national interest is determined by political leaderships and reflects their prejudices and policies. These can be wildly divergent, ranging from hyper-aggressive and genocidal – such as with Adolf Hitler – to more passive or domestically focused.

Of course, leaders don't operate in a vacuum. Another whole set of shaping variables includes a state's society and its political structure. Certain societies at different times will applaud war, while others will oppose entering a conflict. Certain political structures will place limitations on what a leader can do; others will allow leaders practically untrammelled opportunities to act. Society and political structure also interact and shape power in areas such as morale and corruption. There is also no easy categorization here. Democracies can have certain advantages in terms of flexibility and creativity, and yet we are also seeing right now how vulnerable democratic societies are to outside penetration.

If the foundational element of national power is economic/technological strength, which is shaped by leadership, society and political structure, there are two important tests for that power: what kind of military does it create, and what kind of international relationships does it produce? A military must always be understood as a product of the factors above, not some sort of physical end in and of itself. The Russian military has punched well below its weight in Ukraine, and at times in the twentieth century too, because its shaping variables have tended towards corruption and a lack of efficiency. On the other hand, the US military of World War II reflected the personal views of the US leadership (Franklin Roosevelt's obsession with sea and air power) combined with the technological and mass productions provided by the nation's economy. Don't look so much at the number of tanks in an army, but rather at the elements that create those tanks.

Beyond a nation's military, its international relationships play a massive role in the exercise of its power and influence. Another of the failures of the great power paradigm is its focus on the nation state as an individual actor. However, even the most powerful states are far more limited than people often realize. They all work with and indeed need allies to ensure their security and buttress their influence in peace and war. Often, international politics is presented as oppositional, and states are defined by their supposed enemies. Actually, a state is more easily judged by its friendships, and the skilful operation of those friendships can amplify national power significantly. On the other hand, the creation of weak international relationships can hobble even the strongest of powers.

After looking at power, the next five chapters will look at how power operates in war. In other words, what are the key variables that need to be considered in assessing what determines the course of a war once a state gets involved in one? The disconnection between assumed and real power becomes exposed when a state goes to war, and assumptions face the test of reality that only a conventional war can present. To understand the test of war, it is crucial to start with the process of war-fighting, which is very different from the process of battle-fighting. War is a test of various systems in a multitude of different ways; it is not a test of armies, and certainly not something that is determined by supposedly decisive battles.

These systems run from the highly advanced and technological to the very human. Complex operations involve the operation of many different weapons, sensors, and even means of transport in concert with each other, for maximum impact. They are not determined by weapons per se, but by the operations of weapons systems in constant combination, where speed, reliability and technological sophistication all influence the outcome. In the twentieth and twenty-first centuries, no complex systems have been as important as those needed to operate

air power and logistics. The ability of a state to provide for its military
in order to apply air power effectively and supply itself through logistical systems separates the truly powerful from the imposters.

A key element in the success of complex operations and all other
elements of war-fighting is human influence. It's easy to count tanks;
it's much harder to assess how well those operating the tanks have been
prepared for combat, and whether those operating the tanks really
want to operate them in combat. Militaries (at least for now) still must
be controlled by human beings, and often it is their learned skills and
continuing ability to take risks that determine the course of wars. Of
course, human abilities need to be backed up by constant operational
sustainment. When the myth of the short, decisive war collapses,
as it usually does, what is left is a long-term struggle to constantly
regenerate – and even grow – military force as it is being destroyed in
combat. The military equipment with which a country starts a war is
normally eaten up in short order, and the war becomes a desperate test
to make, repair and recreate military force.

Finally, even more so than in peace, alliances often determine the
outcome of a war even for the most powerful states. Allies play an
enormous role in providing aid, and can even take over a significant
amount of the fighting burden. The two world wars were decided
by alliances acting in concert, not individual states fighting their
own wars. Or, to put it more bluntly, the states that acted most
like individual actors – such as Nazi Germany or Imperial Japan in
World War II – were doomed when faced with the Allies, who were
willing to act far more cooperatively. In other words, those states that
try to act like individual great powers, like Germany in both world
wars, ended up defeated; while those nations that were able to work in
larger coalitions – such as Britain – had their victory parades.

The importance of alliances also underlines one of the purposes of
this book, which is to explain the different elements, beyond military
forces, that make up a country's power and help determine how it will
perform in war. Returning to the start of this introduction, the more
complex nature of power means we should dispense with the phrase
'great power', as very few powers are great, and those that are not
considered 'great' are often surprisingly successful at achieving their
strategic goals. Correspondingly, rarely if ever have 'great powers'
won wars on their own. What is far more sensible is to understand

power as a construction in which a number of different elements play a role. The economic/technological strength of a power can be shaped by leadership, society and political structure – and can be reinforced by alliances. A 'full spectrum' power has elements of strength in all these areas.

Hopefully we won't have to worry soon about which of the two most powerful states on the earth today will have a victory parade or not. A war between the US and China would far eclipse any conflict we have seen – other than the world wars – in terms of its potential to kill and destroy, and it has the possibility of surpassing even them. And yet, it must be understood that a war between them is a very real possibility. This book will end by using the methodology outlined on war and power to assess what would matter if these two states (and their allies, of course) end up at war. Perhaps, just perhaps, a proper understanding of the limited nature of power and the disastrous consequences unleashed by the decision to go to war might lead states and leaders to think twice before making a fateful decision.

PART ONE
Power

1. Economic/Technological Strength

Power in both times of peace and times of war depends on the ability to design, build and manipulate 'stuff'. The stuff in question has to be the most technologically advanced for its time, well made, produced in substantial quantities (especially during wars), and at a cost that is sustainable and competitive. This matters more than geographical size or population numbers when it comes to national power. Indeed, looking at which states have been the most powerful over the last two centuries, it has been the economically largest and technologically most advanced that have dominated.

The size of a state in area or population terms plays a comparatively marginal role. The two largest countries today in terms of geographic size are first Russia and then Canada, neither of whom would qualify as a full-spectrum power. In 1900, the largest countries would have been Great Britain (with the British Empire), Russia and China – and in this case only one, as World War I would show, was a full-spectrum power. The United States, on the other hand, has never been more than the fourth-largest country in the world in terms of area, though it has dominated global power for more than a century.

The same holds true for population. Looking at the ten largest countries in the world by population now, it's interesting to see that the two full-spectrum powers of the moment (the US and China) are in the top three, with India above both, and a large range of less powerful states grouped below.[1] Some of these latter states are very close to the US in population, including Indonesia, whose population is more than 80 per cent of that of the US, and Pakistan, at 70 per cent.

It's worth realizing just how out of balance international power is with population. Though the US has been the greatest power in the world for well over a century, its population has only made up about 5 per cent of the globe's total. Yet at the same time, the US has been labelled, successively, a 'great power', a 'superpower' and even a 'global hegemon'.[2] What seems to be the case is that a state needs enough people, but certainly not the most people, to be a significant power. Indeed, if pressed, long-term demographics could be said to matter more than raw numbers. A state needs enough people at the right ages to support future growth. When a nation's population ages rapidly, such as Japan after the 1990s and China today, it presents serious challenges to a country's future development as a power.

The same is not the case with economic/technological power. Economically there have been three states that have been dominant since the mid-nineteenth century. Britain and the British Empire industrialized first and led the world in production and much of high technology until the late nineteenth century. Then Britain was surpassed rapidly by the United States, which became the largest economic power in the world sometime in the 1890s (in both overall and per capita terms) and by 1914 was an economic powerhouse the size of much of Europe.[3] The recent rise of China economically and technologically has posed the first legitimate challenge to US dominance since the 1890s.

Looking at what mattered in the nineteenth century, before the two world wars and today, one of the best ways to see the differences between what the powers were able to accomplish is by examining variables such as gross national product (GNP) and gross domestic product (GDP). There has been one constant since the beginning of modern statistics: the dominance of the US. Now there is a situation where the US and China are in a league of their own. The US is still the largest country in the world in absolute GDP size, however if GDP is readjusted to take into consideration the purchasing power of capital in the different countries, China's GDP is now larger.

In fact, when it comes to economic size, the US was a rival or superior to most *continents* in the twentieth century, and even into the twenty-first. At the end of World War II, the United States even rivalled the rest of the world – about 50 per cent of world GDP was contained within its borders, and it possessed 80 per cent of the world's currency reserves.[4]

Of course, looking at economic size alone is a rather blunt way of gauging relative power. That is because in basic terms what makes a state powerful (both in peace and war) is how its economic/technological strength can be translated into military power – and, as such, economic size can mask different capabilities. For instance, a state such as Russia, which creates much of its wealth through resource extraction, can struggle with many of the technical and complex operational parts of war-fighting. Similarly, over the past few decades, many western states whose wealth is derived from services have lost the ability to create military force quickly and efficiently in times of need. This has left Russia and large European economies in particular (economies far larger than Russia's, such as Germany's) punching below their economic weight. A nation needs the economic/technological strength not just to buy the military systems it needs, but to make them itself – and if needs be, significantly scale up their production in times of war.

Thus, how economic/technological strength can be used to *create* military power matters most in relative power balances – and in many ways this separates the very small number of full-spectrum powers from the pretenders. The act of creating military power requires a range of abilities. First, the state must have the ability to tap into the most important and potentially disruptive technologies of the day, and to use those in the creation of its military equipment. It must also have the ability to integrate these weapons with others by creating and operating complex systems. Having a weapons system is very different from having the ability to integrate it into a complex operation to extract its greatest impact. Finally, the state must have the ability to increase production of such systems and refine and improve their complex operations in times of great crisis or outright war. Essentially, military power depends on having the best and the most – and only the very top of the economic/technological pyramid can possibly do this.

To see how the need for the best and the need for the most have worked together in the modern age, we can look at the construction and operation of some of the defining weapons systems of their time – weapons that determined the course of World War I and World War II, and which today are seen as crucial to any war that would break out between the two full-spectrum powers. These are dreadnought battleships and battlecruisers before and during World War I; four-engine bombers before and during World War II; and, more recently, large aircraft-carrier battle groups. Though many states aspired to create and operate all of these, only a very small number could do so effectively – and as such they separated themselves from the pack.

Dreadnoughts

Dreadnought battleships and battlecruisers were the most complex and expensive creations on the globe in the decade leading up to World War I. The specific ship which started the class designation, HMS *Dreadnought*, was launched by the British in 1906 and represented an important milestone in the construction of modern navies. A century earlier, in 1805, British maritime dominance had been established by the Royal Navy's victory over the French fleet at the Battle of Trafalgar. Then, the Royal Navy's largest ships, under the command of Admiral Horatio Nelson, were powered by sail and built of wood. They engaged and defeated the French fleet at point-blank range.[5] At times during the Battle of Trafalgar, the largest warships on each side were so close that they collided, and Nelson himself was killed because of the close-quarters nature of early nineteenth-century naval combat. When his flagship, HMS *Victory*, got tangled up with the French vessel *Redoubtable*, Nelson was so close to the enemy that he was shot by a French marine with a smoothbore musket. The bullet that killed him was tiny, weighing only twenty-two grams.[6] The French marksman, up in the rigging of *Redoubtable*, was able to put this bullet into Nelson's shoulder. It then passed through his lungs and spine, causing such catastrophic internal damage that it quickly led to death.

By the start of the twentieth century, however, naval technology had so transformed warships that Nelson's fleet was closer in capabilities to the Athenian triremes in the Peloponnesian War more than two millennia earlier (also fought at point-blank range) than those cruising the oceans before World War I. This was particularly the case for the largest, best-protected and most powerfully armed vessels of the day – usually referred to as battleships. These were the technological marvels of the early twentieth century, the highest expression of industrialized economies, and cost more than any moving thing on earth (and most immobile things as well). They were made of steel and iron, propelled by enormous yet finely engineered engines, and sported guns of immense weight and precision, capable of firing shells for many miles. Building such battleships was a supreme test – one that taxed every power that had pretensions to a modern navy. This was the test the British set for the world when they launched HMS *Dreadnought* in 1906.[7]

Dreadnought was the most powerful and the most well-defended vessel in the world. Its sides were belted by almost a foot of the highest-quality steel, which provided excellent protection against all but the largest naval guns in existence. However, it was in its armament that *Dreadnought* really stood out. Battleships before *Dreadnought* had mixed batteries with often just one or two large guns and a larger number of smaller-calibre ones. *Dreadnought* dispensed with all the smaller guns and mounted ten of the largest guns in the world, eight of which could fire broadsides on either side. These batteries of heavy guns could hurl an unprecedented weight of shells an unprecedented distance. A full broadside from *Dreadnought* involved hurling shells weighing a combined 6,800 pounds (more than 3 million grams, compared to the measly twenty-two which killed Nelson) approximately ten miles.[8]

The change wrought by *Dreadnought* was so great that the British did not comprehend fully what they had done. In making all earlier battleships (which were quickly labelled 'pre-dreadnoughts') obsolete, the British threw away their own large numerical advantage in the capital ship category, and replaced it with a time advantage as the first state to have designed and successfully built one of the new vessels. In levelling the numerical playing field, however, the British started an entirely new race for naval dominance – one in which any state in the world could compete, if their economic/technological might allowed it.

As it turned out, the British had basically separated the men from the boys economically and technologically, and almost all other states found themselves floundering far behind in the dreadnought-building stakes. The French and Russians, the second- and third-largest naval powers in the world in 1900, lacked the economic/technological might to compete. Whereas the British built the first dreadnought in only sixteen months and averaged a normal construction period of approximately two years from that point on, the Russians and French took three, four or even five years to do something similar. Neither would have a first-rank navy at the start of World War I.

Only the US and Germany could think of competing with Britain, and the three of them, not surprisingly, were the three largest industrial economies with the most advanced technological capabilities and the best shipbuilding industries in the world at the time. The three of them produced more steel than the rest of the world combined.

This kind of economic muscle was crucial in the building of dreadnoughts. The turrets needed to house the heavy guns were in many ways the most complex and expensive parts of the vessel to create. They needed to be strong enough to both house and protect the guns (the turrets alone also had almost a foot of armour on their sides), and yet at the same time be so precisely constructed and finely engineered as to allow those guns to be quickly moved both up and down and side to side, depending on where they were to be fired. It was the kind of advanced and large-scale engineering that only the British, Germans and Americans could undertake at scale.

Thankfully for the British, the Americans had no political will to engage in a dreadnought-building race. Though Theodore Roosevelt, president when HMS *Dreadnought* was built, was the greatest supporter of the US Navy to have occupied the Oval Office to that time, the American people, and crucially Congress, were less committed to being a great sea power. When Roosevelt sent large requests for new battleships to Congress in 1907 and 1908, the number eventually approved was much smaller than the president had wanted. The US would leave the British unchallenged in naval supremacy until World War I was well underway.[9]

The situation in Germany was different. When the Germans had started constructing a modern navy just before 1900, their plan was not to challenge the British directly. Instead, the intention was to create a fleet strong enough that it could tip the naval balance between what the Germans believed were rival naval competitors: the British on the one hand, and the French and Russians (who were allied) on the other. However, in building the dreadnought, the British had exposed the economic/technological shortcomings of France and Russia to such a degree that the German plans lay in ruins. Germany was therefore faced with the prospect of having a fleet with no strategic purpose, or competing directly with the British for dreadnought supremacy.

It opted for the latter, and the result was one of the most famous arms races in human history. The Germans represented a far greater threat than the British first understood. Even though Germany had little in the way of naval tradition or an institutional memory of sea power, it had an industrial and technological base that rivalled – and in some ways surpassed – that of Britain. This was particularly true when it came to steel production and the machine tools industry. The Germans had taken the global lead in high-quality steel manufacture – so much so that the best steel in the world, the type that was used to build dreadnoughts for instance, was often referred to as Krupp steel, even by the British.[10] Krupp was the name of the German manufacturer who had designed the process for its purification. When Krupp steel was added to German engineering expertise, the results were impressive.

When news of the construction of HMS *Dreadnought* reached the continent, the Germans soon stopped production on their existing battleships and decided to retool to make dreadnoughts. They did so with remarkable speed. HMS *Dreadnought* was commissioned in December 1906; by July 1907 the Germans were ready with their own design, which would be launched as SMS *Nassau* less than a year later.*[11] It was only one sign that Germany was an industrial competitor in a separate league from anyone else on the continent. As the British discovered to their horror in 1909, if the Germans devoted themselves fully to naval construction and threw all caution to the wind, they had the economic and technological might to build more dreadnought-type turrets than even the British themselves. The British government estimated in 1909 that the Germans had the industrial capacity to turn out fifty-four large turrets a year. They then calculated that the Germans, hypothetically, could manufacture up to eleven dreadnoughts a year if they didn't worry about cost – a number larger than the British could build at the time, even if they also threw all caution to the wind.

Now, thankfully for the British, the Germans could not devote all of their resources to dreadnought construction, as they had a rather large army to equip and supply at the same time. However, this did not stop the two nations from significantly increasing their dreadnought construction rates between 1909 and 1914, separating them from all the other naval powers in the world. This race saw the two even start to make HMS *Dreadnought* itself obsolete. They built ever-larger

* The *Nassau* was originally to be built as a pre-dreadnought (as these battleships would soon be known), but its construction was halted when news of *Dreadnought* emerged, and the Germans converted it into their first dreadnought class.

dreadnought battleships, and even invested in a sister type – the battle-cruiser. Battlecruisers were also capital ships, but they sacrificed much of the battleship's protective heavy armour, and their decreased weight allowed them to be faster than any other vessels afloat while being armed with the largest guns possible. Indeed, the cost and size of dreadnoughts were so great that there was much discussion in France, for instance, about whether it would make sense to invest in small torpedo boats or fleet submarines instead of just super-large dread-noughts going forward.[12]

By the early stages of World War I, the battleships and battlecruis-ers Britain and Germany were producing were such extreme creations they could even be referred to as super-dreadnoughts. HMS *Queen Elizabeth* was such a battleship, ordered and laid down by the British in 1912 and launched a few months after the start of World War I.[13] *Queen Elizabeth* weighed approximately 33,000 tons fully loaded (HMS *Dreadnought* weighed approximately 20,000 tons in a similar state), had more than a foot of armour plate for protection in its main belt, and carried eight 15-inch guns, in comparison to the 12-inch guns with which *Dreadnought* was equipped. These larger guns could fire a broad-side which weighed more than 15,000 pounds – more than twice as heavy as that fired by *Dreadnought* – and they could fire that massive weight for more than 20,000 yards, or up to about thirteen miles.[14] Even with all this weight, *Queen Elizabeth* could cruise at twenty-five knots – four knots faster than *Dreadnought*. In approximately eight years, naval construction had more than doubled the fighting power of British battleships. The same had happened with the Germans, who were building their two greatest battleships when the war started, *Bayern* and *Baden*, both of which would enter service in 1916.

Not only were the dreadnoughts powerful and expensive, they also possessed some of the most advanced technology on earth. One of the greatest examples of this was the rangefinders developed by the Ger-mans and the British.[15] As the guns on the battleships grew ever more powerful, the range at which they could engage enemy vessels length-ened. Accurately hitting the enemy from such a distance was no easy task. Dropping a shell from more than ten miles away on an enemy target that was somewhere between twenty and thirty yards in width would be a similar ratio to a golfer making a successful putt from well over 140 yards. This opened up another area of intense technological competition as Britain and Germany engaged in a struggle to develop the rangefinders (complete with calculation devices) needed for the guns to be fired with as much accuracy as possible.

The cost of these vessels made them stand out not only from other war materiel, but also from the construction of practically anything else on earth. When work started on HMS *Queen Elizabeth* in 1912, the most famous passenger liner of the era (or indeed any other era) was making its fateful inaugural voyage. RMS *Titanic*, opulently fitted out, weighed over 50,000 tons and could carry more than 2,000 passengers and crew – making it one of the supposed marvels of the era.[16] All of this size and extravagance meant that it cost £1.5 million to build (a little less than $8 million at the time). Which might sound like a lot, but it was only a fraction of the expense needed to build *Queen Elizabeth*, which cost an eye-watering £2.5 million (more than $13 million).[17]

The great expense of one dreadnought might also be seen by comparing it to the tallest and most dramatic skyscraper built in the world before World War I – the iconic Woolworth Building in Lower Manhattan. Wonderfully decorated, it soared sixty storeys high, and would remain the tallest building in the world until 1930 (it is still one of the 100 tallest buildings in the US today). Yet the construction cost of the sixty-storey Woolworth skyscraper was approximately equal to the cost of building just the *Queen Elizabeth*, at $13.5 million.[18]

By 1914, with the cost of one dreadnought battleship being more than 60 per cent higher than *Titanic* and the equivalent of the whole Woolworth Building, the Royal Navy's total dreadnought force of twenty-five battleships and ten battlecruisers represented the most expensive assembly of machinery anywhere in the world.[19] It was a testament to Britain's economic/technological strength – and Germany's for that matter, as the two of them had built far more dreadnoughts than the rest of the world combined.

And the expense for Britain was decisive in determining the course of the war. The victory over Germany in the dreadnought-building race was so clear-cut that it distorted our understanding of the naval war in World War I. From the moment the war started until the end, the dreadnought advantage that the British had built up over the Germans was so pronounced that Germany could not hope to challenge it. The financial and technological costs of trying to match Britain were beyond a Germany that also had to support a large army; and as British dreadnought construction grew, the Germans flatlined. By the start of the war, therefore, the British had 'won' the naval race by a large measure. In January 1915, when the Royal Navy could call on thirty-five capital ships, the Germans had only twenty-one in service – sixteen battleships and five battlecruisers. At the same time, the British had more on the stocks as well.

Though it needs to be said that in comparison to the rest of the European continent, the Germans were a naval behemoth. The dreadnought revolution placed the technological and economic resources of the other 'great' European powers under extreme duress, and their corresponding response was second- or in many cases third-rate. By the end of 1914, France had only completed four dreadnought battleships and battlecruisers; Italy had built three, Russia two, and Austria-Hungary just one. And all of these vessels were completely outclassed by *Queen Elizabeth* and the most recent German ships, being much closer to the now outdated HMS *Dreadnought* in specifications than anything the British and Germans were building. Taken together, as first-rate naval powers (those with the ability to build and deploy dreadnought ships), all of Europe combined could not match up to Germany, while Germany could not match up to Britain.

In fact, the British had won the race to such a degree that it made no sense for the Germans to even try to build more. Not one new German battleship went from design to completion during the years of the war. What this meant was that the dreadnoughts of the German Navy spent World War I running away from the Royal Navy, doing everything possible to avoid a large naval battle. The one time the British and German dreadnought fleets met in mass combat – the Battle of Jutland in 1916 – happened because the Germans had miscalculated, and the British were able to catch them at sea. During the battle, even when it was shown how well made the German dreadnoughts were, the German Navy was forced to execute a complex manoeuvre and flee to save itself.

The two dreadnought-based surface fleets would never engage in pitched battle again. The German reliance on submarine warfare, on the other hand – which receives so much discussion – was also the result of the British triumph in the dreadnought race. Shut out from competing on the surface of the seas, the Germans had to resort to trying to deny that surface to others. The results were disastrous – for Germany. Its submarine policy ended up antagonizing the US and played a huge role in getting the latter into the war in 1917. Then, when the Germans basically dropped all restraint and used submarines in the most aggressive way possible, they were again quickly outclassed by the British. After a few months of German success in the summer of 1917, the British mastered the submarine threat with the introduction of the convoy, and for the rest of the war drove the German submarines into submission.

In the end, it was Britain's technological/economic strength that allowed it to triumph in the dreadnought race, which set the contours of the whole of World War I at sea – a key element of the Allied victory. Much the same happened in the run-up to World War II, though in this case the struggle was over designing and building aircraft – and, like the dreadnought, equipping them with the systems that would allow them to operate.

'The Bomber Will Always Get Through'

Aircraft had started to show their potential value as war-fighting tools during World War I. Though they remained very primitive machines by the standards of World War II, by 1918 aircraft were being used to try to fulfil many of the roles that they would come to dominate between 1939 and 1945. Particularly with the Allies, aircraft in the last year of World War I were used for everything from scouting ahead of armies, to flying combat air patrols to clear out enemy aircraft from operating over battlefields, to attacking enemy forces on the ground.

The growth of aircraft as a weapon of war led a number of people to theorize in the 1920s and 1930s about the role of planes in any future war.* One of the most discussed issues was whether aircraft could (or even should) be used to bomb targets behind the front lines – such as cities, factories, or other infrastructure targets such as railroads and

---

* The three most famous of air power thinkers of the interwar period were arguably Giulio Douhet, Hugh Trenchard and William (Billy) Mitchell. They all believed that the introduction of aircraft had revolutionized warfare and they believed that in any future war aerial bombing would play a crucial role in determining the outcome.

canals.[20] These kinds of attacks, carried out by aircraft that were soon to be known as bombers, later became grouped together under the rubric of 'strategic bombing' and caused a great deal of public and private speculation. It was British prime minister Stanley Baldwin who ended up making maybe the most famous comment about strategic bombing. In 1932, speaking on the eve of Armistice Day, he tried to warn his fellow citizens that they would be targets in any future war and they therefore had to prepare themselves: 'I think it is well also for the man in the street to realize that there is no power on earth that can protect him from being bombed, whatever people may tell him. The bomber will always get through . . .'[21]

Baldwin ended up being rather too gloomy about the ability of bombers to always get through. As it turned out, during World War II strategic bombing was exceedingly difficult to execute effectively for many reasons. Bombers could actually be shot down by a number of defensive systems, from fighter planes to anti-air guns – both of which could be produced in large quantities.* Even if a bomber did survive until it got over a target and dropped its ordnance, this still did not mean that it had done its job effectively. Hitting a specific target on the ground from an aircraft was very difficult – particularly if the aircraft had to stay at a high altitude for safety.

In other words, a bomber had to be a very advanced and robust aircraft if it was to have any chance of fulfilling its mission. It had to be able to fly long distances and carry a great deal of ordnance. It had to be strong enough to give it a chance to survive in an environment replete with systems trying to damage it, and it had to fly smoothly enough to drop its ordnance with the highest chance of hitting its target. In short, the bomber had to be one of the most advanced warfighting machines developed to that time – and by the end of World War II it could be argued that it was the single most advanced.

However, in a very similar process to that of the dreadnought-building competition, in reality only a few countries could design, refine and then build effective bombers in large numbers. When the dust settled it was really the same three as in World War I: Britain, Germany and the US. But the results in the strategic bombing competition

* For the sake of consistency and clarity, anti-aircraft systems of all types will be referred to as 'anti-air'.

were quite different, as the Germans, who were able to build some of the sturdiest dreadnought battleships, struggled to produce an effective heavy bomber.

The German quest to build a heavy four-engine bomber resulted in their most expensive production fiascos of the interwar and World War II periods. No matter how much money they threw at the problem, they could not devise a workable answer – until it was far too late. The focus of their extraordinary effort was the design and production of the Heinkel He 177 (known as the *Greif* or Griffin). The quest to build the He 177 began back in 1936, when the Nazi government put out a call for the development of new generation of fast bombers – which, it was hoped, would be able to outrun enemy aircraft. As one of the most technologically advanced German aircraft manufacturers, Heinkel started work right away and produced its first mock-up in 1937. However, it was still years until an effective flying version could be built.[22]

It was soon discovered that making a bomber fast enough to outrun fighters would be practically impossible, so the He 177 started getting much heavier defensive armaments. For a while there was also an attempt to design the aircraft as a dive bomber. Dive-bombing was a more accurate manner of delivering ordnance on target, but any aircraft dive-bombing had to hold a straight course for an extended period as it moved from high to low altitude – making it extremely vulnerable. The most famous German dive bomber of the war, the gull-winged Junkers Ju 87, or Stuka, was so easy to shoot down that by the summer of 1940 it had lost almost all of its value fighting the British (though it continued to be used with some effect against the Russians on the Eastern Front until 1945).[23] It eventually became apparent to the Germans that making a large and expensive aircraft like the He 177 into a dive bomber was completely impractical.

However, the greatest problem with the He 177 was the engines. All aircraft represent a balance between the airframe (the structure that is being propelled through the air) and the engines that do the propelling. An under-engined or poorly engined aircraft, even with the most brilliant airframe, is a flying turkey, which makes the He 177 the Thanksgiving dinner of World War II. Its airframe shape was advanced, with an aerodynamic domed front and top that reduced drag, and a large fuselage capable of holding a lot of ordnance.

However, getting the engines to propel this excellent airframe ended
up being a nightmare for the Germans. For years, Heinkel opted to try
to link two engines, front to back, on each wing. They were hoping
this would provide great power while also increasing performance. It
was a design innovation, and the US and UK four-engine bombers
were built with two engines side by side on each wing.

Unfortunately for the Germans, it was a terrible innovation, and
the design did not work. The linked engines' actions led to intense
vibration, and they were known to leak fuel. They were also placed
on wings that were not strong enough to lift the concentrated weight,
and these frequently developed cracks.[24] The engines produced so
much power in such a narrow space that they often caught fire or
exploded. The result was years of crashes and lost pilots as the Germans tried to make the configuration work. By 1944, even Hitler lost
faith, and called the plane 'garbage'.[25] Trying to calculate the cost the
Germans spent on developing the He 177 is impossible – but it might
easily have matched the total Germany spent building tanks during
all of World War II.[26]

Where the Germans failed, the British and Americans succeeded.
The most famous British bomber of the war was the four-engine Avro
Lancaster, an excellent flying platform capable of carrying a great deal
of ordnance. The design and building process also took years, but it
worked out much better than the He 177. The Lancaster emerged out
of an aircraft programme in 1936. The first version was the Manchester,
a two-engine bomber, which made its first flight in 1939 and was put
into service in 1940. However, like the He 177, the Manchester suffered
from serious engine troubles at first, and being a two-engine bomber it
was incapable of carrying the weight of bombs the British wanted for
a strategic bombing campaign against Germany. Plans were thus put
in place to take the design, enlarge it, and equip it with four (better)
engines. The result was the Lancaster, which started operational duty
in 1942 and would be the backbone of the Royal Air Force's strategic
bombing of Germany for the rest of the war.[27]

If the British did better than the Germans when it came to designing and building strategic bombers, partly by being more deliberate
and less adventurous, the US outdid them both – which was hardly
surprising as the US was now the economic/technological powerhouse of the world. Like the British and the Germans, the Americans

started conceiving of a new class of bombers in the 1930s, but unlike the British and Germans they were able to bring a design to active use far earlier. The famous Boeing B-17 Flying Fortress, which would still be flying missions over Germany in 1945, went from design to operational use before Hitler invaded Poland. Its origins came from a call in 1934 by the USAAC (United States Army Air Corps, which became the USAAF in 1941 – there was no separate US Air Force at the time) for a next-generation bomber capable of flying long distances. The US, because of its relative isolation from possible enemies, always had to think about range more than any other power. While London was just over 200 miles from the German industrial heartland in the Ruhr, the US, even from its extreme western (Hawaii) and eastern (Maine) parts, was thousands of miles from Japan and Germany.

Maybe for this reason, the US invested the resources and had the technological expertise to develop the first true four-engine bomber before anyone else. The B-17 was everything an interwar-period design could have hoped for – and possibly more. It was notoriously robust, long-ranged with the ability to fly for approximately 2,000 miles carrying a significant bombload, and equipped with some of the finest engines in the world. The USAAC was determined to get as many as possible, though at first it struggled to convince Congress to fund the purchase of large numbers.[28] However, once war broke out in Europe, funding was made available in much larger amounts, and as there was already a working design, the US was able to start producing the B-17 in quantity. It would become the mainstay of the US strategic bombing of Germany, preferred even over later-generation four-engine bombers such as the Consolidated B-24. By 1944, later B-17 designs had the range to fly very deep into Germany, and were known to reach Leipzig or even Danzig (modern-day Gdańsk) in far eastern Germany.[29]

Though by that time the US had taken four-engine aircraft technology and made another major developmental leap with the most expensive and complex weapons systems programme in the war, resulting in the Boeing B-29 Superfortress. Though often people assume that the Manhattan Project, which resulted in the atomic bomb, or even the German V-2 programme, which resulted in the world's first 'space rocket',[30] were World War II's most expensive weapons programmes, they were both outstripped by a considerable amount by the US programme to develop a Very Long Range (VLR) bomber. It was so expensive that it was eventually labelled the 'three-billion-dollar gamble'.[31]

The idea that the US would need a bomber of super-range went back to 1938 – and was accelerated by the Fall of France.[32] At that point the US needed to imagine fighting a war with Nazi Germany by itself – and believed that American technological advances could still lead to victory. Key to this was extending the range of aircraft. Even if Britain fell or was driven out of the war, so the US reasoning went in its famous Rainbow war plans, the US should have the ability to strike Europe from Iceland.

The B-29 was to provide the US with the ability to fight such a long-range war against Germany. Considering the extreme technological demands placed on the aircraft, it moved relatively rapidly through the design process, making its first flight in 1942. The B-29 could fly for 3,000 miles in comparison to the B-17's 2,000 miles, and was almost a third faster, all while carrying 20,000 pounds of ordnance.[33] However, this was just scratching the surface of its advances. It was also all electric and completely pressurized, allowing it to fly at 30,000 feet but for the crew to operate as if they were at 8,000 feet.[34] Maybe most remarkably, it had automated defences – basically guns linked by an early computer, so that one gunner inside the plane could control a number of guns at the same time. In fact, the B-29 had so many technical advances that some of the technicians at Boeing were 'uncomfortable with the aircraft, feeling that they were going too far forward into the technological unknown'.[35] Amazingly, the US had a flying version deployed to war in 1944, and by 1945 the Superfortress was the main weapon used in the air campaign against Japan.

So, making four-engine bombers ended up being an operation of great complexity, and doing so cost far more than any other weapons programme of the war. Designing and building the B-29, for instance, cost a minimum of $3 billion and might have reached $3.7 billion.[36] In comparison, the designing and building of the atom bombs under the Manhattan Project cost $2 billion. And the total costs of the four-engine bombers, including those that never made it past the drawing board, would dwarf the cost of all other weapons systems.

In terms of successfully harnessing technological development, the Americans not only won the war; they won the production battle as well. The US ended up developing three successful models of four-engine bombers that were flown in combat before the end of World War II: the B-17, B-24 and the very long-range B-29. The British built one real success, the Lancaster, and the Germans struggled to build the He 177, which was not particularly effective. In overall production terms, the competition was not close, with the US building approximately 30,000 B-17s, B-24s and B-29s, the British just over 7,000 Lancasters, and the Germans just a few hundred He 177s.

Of course, these figures obscure the real level of US technological/economic dominance. One B-29, for instance, cost the same as five Lancaster bombers.[37] In winning this competition, the US set much of the strategic course of the whole war. The Germans, as time went on, spent more and more of their resources – not in the land war, but in the air war as they tried to blunt the US and UK strategic bombing offensives. By 1943 not only were they spending half of their economy to building aircraft (overwhelmingly fighters, to confront Allied bombers), but German expenditure on anti-air weapons and ammunition (once again, overwhelmingly directed at the British and American bombing campaign) was approximately equal to the amount spent building all German tanks and self-propelled guns.[38] At the same time, these Allied bombing offensives dislocated and then seriously degraded German production. Factories were dispersed, then at least partially destroyed, and in the end the transportation network linking them was dislocated. The result was that the German economy was basically ground down trying to fight (or directly by) the strategic bombing campaign. Meanwhile, in the Pacific, by the end of 1945 the B-29 was unchallengeable in the skies over Japan. It was the only platform capable of carrying and dropping the atom bomb – and it ended the war as basically the prototype for all future bombers.

So, the four-engine bomber, like the dreadnought before it, stands out as a key weapon of war, because it not only engaged the Germans and Japanese directly in battle, it also greatly affected their whole power creation system, limiting the ability of those countries to generate more armed forces and materiel as the war went on. In the end, a state needed not only to make the best equipment, but also the most, and to support that equipment and use it in complex operations in order to effectively exercise power in peace and war.

Aircraft Carriers since 1945

If the naval vessel was the main point of competition before World War I and the bomber aircraft before World War II, arguably it is the combination of the two in aircraft-carrier battle groups that best demonstrates how economics and technology have separated the powers since. A fully stocked aircraft carrier is not just the largest warship afloat; it contains one of the most advanced and expensive stores of aircraft. It must also be supported and protected by a small fleet of its own. Indeed, it is so expensive today that the long-term viability of the large fleet carrier is being questioned.

During the Cold War and for two decades after, however, building, equipping and deploying aircraft carriers separated the most advanced powers from the others. However, in this case, the difference was even greater than with the dreadnought and the four-engine bomber. Essentially, there was the United States, who could build and deploy a large number of fully equipped carriers at the same time – and everyone else. Many states, from the USSR to France and Britain, had pretensions to being aircraft-carrier powers. What they built, however, was small in number, small in size and limited in abilities. The Soviet Union, the other supposed superpower of the Cold War, never built what could be considered a true fleet carrier, opting for more of a hybrid carrier/cruiser in the *Kiev* class.[39] These were small vessels, less than half the size of US carriers of the time, with deficient aircraft, and they suffered from a huge number of teething issues. Only four of them were built in the 1970s and 1980s, and half of these today are theme parks. The French built two carriers in the early 1960s, *Foch* and *Clemenceau*, but these were smaller than *Kiev*-class vessels, could accommodate half the aircraft (at most) of US carriers, and lacked integrated radar. The British ended up with the smallest carriers of the lot by the end of the Cold War, and officially they were not even carriers. For the first decades of the Cold War the largest British carrier, *Ark Royal*, was a World War II-vintage vessel – construction started in 1943. When plans were made to scrap *Ark Royal* in the 1970s, the British opted for the mini-carriers of the *Illustrious* class (they were even called through-deck cruisers), from which could fly only a handful of jump jets.

The United States had developed carriers of a completely different proportion. From the mid-1970s, while the USSR was struggling with the small *Kyiv* class, the US started producing *Nimitz*-class carriers. Two and a half times the size of the *Kyiv* class, *Nimitz*-class carriers could house up to ninety of the most advanced aircraft of the time. They were also equipped with the most sophisticated support systems, from integrated radar to missile defences. Before the end of the Cold War in 1989, the United States was able to launch five *Nimitz*-class carriers. These formed the backbone of the US carrier force in the 1980s, which would have crushed all the rest of the world's fleets combined. During every year between 1982 and 1989, the US deployed at least ten large aircraft carriers overseas – giving it an unparalleled ability to project power.[40] Each one of these carriers would have been the equal of the carrier force of any other nation.

This US carrier dominance remains today. But the rise of China has led to the appearance of another country that is attempting to build and equip a large fleet carrier of approximately the same size and carrying the same air-wing as the largest US vessels. Though they have not yet put it into production, the Chinese do have one currently undergoing sea trials, *Fujian*, which is as large as the newest US carriers.[41] The fact that the Chinese can do this speaks to their economic and technological might.

The irony is that the future of both *Fujian* and the very large American carriers of today is being debated. Changes in the technology of warfare have led some to wonder whether such massively large, technically advanced and extraordinarily expensive vessels are worth the investment, in an era with much cheaper and ever longer-ranged anti-ship missiles and even UAVs (unmanned aerial vehicles, or drones).[42] It's a question that needs to be asked. If a newer, disruptive technology appears that can destroy an older, more expensive one, then trying to hold on to the old for too long risks military failure.

One of the key areas for any such disruptive technology will be the race for autonomous systems, which can be put within the larger race to develop artificial intelligence (AI). If one nation – or alliance – can develop workable autonomous weapons that can be sent out to identify enemy targets and then attack them without relying on human control, it could change the balance of deterrence and even the outcome of wars. Both the US and China, for example, are working on a range of AI technologies. Though the US first looked to have a significant lead in this area, in early 2025 the Chinese showed that they could devise a cheaper, simpler AI system that used less power (which is a key development in using AI for weapons systems). Though we are still a long way from having this competition decided, it could easily be the ultimate test of economic technological power in the mid-twenty-first century.

One thing we can say now, however, is if one technological era is ending and another is starting, then in the competition to dominate military technology in the new era, the most economically powerful states with the most advanced technology will rise to the top.

They can always make the best and most stuff.

2. Leadership

Adolf Hitler wanted to invade Poland for a long time before he ordered the German Army to cross the Polish border on 1 September 1939. For years he had believed that Germany needed to go to war by 1943, which is when he expected the balance of military production and preparedness would turn against Germany.[1] Also, Poland was always going to be one of his targets. He viewed the Poles as racially degenerate and, even worse, as squatting on land he lusted after as an integral part of the 'greater' Germany he wanted to create.

The question Hitler faced was when to do the deed. By the spring of 1939 he was ready to put his plans into action.[2] As he told his leading henchmen, including his deputy Hermann Göring, in his typically rambling and repetitive way: 'There is therefore no question of sparing Poland, and we are left with the decision to attack Poland at the first suitable opportunity . . . There will be war. Our task is to isolate Poland. The success of the isolation will be decisive . . . The isolation of Poland is a matter of skilful politics.'[3]

For the next few months Hitler would do just that – isolate and then invade Poland. The first part of the process would not be easy. Poland had security guarantees from the British and the French and even the possibility of support from its large neighbour to the east – the USSR, led by Joseph Stalin. Hitler sought to weaken that group of allies and possible allies, and on 23 August he believed he had achieved his dream. He signed a deal with Stalin, gaining Soviet support for an invasion of Poland by promising to turn half his booty over to the Soviet leader. By signing this dictators' pact to divide Poland, Hitler believed (wrongly) that he could keep Britain and France from going to war.

Within a few days, Hitler's hopes were proven to be false. First, he was abandoned by his closest ally, Italian dictator Benito Mussolini – whom Hitler had assumed would go to war alongside him. The threat of Italy going to war, so Hitler believed, would further dissuade Britain and France. However, when Hitler let Mussolini know on

25 August that Germany would soon invade Poland, the Italian dictator replied with a letter saying the diplomatic equivalent of 'Best of Luck, Adolf, you're on your own'. Even if Britain and France went to war against Germany, Mussolini lamented, 'it would be better if I did not take the initiative in military activities in view of the present situation of Italian war preparations'.[4]

Hitler panicked when he received Mussolini's unexpected rebuff.[5] Things were made worse when it became clear that Britain and France would go to war for Poland – even after the Nazi-Soviet Pact. Many of those around Hitler, including Göring, wanted nothing to do with a large European war. Hitler, however, was too far committed to back down. After postponing the attack for a few days, he decided he could not turn back, and on 1 September 1939 he ordered the German Army to cross the Polish border.

World War II had started in Europe.

Hitler was undoubtedly trying to maximize Germany's power in a chaotic international system – just in a hyper-aggressive, entirely personal, unnecessary and ultimately self-destructive way. Yet, far from maximizing Germany's power, he ended up setting off a series of events that led to the deaths of millions of Germans, the dismemberment of the country and the welcome demise of Hitler himself.

As Hitler's example shows, simply having the power possessed by a state because of its economic/technological dominance doesn't mean that this power is used effectively – or even non-disastrously. There is not, has never been and I wager never will be one idea of how a state should maximize power. There is also no clearly defined national interest – even though the phrase is widely employed to try to provide a template to rationalize and de-personalize state behaviour.

Looking at the twentieth and twenty-first centuries, it becomes clear that how states use and create their power is actually an unstable, even pernicious, process. This is often the case because power usage is dominated by national leaders (and a small group of advisers around them). Power is easily mishandled by the whim, prejudice or even indolence or indecision of leadership; the specific outcomes of international affairs, and even the wars that are waged, are written by the choices leaders make. Some make disastrous choices, even for powerful states, and head down paths that lead to disaster and dismemberment. Other, more thoughtful leaders have exaggerated a state's influence and amplified its standing in the international world. In some cases, major wars that people would have thought likely, never occur because of leadership or the manner in which a political system moderates behaviour. The end of the Cold War might be the best example of this. The leadership of the USSR, under Mikhail Gorbachev, accepted the collapse of the Soviet Empire in Europe without resorting to a war that most would have thought was inevitable.

No international power confrontation – indeed no war – is inevitable. Neither World War I nor World War II, for instance, had to happen when and how it did (indeed, the second was doubly uncertain, being influenced a great deal by the first). Each could have broken out years earlier, years later or not at all, and a change in the timing of the start would have altered the duration, the actors involved and the overall impact. The reason that both wars started when they did was to a large degree down to the interaction of the decisions of different political leaders.

For instance, World War I broke out in 1914, after the heir to the Austro-Hungarian throne, Archduke Franz Ferdinand, was assassinated by a small cabal of angry crackpots (mostly through happenstance when his car went down the wrong road). Europe transitioned from peace to war at astonishing speed – within just a few weeks. It was a war that hardly anyone had imagined a decade earlier. One of the best ways to understand how leadership matters is to look at how and when Britain and Germany went to war in 1914 and 1939 – and examine how, in both cases, individual leaders did a great deal to shape the process.

World Wars: Determining When and With Whom to Fight

Joseph Chamberlain, the powerful British Colonial Secretary between 1895 and 1903, believed that Britain and Germany should be firm friends – even allies. He saw Germany as a natural ally, with its small overseas empire and tiny navy, but powerful army that could keep the French and Russians in line. When he surveyed the world from his august and nerve-racking perch in charge of the British Empire, he understood that the era of British dominance was coming to an end. The British economy was slipping from the position at the top that it had held for much of the nineteenth century. This meant that, more and more, Britain would have to work with other states to secure its international position. And the states that Chamberlain saw as most threatening were France and Russia, both trying to expand into areas of great importance to the British Empire.[6]

At the same time, Chamberlain saw the United States, rising even more quickly than Germany, as another natural ally. This was as much because of background and (assumed) natural sympathy as anything else, as he believed that Britain and the US were drawn together by a common (genetic) heritage. It was inconceivable to him that the two great English-speaking powers would ever go to war – and as such, an alliance, or at least a strong friendship between them, was desirable.

Chamberlain made his preference for good relations with Germany and the United States open news in one of the more famous speeches of the pre-1914 years. In 1899, he waxed rhapsodically about the 'new Triple Alliance between the Teutonic race and the two great branches of the Anglo-Saxon race'.[7] For Chamberlain, the alliance with Germany was only 'natural' as the two states had few areas of conflict.

That arguably the most powerful British statesman of the time would suggest an alliance between Germany and the UK was no one-off. In 1902, Lord Lansdowne, the Foreign Secretary, engaged in detailed negotiations with Germany about an Anglo-German alliance. In the end it was the Germans who nixed the idea – concerned as they were about alienating the Russians. They wanted to remain on relatively good terms with Russia, and felt that the animosity between Britain and Russia would make that impossible if they agreed an alliance with the United Kingdom. Ironically, the British would soon hoist the Germans with their own petard, by negotiating their own strategic agreement with the Russians in 1907.

The idea that Britain and Germany, the two leading European full-spectrum powers that would go to war in 1914, almost became allies just a few years earlier, and that the war between them was far from inevitable, can be jarring to some. However, had their leaderships acted differently at the time, a formal alliance might very well have been agreed – and this could have transformed European relations. The Triple Entente would have had no time to form. Britain only turned to negotiate its entente with France in 1904 and agreement with Russia in 1907 (neither stated as a formal alliance) after the negotiations with Germany did not secure an agreement.

In fact, even after the failure of the Anglo-German alliance talks, it was not inevitable that the two states would go to war – that too was mostly down to leadership decisions and perceptions. Drilling down into the decision-making, and looking at the long-term and short-term processes, two people stand out for making World War I happen as it did.

Maybe the most important personality in creating the preconditions for war between the two was the German Kaiser, Wilhelm II. When he became the German emperor, military commander-in-chief and head of state in 1888, Wilhelm was in a position to influence German foreign and strategic policy a great deal. Crucially, he had the power of appointment – the ability to select a chancellor of whom he approved and who would implement his chosen policies. As such, government ministers were responsible only to him – even if their policies lost votes in the German parliament (the Reichstag). He was also deeply emotional and impulsive, and ended up destroying the policy that had helped secure German unification and the rise of Germany to become the greatest land power in Europe.

What Wilhelm did was break with the long-time policy of the legendary Prussian/German chancellor Otto von Bismarck, who favoured an alliance with Russia and a small German Navy.[8] Bismarck believed in isolating France, not threatening Britain, and also in maintaining good relations between the emperors of Central and Eastern Europe, which naturally included Austria.[9] Wilhelm, however, had very different ambitions, and being a monarch with a great deal of power over the German state and people – particularly when it came to military and foreign policy – he was able to push Germany down a very different road.

In 1890, Wilhelm did not renew Germany's Reinsurance Treaty with Russia.[10] This was a defensive alliance that meant Russia could not support France if Germany and France went to war. Wilhelm seemed to believe that ideological differences would keep the French and Russians apart – and that he could let the treaty lapse on the assumption that the other two would not gang up against him. He was wrong. The Franco-Russian Alliance was negotiated in stages between 1891 and 1894, and it proved durable until Germany ended up going to war against both in 1914. Wilhelm thus ended the French isolation that Bismarck had engineered since the Franco-Prussian War, while making sure that the second- and third-most powerful land armies on the European continent were now surrounding Germany.

However, that was only the beginning. In the coming years, Wilhelm would antagonize the British by pushing the creation of a German fleet that would threaten Britain's very existence. Wilhelm's desire to make Germany a naval power was deeply personal. As a young boy he had fallen in love with warships, and could often be found 'lovingly' sketching the great battleships with the largest guns.[11] After being captivated by the works of American naval theorist Alfred Thayer Mahan as a young man (it was said he 'devoured' Mahan's *Influence of Sea Power upon History*), he came to believe that the only way Germany could become a global force was if it built one of the largest fleets in the world.

From the late 1890s until 1914, strengthening the German fleet was one of Wilhelm's greatest ambitions. He used his power of appointment to make the legendary (and legendarily dangerous) Admiral Alfred von Tirpitz the Secretary of State for the Navy in 1897.[12] For a few years later (until they fell out) Wilhelm worked closely with Tirpitz – who was convinced that Britain was Germany's greatest enemy and the great block to Germany becoming a world power – to see appropriations for naval construction raised and ensure that Germany built more naval vessels.[13] It was Wilhelm's efforts that caused Germany to build the very expensive and technologically advanced German dreadnoughts that would feature so prominently in the Anglo-German naval race.

What Wilhelm had done, though he did not entirely understand it, was present such a threat to British independence that Britain's political leadership moved decisively to see Germany as a threat to its existence. The basic issue was one of food and raw materials. Being an island with a large manufacturing base and a population larger than its own agricultural output could feed, Britain needed to trade to exist. If any naval power could threaten its seaborne commerce, Britain's factories would cease functioning and its population would starve.

Thus, in a matter of years, Britain's leaders moved from the policies of Chamberlain and Lansdowne – who had sought an alliance with Germany – to aligning with France and Russia in an anti-German grouping. This switch was made easier because the leadership itself changed. In 1905 the Conservative/Unionist coalition that had been considering an alliance with Germany was replaced by a Liberal government that would rule until after the outbreak of the war. The only Liberal Foreign Secretary during that entire era was Sir Edward Grey, and he ended up playing a crucial role in Britain entering the war in 1914.

Grey's appearance belied the man. Though he was a quiet and bookish figure, with a penchant for weekends in the country spent reading and birdwatching, he could be surprisingly aggressive when it came to the application of national power. He was more worried about the growth of Kaiser Wilhelm's navy than most of the British government, and it could be said that he led an anti-German grouping not only in the Foreign Office, but in the entire cabinet.[14] He made sure that voices calling for improving relations with Germany were marginalized, and at the same time he was instrumental in improving relations with France and Russia – even pushing forward with military discussions between the states. He was a big supporter of the Anglo-French entente, which was negotiated before he became Foreign Secretary, and used it as the first step towards the creation of the great British-French-Russian alliance that would start World War I. [15] He remarked after the creation of the entente that henceforth he would be ever vigilant against Britain 'relapsing' into favouring better relations with Germany.[16] He was as good as his word, and from then on fought those who wanted good relations between Britain and Germany.[17]

He was careful to keep much of this quiet, and he never spoke of a military alliance coming into being, but Grey was personally responsible for pushing Britain closer to Germany's enemies and further away from Germany. When the British first started worrying about the growth of the German Navy, far from trying to dampen down the concern, Grey fanned the flames. He deliberately mis-stated different threats to make the situation worse than it was, and because of him the naval race between the British and Germans became a far nastier and more contentious affair.[18]

In some ways Grey had accumulated the influence to prevent or precipitate a British entry into war. In 1912 he played an important role in working out a peaceful settlement to a serious crisis in the Balkans that could have resulted in World War I occurring two years earlier.[19] Essentially, the decline of the Ottoman Empire saw the formation of a Slavic League under Russian guidance, to help gain independence for different Slavic nationalities. This brought immediate tensions with

Austria-Hungary, and through them Germany, who were suspicious of anything that would increase Russian influence and potentially threaten the stability of the multi-ethnic Austro-Hungarian Empire. With the threat of war looming, in this case Grey convened a peace conference in London and with real skill helped defuse the situation – even, perhaps to his chagrin, temporarily leading to better Anglo-German relations.[20]

In 1914, however, Grey was more bellicose. By this time believing that Germany was too much of a threat, and that France and Russia needed British aid if they were to have a chance of surviving a war, Grey pushed for Britain to stand up to Germany all the way to the outbreak of hostilities. He played a rather dangerous game of preparing Britain for intervention even though the British cabinet as a whole was not set on it.[21] In the end, the German invasion of Belgium was used by Grey to get Britain into the fighting on the side of France and Russia, even though the German government was clear that it had no intentions of taking British or French territory (except possibly for parts of the French Empire). Grey is often remembered for the evocative phrase he uttered when war started that 'the lamps are going out all over Europe, we shall not see them lit again in our lifetime', which makes it seem like he was devastated at the outbreak of the conflict.[22] However, Grey was as responsible as any policymaker for bringing Britain into a war that it did not have to fight.

Thus the personalities of the German and British leaders helped move the countries from a position where they were considering an alliance at the start of the twentieth century to one in which they went to war in 1914. Germany's leadership played a large role in making an avoidable war unavoidable, while a specific British policymaker was influential in determining exactly when the war started. This was a process that would be repeated in the interwar period, with different actors causing a similar outcome in the run-up to World War II.

The 1920s revealed that enmity between Britain and Germany was not some natural state and that war between them was not inevitable. While Britain and Germany were hardly the best of friends, they were cooperative powers. A great deal of effort, on both sides, was put into trying to establish a productive bilateral relationship in the decade after World War I, when the two worked together on initiatives such as the Locarno Pact and the Kellogg-Briand Pact. German leadership during the somewhat anarchic Weimar period was democratic and, while wanting to redress what it saw as the iniquities of the Versailles Treaty, arguably as liberal as Britain's own – if not more so.

The change to the expansionist, bloodthirsty, hyper-militarized leadership of Hitler, which set Germany and the rest of Europe on the road to World War II, only happened because of an economic calamity of the highest order. The Great Depression, which began because of a 1929 stock market collapse in the US, led to an economic contraction of almost unimaginable proportions. By 1930, the New York Stock Exchange had lost approximately 90 per cent of its value.[23] The repercussions of this collapse spread outwards quickly, and Germany – which had boomed because of a flood of American loans – was one of the worst-hit countries when the US imploded. And the man who benefited most from this confluence of historic events was Hitler.

Until 1929, Hitler had been a fringe figure in German politics, bordering on a crank. His cocktail of antisemitism, anti–Versailles Treaty and pro-nationalist stances had led his National Socialist Party to loss after loss. In the 1928 German elections, the last before the Great Depression hit, the Nazi Party received just over 2 per cent of the vote – making them only the ninth-largest party in Germany and one whose vote total was barely a quarter of that of the German Communist Party – and less than a tenth of that of the moderate Social Democratic Party, which won the election. In a Reichstag of 491 seats, the Nazis had 12.

But the Great Depression provided an entirely unexpected and unpredicted transformation. Suddenly Hitler's rhetoric of anger and blame appealed to masses of the population, of all classes, who were deeply fearful for their own future. By the election of July 1932, with the Great Depression in full flow, the Nazi vote total had risen astronomically to just over 37 per cent of all votes – making them the largest party in the country. When another election four months later confirmed that they were now the largest party in Germany (though their vote share actually declined, to 33 per cent), Hitler was invited to lead a coalition of parties as the new chancellor.[24]

Hitler's individual psychopathology was perfectly placed to cause, and then determine the course of, the most destructive war in human history. Though there has been some deliberately provocative discussion about whether Hitler was doing anything other than following a slightly exaggerated version of traditional German foreign policy, this is wrong.[25] Hitler was always planning on war breaking out under his leadership – the question only being the *when* and not the *if*. Having been a soldier in World War I, he was determined to 'save' Germany in the future through military conquest.

In his famous book *Mein Kampf*, dictated after his arrest in 1923 after a failed putsch, Hitler went to great lengths to explain why Germany had to expand. It needed more territory to settle Germans, grow food and provide markets for German goods, he stated. That territory would never be given to Germany – so the nation would have to take it.

> At this point the right of self-preservation comes into effect. And when attempts to settle the difficulty in an amicable way are rejected the clenched hand must take by force that which was refused to the open hand of friendship. If in the past our ancestors had based their political decisions on similar pacifist nonsense as our present generation does, we should not possess more than one-third of the national territory that we possess to-day and probably there would be no German nation to worry about its future in Europe.[26]

As the first part of his plan to unleash a war of expansion, Hitler had to first subjugate the Weimar political system to his personal wishes, which he did remarkably quickly. The Nazis blamed a Dutch communist for an arson attack on the Reichstag and called for a referendum giving Hitler dictatorial powers. It passed, and at that moment German democracy died.

Hitler then personally drove the process of rebuilding the German military and repudiating major parts of the Versailles Treaty that had ended World War I. He ordered the remilitarization of the Rhineland, which under the Versailles Treaty was to be left undefended so as to allow the French to march in quickly. Hitler also determined the course of the Anschluss (the militarized incorporation of Austria into Germany) and the annexation of the Sudetenland from Czechoslovakia, followed not long after by the seizing of the rest of the Czech Republic. Most of the time it was Hitler pressing the rest of the German government to put into action his schemes for expansion. When it came time to attack Poland in the summer of 1939, it was once again Hitler who was at the far edge, driving German policy down a road that he personally wanted.

While Germany was having its foreign policy choices determined by the prejudices of one extreme individual, the British response to these moves was being decided by a small group, in particular Neville Chamberlain. He was the youngest son of Joseph Chamberlain, the British leader who had talked about an alliance with Germany before World War I. Born into British political power, by the 1930s Neville was the one of the dominant figures of his time. Sometimes lampooned as weak because of his tremulous voice and fondness for dressing in old-fashioned winged-collar shirts, he was actually a tough and very successful political leader.

Prime minister from 1937 to 1940 (and very influential as Chancellor of the Exchequer for the six years before that), he became a byword for a political leader who is willing to make enormous concessions to avoid war – or an 'appeaser'. In some ways this charge is extreme, as Chamberlain was not as exceptional in avoiding war as Hitler was in pushing towards it. That being said, Chamberlain was personally and passionately convinced that Britain needed to avoid war throughout the 1930s for economic and domestic reasons. He believed that the impact of the Great Depression made war far too expensive to contemplate, and he was worried about whether the British population really had the stomach for another large conflict. Because of this, Chamberlain was willing to antagonize the United States by improving Britain's relationship with Japan, as he was convinced that the Japanese were more reliable allies than the Americans.[27]

When Hitler started pressing even more forcefully, breaking the Versailles Treaty and eventually taking over parts of other countries, Chamberlain decided at first that it was preferable to cut deals with the German dictator rather than oppose him. In 1938, for instance, Chamberlain *could* have threatened Hitler with war when the latter started agitating to take over the Sudetenland, which was populated mostly by ethnic Germans but had never been a constituent part of Germany. A territory of the Austro-Hungarian Empire until the end of World War I, it had been included in Czechoslovakia by the Versailles Treaty.

The Sudetenland was a crucial border region for the defence of Czechoslovakian independence. Moreover, Britain was pledged to fight for Czechoslovakia, and if it had chosen to do so then France and probably the USSR would have been willing to do so as well. While the Czechs were willing to fight, Hitler's only European ally who could have joined him – Mussolini – was not. Had World War II started in 1938, Germany would have found itself in a far worse strategic position than it ended up in when war broke out in 1939. Its army would have been bloodied, as Czechoslovakia was so well defended (which Hitler was a little stunned to find out about, after Chamberlain had betrayed the Czechs).

Chamberlain, however, was willing to trust Hitler enough to reach a deal and to compel Czechoslovakia to hand over the Sudetenland to Germany. This happened during the famous Munich Conference held at the end of September 1938. Chamberlain even thought it mattered that he and Hitler signed a meaningless pledge not to go to war with each other – a thin piece of paper that Chamberlain showed to the world as if it were some legally binding commitment. Hitler, by contrast, stated this 'piece of paper is of no significance whatsoever'.[28]

In trying to appease Hitler, Chamberlain had personally taken a major gamble with Europe's security. Some have argued that it made sense, as it allowed Britain about eleven more months to rebuild its military. The time gained, however, was not worth the strategic cost. Less than a year of extra preparation led to the end of the existence of Czechoslovakia, the Nazi-Soviet Pact and the isolation of Poland. Had war broken out at the end of 1938, Britain would have had more support to fight for Czechoslovakia, while Hitler would have been on his own.

Chamberlain had gambled and lost. Almost immediately after the Sudetenland was handed over, Hitler made it clear that this was only an appetizer. Even though he had solemnly told Chamberlain at Munich that he had no designs on the rest of Czechoslovakia, on 15 March 1939 he had the German Army march out of the Sudetenland and take the remaining Czech lands, including the capital, Prague.* This was too much even for Chamberlain, who decided that if Hitler made another attempt to expand Germany's borders, this time Britain would fight. When it came to Poland a few months later, Chamberlain was as good as his word. Hitler invaded on 1 September, and Chamberlain declared war two days later.

---

* Slovakia was allowed to break away and become an independent country, which promptly allied with Hitler.

So World War II, like World War I, started when and how it did because of the interaction of specific German and British leaders with their idiosyncratic (even sociopathic, in the case of Hitler) views of the world.

Leaders and Economic Power: Great Leaps Backward and Forward

China is today one of the two most important full-spectrum powers in the world, exercising influence over significant parts of the globe. With either the first- or second-largest economy in the world, depending on whether you are measuring GDP by raw terms or purchasing power,* China is the only nation that can challenge the US directly as an economic/technological force. China also has a large and growing military that is a unique competitor to American forces, which have dominated the globe since the collapse of the USSR between 1989 and 1991.

This rise, or more accurately re-rise, of China as a global power is something that outsiders speculated about for more than a century. From the nineteenth century onwards, European and American thinkers and policymakers wondered about the question. One of the people who speculated about the rise of China the most was Franklin Roosevelt. After World War II, the American president made sure that China was included as one of his global 'four policemen' who were to organize the post-war world – in part because he was convinced that China would soon become a global power.[29] China was given one of the few permanent seats on the United Nations Security Council as a sign of what it would become, not what it was at the end of the war.

Yet, in economic terms, China's rise kept being delayed. Though it was the most populous nation in the world, with large fertile areas and access to a wide range of natural resources, in per capita terms China remained one of the poorest countries in the world until the

---

* Raw GDP is the calculation of the total value of goods and services in a country. When it is adjusted for purchasing power parity (PPP), the difference in cost of different goods is used to alter the calculation. A country like China, in which things generally cost less than in the US, will end up with a higher relative GDP under PPP.

1990s. In 1976, for instance, China's per capita GDP income was a tiny $165.[30] It was far less wealthy than many African countries – including Nigeria, which was much richer at $562 per capita, and Kenya at $246 per capita.[31] The United States was in an entirely different economic league from China at this time, with a per capita GDP of almost $8,600 – a figure over fifty times as great.[32]

The rise of China economically since then has been astounding. By early 2024, its per capita GDP had grown by almost eighty times – to over $13,000.[33] The reason for such a remarkable change is at least partly down to the very different policy choices of China's two most important twentieth-century leaders, Mao Zedong and Deng Xiaoping.

Mao and Deng are both remembered positively in China today – heralded for helping build modern China up under the control of the Communist Party – and Mao is arguably more popular now than he was in the years immediately after his death.[34] Though Mao and Deng were both Communists, and willing to do brutal things to enforce their authority, when it came to economic policy they ended up taking China down very different roads. Mao sabotaged Chinese growth for decades, and when he died in 1976, China was one of the poorest states in the world. It was Deng who instituted the policies that helped create the economic powerhouse that either is or soon could be the largest economy on earth.

Mao Zedong was arguably the most successful and at the same time most destructive leader of the twentieth century – a century that saw many terribly destructive leaders. He was a charismatic figure who excelled at taking and exercising power, and he used these skills to dominate the Chinese Communist Party for almost all of his life. A founding member of the party, Mao helped devise the military and political strategy that saw them grasp power over all of mainland China by 1949.

At this point, however, Mao revealed himself to be economically and socially catastrophic. He seemed motivated by two things in particular – both reinforced by his decades of struggle to control the Communist Party and seize power in China. The first was a predilection for extreme Communist Party ideology – a form of utopianism, and control over the nation.[35] The second was a powerful desire for self-preservation and the eradication of those he thought were his enemies. The result was periods where he enforced extremely destructive policies that delayed Chinese economic modernization, killed millions, and left China lagging behind as other states grew.

The two most famous of Mao's periods of national self-harm were the Great Leap Forward and the Cultural Revolution. The Great Leap Forward was his attempt to show the world that China was ready not only to overtake the Soviet Union economically, but also to compete with advanced western states.[36] It saw him press the country into mass collectivization in agriculture and the establishment of small light industries wherever possible, in a fantastical attempt to supercharge Chinese growth.

The result was human misery on a grand scale. Completely untrained peasants were instructed to create small factories, and many villages built primitive blast ovens to try to smelt metals. In many cases they simply melted down all the pots and pans and miscellaneous pieces of metal, such as door handles, that they could find. The steel they usually created was a useless blob of poor-grade metal that had no purpose in a modernized industrial economy.

At the same time, the push to create mass agricultural communes ended up seeing food production slashed (a situation made worse as many places no longer had pots and pans in which to cook their produce). Transport also broke down under the strain of all the different upheavals. Soon the countryside was gripped by widespread starvation as Mao's economic masterplan unravelled spectacularly. It is estimated that as many as 30 million Chinese citizens died through starvation and deprivation during the Great Leap Forward (which lasted from 1958 to 1962), making it one of the greatest man-made catastrophes in human history.[37]

When the Great Leap Forward ended, China had, if anything, fallen further behind. This set the stage for the second of Mao's periods of personal-rule disaster. The Great Leap Forward was such a failure that he had temporarily lost influence within the Communist Party. A new, modernizing group (including Deng Xiaoping as one of its leading figures) tried to relieve the terrible situation Mao had precipitated. They loosened some state control and brought some calm after Mao's enforced chaos. In a very short period of time, Deng and this less radical group became dangerously popular in Mao's mind; so powerful that they represented a threat to his control over the party.

Mao decided to restore his position and influence by unleashing another period of profound ideological insanity, the Great Proletarian Cultural Revolution – usually called the Cultural Revolution.[38] Starting in 1966, he empowered a mass of mostly younger cadres in the Communist Party to call for ideological purity, and let them loose to purge those who had shown dangerously moderate tendencies during the period when Deng and his group had influence – and many others besides.

Over the next ten years, the Cultural Revolution saw teachers, scientists, engineers and other educated people who were crucial to the functioning of the Chinese economy denounced, tortured and even killed because they were considered to lack ideological conviction. Often labelled reactionaries by roving packs of young party cadres whose only guiding principle was devotion to the works of Mao himself, those persecuted might be singled out because of how they looked, what they had supposedly said, or simply because they seemed too well-off. The results were monstrous. Though the amount of people directly killed by the Cultural Revolution is still debated, at least 2 million seems the best estimate.[39] And tens of millions, maybe over 100 million, were greatly affected by the extremist events.

One of those targeted was Deng himself. A Communist Party member since his teens, Deng had studied in Moscow and become a devotee of Zhou Enlai, who was second in command under Mao and generally believed to be less bloodthirsty. Deng was also a strong supporter of Mao's party, but he tempered this with a streak of pragmatism – never an easy balancing act in the early decades of the People's Republic of China. Having had to 'pick up the pieces' after the Great Leap Forward, Deng became suspect in Mao's eyes.[40] He thus swiftly fell from power when Mao launched the Cultural Revolution,[41] and was packed off to work in a tractor factory in rural China, disappearing from public view. Deng's son was also mercilessly targeted, eventually leaping from a window in a possible suicide attempt which left him a paraplegic.

For Mao this was all to the good. He intended to use the Cultural Revolution to regain power – and if millions had to suffer and the Chinese economy crumble, so be it. And regain power he did. From 1966 until his death in 1976, Mao was the unchallenged leader of the Chinese Communist Party and the state. Even in his last years, when his mind was clearly failing, no one represented a serious threat to his rule. He had won, and died from natural causes in his bed – to be lionized as one of the greatest figures in Chinese history. Today, when you visit the Forbidden City, the great imperial palace that dominates Beijing's central Tiananmen Square, you will be greeted by an enormous portrait of Mao, slaughterer of millions, looking down at you with the most self-satisfied of smiles.

The reality was China had suffered greatly because of Mao's rule, and its development had been severely delayed. When he died, China was one of the poorest societies in the world with a dysfunctional ruling Communist Party and a surprisingly weak military. But Mao's death would allow the implementation of an entirely different set of economic policies, under a new leadership dominated by Deng Xiaoping. This change in leader would go a long way towards creating the Chinese economy that we see today.

After years of keeping his head down, Deng was brought back to Beijing under the protection of Premier Zhou Enlai in 1973. However as long as Mao was still alive, Deng's position was tenuous. When Mao died, Deng moved with great speed to take over control of the Communist Party. By 1977 he was back as a central figure and would soon come to dominate over Mao's chosen successor, Hua Guofeng.

As Deng accumulated power, he was careful to destroy much of the impact of Mao's policies without destroying the reputation of Mao the leader.[42] He discredited the Cultural Revolution while praising other elements of Mao's rule, famously saying that in retrospect Mao's leadership had been 70 per cent good and 30 per cent bad. In reality, Deng acted more like it had been 70 per cent bad and 30 per cent good. What he started doing almost immediately, and then accelerated greatly, was to open up the Chinese economy in ways that would have been inconceivable to Mao. Deng allowed trade with the outside world to grow and interjected market forces into economic relationships, both within China and via trade with the outside world. He helped upgrade Chinese technology through imports, and even allowed foreign investment into the country – thus beginning the process of ending the Communist Party's direct control of all economic production.

On the other hand, what Deng maintained was the dominant position of the Chinese Communist Party politically. If he was not the slaughterer of millions that Mao had become, he was still determined to preserve control and ruthlessly clamped down when the party's rule seemed threatened by pro-democracy forces. This happened most famously in the Tiananmen Square crackdown of 1989.

It was a moment when much of the world seemed to be about to embark on the process of liberal democratization. Soviet control over its Eastern European neighbours was weakening. Oppressed by decades of Communist rule, the peoples of Poland, East Germany, Czecho-slovakia, Hungary and Bulgaria started challenging their rulers. Something similar seemed to be happening in China. Starting in April 1989, tens of thousands of protestors, many of them students, started gathering in Tiananmen Square and calling for greater freedom. By May, it was said that upwards of a million people were participating in the protests.[43]

At first, Deng and the Communist Party seemed uncertain about how to react and did not interfere much with the demonstrations. However, by June, as the protests continued, Deng and the party had had enough. Believing that the activities in Tiananmen Square rep-resented a threat to their ultimate authority, they sent in the army to crush the protests and even kill the protestors.[44] The result was a massacre – not one of Mao proportions, but still mass murder on a ter-rible scale. It is estimated that about 10,000 people were killed when the army moved in.[45]

The crackdown showed the limits of Deng's liberality. It was all fine and good to make money and do business on capitalist terms, but it was unacceptable to threaten the political control of the Communist Party. Deng had instituted a new model that moved beyond Mao and set the stage for the China of today.

It must always be remembered that, in devising his policies, Deng was also motivated by the desire not to make what he saw as the great mistakes of another famous figure of the 1980s – Mikhail Gorbachev, the leader of the Soviet Union's controlling Communist Party. Gor-bachev, like Deng, believed that rigid Communist Party control over his country was leading to relative decline. What he followed was a course of limited intellectual liberalization and openness, centred on the controversial policies known as *glasnost* (openness/transparency) and *perestroika* (restructuring). Gorbachev was hoping that by injecting limited doses of freedom into the USSR and its allies, he could invig-orate their economies. He failed.

Gorbachev and his policies were largely responsible for various

Eastern European states breaking away from Communist Party control, a few months after the Tiananmen Square massacre. Once it was stated that the USSR would no longer exert military force to keep Communists in power, the whole edifice of its imperial rule collapsed. In late 1989, most famously with the fall of the Berlin Wall, revolution swept the Communist Party from power in East Germany, Poland, Czechoslovakia, Hungary, Bulgaria and eventually Romania. Gorbachev could have tried to stop these revolutions occurring with the large Soviet Red Army, but in the end he chose not to.

Such leadership differences are central to understanding the world we live in today. How and why China became as economically developed as it has, and when it changed, while always operating under the control of the Chinese Communist Party, owes a great deal to the specific choices of Mao Zedong and Deng Xiaoping. On the other hand, how and why the USSR, considered a superpower in the Cold War, lost its Eastern European empire and eventually ceased to exist is down to Soviet leadership decisions (which also directly influenced Chinese thinking).

And this reveals one of the poverties of the theoretical understandings of power relationships. Power can be very personal. It can be erratic and selfish; it can be destructive or far-sighted. One thing it is not is consistent. By trying to stress similarities in the behaviour of different states, theorists miss out on this and have provided a bland – and I would argue ultimately simplistic – model of how a state will act at any time. While it might not be fashionable to stress the role of individuals, which has sometimes been denigrated as the 'great man' view of history – fashion is flawed. What we are seeing in the world today is Donald Trump, Vladimir Putin and Xi Jinping determining the policies of their nations to a significant degree, and we would be foolish to ignore that reality.

And what guides the policies of Trump, Putin and Xi is not some shared template to maximize power in an unstable world; it's the basic societal and structural limitations in which they operate. Even very powerful, dictatorial leaders can at times attempt to implement policies that their societies and national political structures either oppose or lack the ability to fulfil. The result of that can be disastrous leadership.

3. Society and Structure

The US and China are the two economic/technological behemoths of the moment. They are the largest two economies in the world, as well as being the two largest scientific powers. They also possess the two largest and most powerful militaries with arguably the most advanced technological equipment. Their relationship is fraught, and they are engaging in a series of dangerous competitions/confrontations. They disagree directly over the Chinese claim to the South China Sea, which China is trying to enforce by militarizing the region and the US is openly rejecting by sailing naval units in the area.* They also seem regularly poised to enter into a trade war, as China exports far more to the US than vice versa, and that has powerful political resonance in Washington. In the 2024 presidential election, the victorious candidate, Donald Trump, made a great play about entering into an economic confrontation with China to reduce this trade imbalance.†

Beyond these issues, the fate of Taiwan looms as a constant flashpoint between the two states. The island of Taiwan is both a territory claimed by China and a long-time ally of the United States. It is also one of the most important parts of the modern world-economy – more than 60 per cent of the world's computer microchips are manufactured there.[1] Its future is of strategic interest to both China and the US, and both are concentrating more and more military force in the Indo-Pacific.

The eventual course of this struggle between the US and China

* The Chinese claim to the South China Sea, sometimes referred to as the 'nine-dash line claim' based on the maps put out by the Chinese government, has been rejected by the World Court. However, the Chinese refuse to accept this ruling and are enforcing their claim regardless.
† At the time of writing, the Trump administration has just taken office and seems to be operating a much less confrontational policy with China than had been talked about during the campaign.

will be determined by many things. Their relative economic performance could be telling if they do end up going to war. The difference between Chinese and US leadership has also had a great impact on the course of events in recent years. Xi Jinping, who became the General Secretary of the Chinese Communist Party in 2012 and president of the PRC in 2013, has played a powerful role in pushing China to assert its claims to both Taiwan and the South China Sea. His rhetoric around the latter has become increasingly more bellicose, and it seems to be such a personal crusade that many believe that Xi, now in his seventies, is determined to bring Taiwan back under direct Chinese rule before the end of his life.

The United States, meanwhile, has had a peripatetic policy towards China. There have been periods of more traditional interaction, under the presidencies of Barack Obama and Joseph Biden, during which the US tried to work with its allies – including Japan and South Korea as well as Taiwan – to deter China from attempting to change the status quo in the region too aggressively. Then there was the first presidency of Donald Trump, which added a fascinating element of instability. Trump was economically far more threatening to China, but when it came to the US military position in the region, much less concerned. Trump during the 2024 election campaign and at the start of his second term articulated an outlook that made Taiwan seem less strategically important to the US and reframed it more as an economic competitor. It made a US military intervention to try to protect Taiwan from China seem far less likely than before.

However, just as important so far and going forward are the fundamental societal and structural differences between China and the US. Both full-spectrum powers have distinct societal characteristics when it comes to education, beliefs, political affiliations and the like, which have created two different societies when it comes to supporting state policy and being appealed to by state leaderships. The structural differences involve how the various elements that make up a governmental system (its bureaucracies, competing power centres, etc.) can at least attempt to influence policy. Even dictators have to see their policies implemented by a political structure – they can't just wish them into operation. Democratic leaders are usually even more constrained, having to operate within a governmental system that has created other power centres.

China's leadership policy is a result of the continuing dictatorial dominance of the Chinese Communist Party (courtesy of Deng Xiaoping) that has allowed for one man, with a particular agenda and a determination to see it through, to stay in power for an extended period. This stands in contrast to the US political system, which can see major changes in tone and substance every four years depending on who is elected president. That being said, their respective governmental systems impact the interaction between China and the US in many ways that are distinct from just the selection of leaders and their tenures in office. The dominance of the Chinese Communist Party can be said to be both a blessing and a curse for China's attempts to assert itself internationally. It has allowed for major decisions – such as the shape and extent of China's military build-up – to be taken quickly and enforced. It has seen, for instance, China going from possessing a small and not particularly powerful navy in 2000, to having more ships commissioned than the US in 2024. On the other hand, dictatorial systems are prone to major inefficiencies and even corruption, as those in power either enforce their prejudices or take advantage of their position to fulfil personal wishes. Having spent massive amounts on China's military build-up, starting in 2023 Xi Jinping launched a new, major crackdown on those responsible for much of the work, imprisoning three major defence department officials and a host of lower-ranked ones.[2] Many were detained for 'serious violations of discipline' – a regular euphemism that the Chinese media uses for corruption.

The US system is certainly far from corruption-free. There are signs that certain elements of corruption, such as direct payments to the family members of presidents, even presidents themselves, are far from uncommon and could be growing. There is also the question of inefficiency in defence spending which means the US spends far more than it must for political reasons. The American political system means defence funding is spread around the country, and this can lead to massive amounts being allocated to very high-end systems such as the F-35 fighter jet. However, at the same time, it can sometimes lead to the relative ignoring of basic sustainment and support capabilities such as the manufacture of artillery ammunition – which was exposed in early 2022 as being far too low.[3]

The US has also allowed certain vital strategic industries to wither, most remarkably shipbuilding. While China has become the largest shipbuilding country in the world, the American domestic shipbuilding industry has all but disappeared. In early 2023, for instance, Chinese shipbuilders had 1,800 ships on their order books, while the US had only five.[4] This extreme imbalance has led to the lopsided situation that while the US fields a powerful force of modern aircraft carriers, it certainly could not quickly manufacture either new carriers or the vessels needed to support them to replace those lost in war. It would be the reverse of the situation in World War II. Then, the US had the ability to manufacture far more new shipping than any other power. Now, China is in that position.

Finally, there is the tricky but important question of societal pressure. Dictatorial states have a way of seeming united in peace, but not always delivering in times of war. We have no idea how the Chinese population would react to a longer-term war – would it be wedded to supporting the goals of the Communist Party and fight hard, as German society did for Nazi Germany? Would it mostly keep its head down and go about its business (a common trait in dictatorial societies that we are seeing now in Russia during the Russo-Ukrainian War)? Or would it turn on its master, as was seen in Fascist Italy in World War II?

For the US, societal pressures also play a massive role. American society seems torn between a strongly populist faction, which supports a form of neo-isolationism that would severely restrict the US deploying military power overseas, and more internationalist elements that still believe that the US has a constructive role to play as an alliance leader and world power.

Overall, structural and societal factors have and will continue to play a major role in determining the outcome of the current stand-off between the US and China. The issue is that determining how the different factors will do this, both on their own and through their interaction with economic and leadership elements, is very difficult to anticipate. One of the best ways to see just how influential these factors can be, however, is to look back at periods of power confrontation and transition over the past 150 years.

The Power Confrontation That Never Was

It is regularly said in international relations that periods of power transition are particularly dangerous.[5] Yet the greatest power transition in human history – when the sole 'superpower' of the nineteenth century gave way and was replaced by the great 'superpower' of the twentieth century – occurred without war or really even the prospect of war.* This was the transition between the period of British dominance and that of the United States. The implications of that peaceful transition at the pinnacle of the power tree are so great that it is commonly ignored in theory or passed off as an aberration (with little or no evidence).

At its high point in the mid-nineteenth century, Britain was the leading economic/technological power in the world. It possessed the largest and most advanced industrial economy, with high-technology leadership in areas such as shipbuilding and railways. It also possessed the most important and efficient financial markets in the world, which meant it could raise and spend funds with greater flexibility than any other nation. Its strength was such that it has been called the 'unchallenged' economic powerhouse of the era.[6]

These fundamentals allowed the British to assemble an impressive and flexible military force to fight for its global position. The key to this was the Royal Navy, the most powerful and technologically advanced military force on the planet, which also had an unparalleled chain of worldwide bases and a communications network that was the envy of the world.

Britain also had the largest empire in the world, with territories on every continent. At its greatest extent at the end of World War I, the British Empire had a population so large that it could not accurately be counted (it was between 400 and 500 million people) and it covered a space approximately equal to a quarter of the globe. At its peak, the British Empire was the largest empire the world had ever seen – by a long measure.[7]

---

* The War of 1812 occurred a half-century before the US was a direct rival of Britain economically and militarily. What is fascinating is that as the US grew in both areas, the possibility of war between the US and Britain declined markedly.

The British were willing to fight both internal and external forces to hold on to their pre-eminence. The empire itself was the scene of regular combat, from insurrections in India to large-scale conflicts such as the Boer War. When the British government looked outward they saw even more threats. They launched a pre-emptive war against Russia in the 1850s (the Crimean War) when they were unhappy with the Russian invasion of the Ottoman Empire.[8] The British also regularly threatened other powers who had the temerity to encroach on land that the British considered strategically important, including the French and Germans. They deliberately shaped the Royal Navy to allow them to triumph against any threat to their global position, maintaining policies such as the two-power standard or 160 per cent ratio to make sure that they could defeat any individual power (or even group of powers) that might threaten their maritime dominance.*

Except, that is, in one case. When it came to the greatest challenge they faced to their pre-eminence – from the United States – the British did nothing of note to try to confound their rival, even when they had the opportunity. It could even be argued that the British became one of the most important *supports* to the Americans as the US rose to global dominance. They allowed the US access to colonial markets and to borrow money liberally on the London exchanges. In other words, the British deliberately abetted the power that ended up displacing them.

And by much of international relations thinking, this should not have happened. The United States was exactly the kind of state the British should have bent over backward to restrain. It is hard to understate the challenge that the US presented to British supremacy. It was a growing economic/technological rival when it came to industrial production; New York's financial markets were a growing challenge

* The two-power standard, which came into being in 1889, meant that Britain should maintain a fleet at least as strong as the next two naval powers. This was aimed primarily at France and Russia. In 1909, this was changed to the 160 per cent ratio, which meant that the British should be at least 60 per cent stronger in naval terms than the second-ranked naval power – which in this case was Germany. These standards meant that the British maintained a comfortable naval dominance over any possible rivals coming from Europe or Asia.

to those in London; and after 1900, the US would even threaten British naval supremacy. The US represented a cultural rival to Britain's standing in the large and expanding English-speaking world. It also bordered the largest part of the British Empire (Canada), and was growing far more influential than Britain in the Caribbean and South America – which held other parts of the British Empire.

Looking at the situation from the US perspective, the British Empire represented an enticing target for national expansion – and the US was one of the most expansionist states in the world, particularly in the nineteenth century. At the time of independence in 1776, the US had been limited to a space north of Florida, east of the Mississippi River and south of Canada – in terms of geographic size, this was between a quarter and a third of the area it would control by 1900. In the intervening 124 years the United States acquired territory by purchase from France (the Louisiana Purchase) and Russia (Alaska), by fighting wars with Mexico and Spain, and by waging brutal military campaigns against numerous Native American peoples to secure more and more land.

Basically, the United States took or acquired whatever it wanted – except, remarkably, Canada. Admittedly, the United States did try this early in its existence, lusting after the vast, resource-rich area to its north. During the American Revolution the United States invaded Canada (unsuccessfully), and in the War of 1812 further attempts were made to seize it from the British Empire. However, at this time, the United States lacked the economic and military power to sustain a full-scale invasion, and the British were able to hold on.

In the second half of the nineteenth century, particularly from the American Civil War (1861–5) onwards, the US had the ability to seize the vast majority of Canada almost at will – but it chose not to try.* Indeed, what happened during and right after the Civil War was in many ways unique in the history of dominant full-spectrum powers – the US and Britain both had opportunities to try to reduce the other as a power and cement their own standing, and neither took the opportunity. It could be argued that this was the moment when the British

---

* Donald Trump in 2025 started talking about Canada as the 51st state, rekindling the idea that the US might incorporate its neighbour to the north. So far, however, signs are that he wants this to happen through economic war, not a military invasion.

decided to ease the process of their replacement as the world's greatest full-spectrum power by the US, and in turn, the US decided to help provide some assistance maintaining British power and the British Empire.

For the British, the American Civil War represented the best and arguably final opportunity to seriously impede the growth of the United States into the world's leading power (and provide security for Canada as part of the package). Had the Confederacy gained independence, it would have led to the breaking up of the US and the formation of North America into a version of Europe, with a number of significant powers balancing each other out: Mexico, Canada, the remaining United States of America, and the Confederate States of America.

There was a serious discussion amongst Britain's political elite about whether to help the Confederacy win its independence or not. The British prime minister throughout the Civil War, Viscount Palmerston, told Queen Victoria at the start of the war that the permanent break-up of the Union was inevitable.[9] The question was how Britain might aid this process (which Palmerston believed was in British interests). Ultimately, there were two potential ways of doing this. The first was full, diplomatic recognition of Southern independence, which would afford the Confederacy great legitimacy.[10] The other was through the provision of significant amounts of military and economic aid. If the British made a major effort to help the South in these areas, they could put enough pressure on the North that it would have to reach some kind of deal with the Confederacy. When the Civil War started, Britain was still by a considerable measure the largest manufacturing and financial power in the world, and could have provided the South with major material support and loans. At the same time, the Royal Navy controlled the world's seas and could have swept Northern trade from the globe and even blockaded Northern ports.

In the end, the British could not bring themselves to take the plunge and only stuck their toe in the water.[11] They provided the Confederacy with useful but far from decisive amounts of support. They sold them weapons, including some of the finest rifles in the world. They also built a number of warships for the Confederacy States Navy, most famously the CSS *Alabama*, and provided the South with modest diplomatic support such as during the Trent Affair. This was triggered in

November 1861, just a few months after the Civil War started, when a US naval vessel, USS *Jacinto*, stopped a British mail ship on the high seas and removed two Confederate diplomats who were travelling to Europe. The British reaction to this move was forceful, and they demanded that the US government, led by President Abraham Lincoln, release the two Confederates. Even though the North had celebrated lustily when the Southerners had been seized, and the two were considered open traitors to the Union, Lincoln thought it prudent not to antagonize the British too much this early in the war. In January 1862, he acceded to British demands and let the Confederates go so they could proceed in safety to Europe. It was a humiliation.

And yet, the British government could never bring itself to step in and fully aid the South to try to help it win. The idea of breaking up the United States, even if it would have been to Britain's benefit as a global power, was not something that appealed to large sections of the British population, including some influential business interests. Even the South's attempt to appeal to the British aristocracy, who they believed would naturally favour the Confederacy due to a shared love of elitism, ultimately fell flat.[12]

It was as if, deep down, Britain was reconciled to the growth of the United States. At the same time, the US accepted that it would not use its now dominant position in North America to try to take Canada. By the end of the Civil War, the power balance in North America had transformed. The United States had a large, battle-tested army and one of the largest navies in the world (if not the largest). It also had a highly efficient and large war industry that was capable of supplying any military force the country was able to raise. As such, if the US had chosen to invade Canada, the British would have found defending the Canadian border impossible. Yet even though there were some voices in the US that were calling for the seizing of Canada, the Americans and British cut a deal which set the stage for a basically cooperative relationship that they have maintained until today.

This cooperative relationship spanned moments which could easily have damaged it. Right after the war, the United States asked the British to pay for all the ships the CSS *Alabama* (built in a British shipyard) had sunk. After her launch in 1862, *Alabama* had gone on to capture sixty-five merchant vessels flying the Union flag (and sink one Northern warship).[13] This made the vessel a cause célèbre in the North, and when the Union won the Civil War, Northern society was determined to enact some revenge on the British who had built her.[14] Soon, the Northern government came calling with a request for compensation for the ships lost to *Alabama* and other Southern raiders.

This request was noteworthy, as the US – with much of its Northern population still angry with the British for their role in the Civil War – could have seized Canada in recompense (a move some senior US politicians might very well have approved). The British, on the other hand, did not believe that they were in the wrong. After years of quite delicate negotiations, the two sides eventually agreed on a financial payment to the US of $15.5 million, in lieu of the lost vessels.[15] The result of this tension showed both powers were keen to get along.

With the Civil War and its immediate ramifications out of the way, US–UK relations improved significantly. The late nineteenth and early twentieth centuries saw the two get along well enough that discussions of a 'special relationship' started to emerge. The two nations would occasionally squabble over issues such as influence in South America (the Venezuela Boundary dispute of 1895–99) or even the border between Canada and Alaska.[16] But although rhetoric could get temporarily heated, the disputes were always settled amicably through negotiation and even binding arbitration. There was often in fact a shared identification of interest – that as two democracies with at least some similarities in ethnic make-up, economic system and even outlook (such as a maritime orientation), their relationship was different than that between competing states.[17]

Over the course of the twentieth century the relationship became even more unusual. During the two world wars, for instance, the willingness of the British to do things to help the US grow to eventually replace them as the dominant full-spectrum power became turbo-charged. During World War I, the UK went on a spending splurge in the US, helping power the American economy to global dominance. They also took out massive amounts of loans from the US – and by the end of the war, London had lost a large amount of its financial supremacy to New York.

Something similar happened in naval power. When in 1916 the US passed a naval act that would make it the most powerful naval power in the world, the British reacted meekly. They publicly shrugged their shoulders and, when the US joined the war a year later, moved with the greatest of caution to try to convince the US that it was not worth it to build such a large fleet. Then, once the war was over, the British relatively quickly moved to abandon their long-held claim to naval supremacy, and were more than happy to negotiate – at the Washington Naval Conference of 1921–22 – an agreement that gave the US parity in the largest class of warships.[18] During World War II, the British went even further and sacrificed their economic independence to the United States. Britain basically abandoned all production for global export, focusing almost entirely on military production.

It might be said that Britain had to do these things because of the war with Germany, though it's worth putting that idea under the microscope. To defeat a lesser rival – Germany – the British were willing to acquiesce to a more powerful state, the United States, becoming even more powerful. This only makes sense if a society's leadership resides intellectually and emotionally in a world where war with the larger power is simply not to be contemplated.

And this illustrates the important role of society and structure, combined with leadership. What is striking is the unanimity showed by both Britain and the US that when it came to their relationship, the idea of a war between them was practically impossible. From Ulysses S. Grant and William Gladstone, to Theodore Roosevelt and Arthur Balfour, to Woodrow Wilson and David Lloyd George, to Herbert Hoover and Stanley Baldwin, and finally Franklin Roosevelt and Winston Churchill, what stands out about all these leaders is the consensus about the possibility, or more accurately the impossibility, of an Anglo-American war. There was an oft-expressed view that the leaderships and societies of Britain and the US shared values.[19] Even if this was romantic nonsense (and it partly was), it was widely believed, and this belief eased the process by which the two powers switched positions in the global hierarchy.

World War I might be the greatest example of this. From the moment the war started, there was amongst the American leadership an instinctive siding with the British, even if they were irritated, frustrated and at times ferociously angered by British behaviour and high-handedness. From President Woodrow Wilson to his closest adviser, Colonel Edward House, to the soon-to-be Secretary of State, Robert Lansing, Britain was seen to be in the right and Germany in the wrong (though the reality was a tad more complex than that). When the war broke out, for instance, Wilson went out of his way to outline his pro-British sympathies to the British ambassador to the US, Cecil Spring-Rice. Wilson told Spring-Rice, who then passed on his statements to Edward Grey, that Germany was to blame and 'everything I love most in the world is at stake . . . If they [the Germans] succeed, we shall be forced to take such measures of defence here as would be fatal to our form of Government and American ideals.'[20] Wilson went on to say that even though the US would remain 'officially' neutral, its sympathies were with the British.

And Wilson was as good as his word. During the war he could get extremely irritated with the British, and even denounce them privately. However, the Germans were always the real enemy. When the Germans started unrestricted submarine warfare, Wilson confronted them with a forcefulness that belied even-handedness. He made them back down, in essence setting a trip wire to get the US into the war on the side of the Allies if the Germans ever reverted. When the Germans did so, the US joined the war not long afterwards. Of course, compared to World War II, this was slow. As soon as France fell in May 1940, President Roosevelt determined to do everything possible to save Britain. In this he was supported by a large part of the US population, who did not want Britain to be conquered.

To see the importance of society and structure in the development of the international power balance, it makes sense to contrast what happened between the US and Britain with what happened the next time two full-spectrum powers confronted each other. This, of course, was the Cold War, which lasted from some time in the late 1940s (I favour 1948 as the starting point) until 1989.

Society and Structure Win the Cold War

The United States was at one of the two heights of its position as a full-spectrum power at the start of the Cold War (the other was at the end). It was arguably the greatest full-spectrum power in human history at these times. In 1945, the US was economically dominant in a way that no state had ever been in world history, or has been since. At the end of World War II, its economy was larger than those of all the other major warring powers combined,[21] and it had hoovered up most of the world's gold supply. To go along with that, the US had relatively strong social cohesion and a political system that shared a consensus view that the US needed to become a global power, and featured competent, skilled leadership at the tops of both of its main political parties. For instance, Harry Truman (president in 1945–53) had a team that included at various times some of the most experienced foreign and strategic policy practitioners in US history, including his Chief of Staff William Leahy (who had been Chief of Naval Operations, ambassador to France, and then Franklin Roosevelt's Chief of Staff and Chairman of the Joint Chiefs), George Marshall (who had been Army Chief of Staff and would serve as the president's special emissary to China, and then Secretary of State and eventually Secretary of Defense) and Dean Acheson (who served as Assistant Secretary of State, Undersecretary of State, and eventually Secretary of State).

The United States possessed and was further developing the most technologically advanced military on the planet. Militarily, it was the only state that possessed the atomic bomb until 1949. It also had absolute dominance over the world's seas, controlling them in a way that was completely new, with more naval power than the rest of the world combined (the second naval power in the world was Britain, who remained committed to working with the US, and there was no legitimate third naval power worth discussing). Meanwhile, in the skies its aircraft had the longest range, heaviest bombloads and greatest armament.[22] Essentially, the US could single-handedly cut off trade almost anywhere – and, if it wanted to, it could literally vaporize any enemy city or military facility on the planet. There would be nothing that the country attacked could do in order to strike back.

It is worth reflecting on that period because, even with this dominance, the United States did not try to maximize its power within the international system. It easily could have deconstructed the domination of the Soviet Union – an aspirational full-spectrum power – in Eastern Europe. At the end of World War II, the USSR controlled Poland, Czechoslovakia, Hungary, Bulgaria and Romania, none of whom wanted to live under Soviet domination and the first two of whom were some of the original victims of Nazi brutality. As the USSR did not have the atomic bomb until 1949, the United States could have used the threat of a nuclear attack to force the Soviets out – however, this was never seriously contemplated.

The restraint shown by the US set up the paradigm under which the Cold War would eventually be decided – societal competition, with no direct war between its greatest protagonists. And for a while, it looked like a closer-run competition than it ended up being. If the USSR was a full-spectrum power, it was an odd and severely limited one. It showed, eventually, it had the capacity for a large, if not always efficient, industrial economy. The USSR became, for instance, the world's largest individual producer of steel during the Cold War. In 1974, the Soviet Union passed the US in terms of national steel production – and maintained this lead into the 1980s.[23] It was also producing huge amounts of coal, pig iron, and oil. Overall, the USSR used its impressive industrial output to produce far more weapons than the US, outbuilding the Americans in tanks during the Cold War by a factor of many times.

The USSR was also a scientific leader in certain areas, particularly theoretical research, and parlayed this scientific excellence – combined with its ability to procure advanced western technology through espionage – to make some notable advances. In 1949 it became the second power to explode an atomic bomb, reaching this milestone years before the US believed it would (though much of technology was learned from spying on US operations such as the Manhattan Project). The USSR then went on to win the first part of the space race by sending a satellite, Sputnik I, into earth's orbit months before the United States, shocking the Americans.

And the USSR was able to translate some of its technological excellence into military hardware too. In the late 1940s it developed arguably the best jet fighter of the early Cold War period. The MiG-15 was the first successful swept-wing jet fighter, and it was fast and highly manoeuvrable. It was also very heavily armed, and when it first met US jet aircraft in combat, during the Korean War (1950–53), it outclassed its American rivals. It could be argued that for the first two or even three decades of the Cold War, the story was one of the USSR closing the gap with the United States.

But then, remarkably, in the 1970s, when the USSR was passing the US in steel production, it was also entering a stage of relative decline. This was probably because while its power was in heavy industry, a new technological era was beginning – the computer revolution. From that decade on, the use of computers at home and work exploded, leading to a wholesale transformation of products of all

types, from automobiles to weapons. It was the computer processor
that really ushered in the explosion of ranged, precision weapons for
instance (the kinds of weapons that would determine the course of
any war in the Indo-Pacific today). Basically, it could be said that the
world – and world militaries – moved from a period where industrial
strength could determine the ultimate power a state could deploy, to
one where processing excellence and technological innovation mattered just as much, if not more.

The USSR simply could not compete in the silicon revolution,
due to a combination of society and structure working together to
hold back the needed economic dynamism. Politically, the rule of the
Communist Party disincentivized the creativity needed for technological change and adaptation.[24] State control of practically all aspects
of economic life meant that the kind of disruptive thinking needed
to create an Apple Computers or a Microsoft simply didn't exist. The
decline of oil prices also deprived the state of funds. Widespread com-
plaints started emerging about 'sloth, corruption and drunkenness' in
Soviet society.[25]

When the political leadership tried to rectify the situation, they
failed miserably. In the early 1980s, the USSR was still under the
control of Leonid Brezhnev, the General Secretary of the Communist Party. His rule has become a byword for ossification, so much so
that Gorbachev later referred to it as an era of 'stagnation'.[26] Brezhnev
spent the last years of his life becoming increasingly frail and lethar-
gic, before dying in 1982. There followed a tragicomic two and a half
years when two more general secretaries rose to power – first Yuri
Andropov and then Konstantin Chernenko. Each was old and ill when
he was appointed, and each lasted a little while before also expiring –
which seemed a metaphor for the Soviet governmental system.

Eventually, the leadership of the party ended up in the hands of someone younger and far more dynamic: Mikhail Gorbachev. Gorbachev
wanted to invigorate the Soviet system, to make it more competitive with
a US-led western bloc that he understood was more dynamic. He instituted the policies of glasnost and perestroika, to spur internal openness.
He also borrowed billions and billions of US dollars to import advanced
goods to try to kickstart the ailing Soviet economy.[27] All that did, however, was lead to unsustainable levels of debt.

No matter what Gorbachev tried, the system could not be saved.

Even when President Reagan tried to improve US relations with the Soviets by negotiating the strictest nuclear arms control agreements in history, it made no difference.[28] Indeed, in opening Soviet society up, all Gorbachev had done was probably hasten its demise.[29] By providing people with hope of a freer future, he released long pent-up resentments in Eastern and Central Europe that led to the collapse of the outer layer of the Soviet empire. In the end, without a shot being fired between the US and USSR (at least in a declared war), the Soviet Union lost the Cold War because socially and systemically it could not keep up with its western rivals.

At the same time, US society was proving itself far more resilient than expected. From the late 1960s, there had been talk of relative economic and strategic decline becoming a major problem for the US.[30] Japan and Western European states were growing economically faster in many cases, and the USSR was catching up as a nuclear weapons power. One of the reasons, for instance, that Richard Nixon wanted to withdraw American forces from Vietnam was his belief that this US decline was leading to national weakness and division. If anything, these worries grew in the 1970s. The rise of other powers (interestingly, the economic risers were US allies Japan and West Germany) coupled with the expansion of communism to different states in the global south made the US seem less secure. And the oil crisis of that decade showed that, economically, the US was far more vulnerable than many had supposed.

On Lagging

Even as the USSR was entering its death phase in the late 1980s, there was a discussion about how the US was also in serious trouble. This debate even had a very important academic element. In 1987, Paul Kennedy published *The Rise and Fall of the Great Powers*, which made very depressing reading for the US. He argued, in a book that became a bestselling phenomenon, that the US was undergoing a process of relative power decline similar to Britain in the early twentieth century and Habsburg Spain in the sixteenth and seventeenth centuries. The reason for this decline, Kennedy said, was the great expense and effort that the US was putting into maintaining its global position.

This expense, which was part of a historical pattern that bedevilled states who reached the top of the power tree, meant that resources were taken away from productive elements and spent wastefully on military adventures – what Kennedy termed a process of 'imperial overstretch'. Imperial overstretch, it was argued, was going to hold back the future growth of the United States, unlike those states such as Japan and Germany, which were not hampered by the need to waste resources on excessive military spending or fighting foreign wars. For Kennedy, the rise of Japan up until the 1980s was down to the fact that its defence was taken care of by the US and thus it was able to 'redirect its national energies from militaristic expansion and its resources from high defense spending'.[31]

And yet, in the end, the US did not decline and Japan did not continue rising, even though the US started spending more and more on defence and Japan hardly spent anything. In fact, from the late 1980s US power saw relative growth. Not only did the USSR collapse, but those supposedly unburdened by overseas commitments – including Japan and Germany – starting lagging behind the US in terms of economic growth. The US was now poised to enter the second period of its greatest relative power: the 1990s. Once again, it would not only have no economic competitors worth speaking about, its military strength was unchallengeable.

This period of relative rise for the US was as societally and structurally driven as was the decline of the USSR. The US, which was frankly lagging in industrial output, took control of the computer revolution, leading to the creation of an entirely new set of industries (which arguably still dominate the world today). From the 1980s onwards, US high-tech began to relentlessly take over much of the world's economy.[32] From computer software and hardware, to the machine learning of today, the US created the companies that defined the new technological era. In 2024, the six largest high-tech companies by market capitalization were all US-based, and all globally recognized: Apple, Nvidia, Microsoft, Amazon, Alphabet (Google) and Meta (Facebook).[33]

The end of the Cold War between the US and USSR, and the results of the subsequent relative economic competition between the US and Japan and the larger European states, demonstrated how society and structure can shape the outcome of power competitions. And the USSR was a stunning example of how these elements can lead to a rapid (and mostly unforeseen) decline in power. However, the post-Cold War era has also shown how various and unstable the different elements of society and structure can be. Arguably all the major powers that determined the course of the Cold War, especially from the victorious US-led coalition, have had their power positions shaped by societal and structural impulses.

One of the most fascinating examples is what happened to the large states of Europe. If one believes imperial overstretch is what leads to relative decline, Europe was poised to be a powerhouse at the end of the Cold War. Except for a small smattering of imperial possessions, European states had spent most of the previous fifty years shedding the empires they had worked so assiduously to collect. They also cut back their defence spending to the bone with the end of the Cold War – so much so that the US, which spent far more, became rather annoyed. Many European states also remained on the cutting edge in many high-technology areas, with educated populations and well-developed economic infrastructures. In Germany, Europe had an economic engine that was one of the world's great trading powers; in London, it had a growing financial powerhouse; and there was the prospect of integrating Central and Eastern Europe into its orbit. To this day all of Europe combined is economically only modestly smaller than the US and is still larger than China.

And yet Europe has consistently underperformed as a power, for reasons of society and structure. While there is a political grouping, the European Union, which contains most of the continent's nations and economic power, it is hampered by a structure that severely limits its freedom of action, particularly in the military sphere. The nation states retain a large amount of their independence and, as Brexit showed, can actually leave the EU in a relatively easy (if self-harming) process. Moreover, much of Europe's population, not surprisingly, prefers to live with the relatively extensive social safety nets, shorter working hours, more vacation time and earlier retirement ages that they possess in comparison to the US. This 'work to live, not live to work' attitude seems significantly more healthy (Western Europeans have longer lifespans than Americans), but seems to have gone hand-in-hand with a relative economic decline vis-à-vis the United States. It has also been accompanied over the last three decades by a massive decline in research and development (R&D) and military spending in comparison to the US, as European nations have prioritized domestic spending in their budgets.[34] The overall result has been that, between 2010 and 2024, European economic growth was more than 50 per cent slower than that of the United States.

The awareness of European decline is well spread. The European Union even commissioned a report on the subject, written by former Italian premier Mario Draghi and published in 2024, which pulled no punches on the perils facing Europe:

> Europe has been worrying about slowing growth since the start of this century. Various strategies to raise growth rates have come and gone, but the trend has remained unchanged . . . For most of this period, slowing growth has been seen as an inconvenience but not a calamity . . . But the foundations on which we built are now being shaken.[35]

This relative decline has led to a pattern of constant strategic failure, with Europe punching below its weight. From a catastrophic intervention in Bosnia in the mid-1990s (which was supposed to herald the Hour of Europe)[36] through a continent-wide split over how to respond to the American-led War on Terror, Europe has been uncertain, divided and often inconsequential when it comes to hard power choices. Politically there has never been clear leadership of the continent, and societally many European states seemed to believe that another real war on the continent was inconceivable. As such, military spending plunged after the Cold War, so that by 2015 many European states were spending only 1 or 1.5 per cent on defence. The impact of European states to undertake military operations deteriorated markedly. It has been estimated that, since 2000, Europe has lost about 35 per cent of its military capabilities.[37] It took the Russian invasion of Ukraine in 2022 to kickstart a noticeable change in the outlook of many Europeans. However, even then, military spending still lags considerably behind that of the US.

These issues of society and structure have also determined how Europe reacted (or in many ways failed to react) to the Russian invasion of Ukraine. Though the results of the Russo-Ukraine War will have greater impact on the future of Europe than that of the US, the European response was hesitant and divided from the start. Having outsourced their strategic thinking to the US, European states were not able to act in unison to safeguard their vital interests (once again calling into question the idea that there is a clearly defined national interest). Some, such as the Baltic states (Estonia, Latvia and Lithuania), the Nordic countries (Finland, Sweden, Denmark and Norway), Poland and the Czech Republic were keen to aid Ukraine to win the war. Some, such as Germany, were generous in providing Ukraine with defensive weaponry, but didn't want to push Russia too much. Many others were in the middle between these two – or even less interested. The result was that even though the European states combined had the economic and technological resources to help Ukraine win the war, their response was halting and uncertain.

If Europe's struggles have been the most dramatic, sometimes the changes can be more gradual. That was certainly what happened with Japan, which in many eyes seemed on the cusp of becoming a direct economic challenger to the US in the 1980s. In fact, fear of Japan became so marked in that decade that the phenomenon of politically attacking the Japanese, or 'Japan bashing', was commonplace.[38] But after decades of stunning growth, which made Japan the second-largest economy in the world by the late 1980s, Japan's relative economic growth slowed remarkably (and unexpectedly) in the 1990s and has stayed relatively low since. Indeed, depending on exchange rates, not only has Japan been passed by China (hardly a surprise) but also recently by Germany.

This relative decline has resisted any attempt by different Japanese governments to change the downward trajectory. No matter how much money has been spent to accelerate growth, or how low interest rates have been kept at different times, the Japanese economy has been slowly but regularly slipping. At least one of the reasons that changing course has been so difficult for Japan shows how one relentless element of societal change has an important impact on power development – demographics.

Starting in the late 1980s, Japan's population has been becoming very old. The large numbers of people born in the early and mid-twentieth century began reaching retirement age and, thankfully for them, living a long time. (By 2023, more than 10 per cent of Japan would be eighty years old or older.[39]) In some ways, they were one of the luckiest groups in the world. One of the longest-lived and healthiest cohorts of elderly people in history, this large demographic bulge could look forward to a long retirement. However, Japan did not have the growing population to compensate for all the people leaving the workforce, and moreover the state had to pay more to keep the retired population going.[40] Japan's birth rate was well below replacement levels – a situation which continues today.

As the Japanese could not or would not countenance utilizing immigration to make up the gap between workers retiring and workers starting, the result was a steady relative decline in economic growth. This societal demographic drop is not limited to Japan. It affects many of the developed countries in the world, from South Korea to various European states. There are even signs that the Chinese economy is slowing as its population ages and the replacement workforce is much smaller than the number of those retiring or dying.

In some ways, the exception to this development has been the US. Because of a strong flow of immigrants, much of the impact of a declining domestic birth rate has been mitigated. US economic growth is usually amongst the highest in the economically developed world, and it has maintained a strong relative economic advantage in terms of major high-tech companies. And yet, the US has become more divided and made a series of disastrous foreign policy decisions – from the War on Terror, which culminated in the shocking and amateurish withdrawal from Afghanistan in 2021, to the bungling of an opportunity to deal with Russia (and through that, China) after Putin's decision to launch a full-scale invasion of Ukraine in 2022.

Looking back at the world over the last 125 years, what becomes clear is that society and structure play a major role in determining power development and relationships – but there is no obvious pattern as to how they do so. There is no easy formula to understand how these factors will shape economic/technological power. It is much easier to count military equipment such as tanks, aircraft, UAVs, etc. – or even to compare economic size or discuss the choices leaders make. However, to do so without taking into consideration the influence of society and structure often leads to the worst analytical flaws.

4. Constructing a Military

Vladimir Putin had built one of the most awesome and effect-ive military machines in the world. It was armed with cutting-edge weapons – including state-of-the-art aircraft, new and powerful tanks, and supersonic precision-guided missiles – that would give it a decisive advantage over its Ukrainian foe. It had honed its skills through excel-lent training and practising military manoeuvres, and had developed new and impressive doctrines to inform its actions.

In February 2022, this force was thrown against Ukraine. The Rus-sians had gathered thousands of tanks, thousands of artillery pieces and hundreds of their most advanced aircraft, and also controlled the Black Sea with their naval forces. This juggernaut was assembled on the Ukrainian border in preparation for what analysts called a Russian 'shock and awe' campaign.[1]

The Russians would surely be showcasing their skills in com-plex operations. First, they would bombard the Ukrainians from a distance, disabling Ukrainian command and control communica-tions. Then, ruling the skies over the battlefield against the outclassed Ukrainians, the Russians would smash through whatever resistance the Ukrainian Army could muster. The results of this campaign were surely a foregone conclusion. The Ukrainian military would be severely degraded in the opening hours; Kyiv, the Ukrainian capital, would be surrounded in days; and the whole campaign would prob-ably be over in weeks.

The Russian military was judged to be so powerful because of all the money that had been spent on it and the excellent equipment it supposedly possessed. Starting around 2008, it had been modernized at vast expense, in what is sometimes referred to as the New Look reforms. The amount spent on the New Look military is not entirely easy to estimate, as the Russian government is not exactly transparent. Still, it is thought that somewhere between $150 billion and $180 bil-lion were allocated to create a more powerful Russian military.[2]

Of course, the invasion of Ukraine did not turn out like this at all.

The Russian Army revealed itself from the moment it crossed the border as considerably less than the sum of its parts. It struggled to execute complex operations, showed itself deficient in basic tasks of military competency such as logistics, and soon foundered, finding itself overextended. The Ukrainians, meanwhile, fought back with intelligence and determination. And though they were not armed with nearly the level of advanced equipment possessed by the Russians, they used what they had to stymie the more powerful force, eventually driving it back from Kyiv and pushing the Russians out of more than half the ground they had seized when the campaign started.

How could the analytical community – from governments to think tanks – so completely misunderstand what the Russian and Ukrainian militaries were capable of doing? These were supposedly deep experts in the field with unsurpassed knowledge of military power. And yet with all their expertise they failed to understand that the Russian military was a deeply flawed institution, and the Ukrainian military was poised to fight with great determination. One of the fundamental problems is that the analysis focused on the Russian military in and of itself, and not on the larger factors that had created that military. A military needs first to be understood as a product of all the other elements possessed by the state that created it – its economic/technological prowess, the choices of its leadership, and the society and political structure from which the military emerges. Indeed, stepping back and looking at these elements gives a better idea of how a military will operate than adding up its tanks or discussing its doctrine or military manoeuvres.

One of the best examples of the importance of these underlying factors, and the problems unleashed by not considering them properly in strategic analysis, is the underestimation of corruption as a factor in the functioning of the Russian military. It has been widely known that corruption is societally endemic in Putin's Russia. With many officials – including those in the Ministry of Defence – owning grand yachts and villas while supposedly getting paid official salaries, it might be said that corruption has been the lifeblood of Russian military procurement. In 2011, the Russian state estimated that 20 per cent of its military budget was lost to corruption.[3] Some have estimated that in reality this number is far higher.[4]

Yet the analysis of the Russian military before 24 February 2022 rarely mentioned corruption, and when it did it was to say that this was a problem that had been corrected. Of course, this was nonsense. You can't simply eradicate something that is societally endemic from an institution as large and well-funded as a military. Indeed, corruption played a significant role in exacerbating the institutional failures of the Russian military. But in the end it was the Russian soldiers who suffered from this corruption the most.[5] In Ukraine, the invading forces were eating food that had expired years earlier, riding in vehicles that had not been maintained, often lacked the basic equipment needed to communicate, and even fought in vehicles whose protective armour had been stripped to sell for profit.

If corruption is one of the reasons that the Russian military punched well below its weight, though its impact was almost entirely discounted by analysts, the opposite was the case when it came to Ukraine. Corruption was seen as a much greater problem for the Ukrainian military – indicative of how, while larger societal, leadership and economic factors were rarely used in the analysis of the Russian military, they figured regularly in the analysis of the Ukrainian military. Ukrainian society was also said to lack the cohesiveness and identity to resist, and this would supposedly be a particular problem in the east of the country. Many Russian-speakers resided in the region (there are fewer now that the Russian military has killed or driven many away), and it was stated that the population would either accept or quickly reconcile itself to Russian rule.

As it was, many preferred to fight and die for their ability to remain Ukrainian.

The totality of the errors in the analysis points to a methodological crisis in the understanding of military power. There never has been an agreed way to judge a military, which is a fundamental problem in judging national power. Many analysts and scholars assessed the Russian military primarily through simple metric understandings: how much military equipment it had, and with what supposed capabilities. This led them to make extraordinarily specific prognostications as to how efficiently and effectively the Russian military would perform.

This is as true of all the large militaries of the last 200 years as it is of the Russian military before the invasion of Ukraine. Indeed, looking at the different national militaries as they were constructed and prepared for the two world wars and the Cold War, and now in the post-Cold War period, it is safe to say that the constituent elements of a power tell us more about how effective a military will be than raw numbers of equipment, military doctrine and the like.

Preparing for World War I

When it comes to the size of armies, for instance, metrics can be downright distorting. If the number of armed soldiers is what matters, then World War I should have been a very short conflict. In the years leading up to 1914, the Allies (Russia, France and Britain) assembled far larger armies and navies than the Central Powers (Germany and Austria-Hungary). Including those on active duty and reserves who could be mobilized, the Russians were by far the largest land force in Europe, and when they were added to the French and the small British armies, the advantage of the western allies was approaching two-to-one. This was a numerical advantage they would retain during the war.[6]

Even within alliances, army size was deeply deceptive. The Austrians during the war maintained an army that was more than half as large as the German Army. However, the Austrian force was poorly led and funded, meaning that when it came to combat, it was considerably less effective, man for man, than that of its German ally.[7] Its losses ended up being close to those of Germany – with a much smaller army.

So, if the numerical balances explain very little about how the militaries of Europe were poised to perform in World War I, what *does* explain it? When it came to the armies, the German Army was *tactically* superior to the rest – particularly when compared to the Russians. And the reason for their success in engagements had much to do with some overall strengths in the structure that created and underwrote the German military.

These areas of strength include the training of soldiers and non-commissioned officers. While training could be harsh, it also stressed the importance of initiative being exercised down the chain of command.[8] The German Army kept its soldiers in relatively good physical shape, and fostered a corps of experienced NCOs who were often given the responsibilities possessed by junior officers in other militaries. The officer corps in the German Army was a high-status profession, with officers often coming from the landed gentry, and it maintained (for the time) a high level of professionalism. The German High Command, though strategically lacking, was well drilled in commanding large numbers of troops and undertaking large operations. Moreover, the training and manoeuvres of troops were an issue that received a great deal of coverage and attention, involving even the Kaiser.[9] Overall, the German military was kept at a high state of readiness to go to war quickly if the opportunity presented itself.

In material terms, Germany's significant economic development provided a number of important advantages. Its rail network, one of the best in Europe, allowed the quick movement of troops from one part of the country to the other (which would prove quite useful a number of times during World War I). Moreover, the army, due to Germany's leading position as an industrial power, was in relative terms well equipped, from small arms to artillery.[10] Compared to other economies (other than the British), Germany could count on manufacturing large amounts of shells and ammunition for its forces.

Overall, the German Army was well constructed to win battles – which it did regularly in World War I. That being said, it suffered from major weaknesses that prevented it from winning wars. These included poor strategic thinking from its top leadership and a severe underinvestment in logistics, which would hamper operations regularly in the war and keep the army from being able to exploit its success in individual engagements.

The Russian military was constructed neither to win battles nor to win wars. Its one great advantage was the sheer number of soldiers, but beyond that it struggled with training, morale, equipment, command and logistics. The average Russian soldier was amongst the least educated in Europe, with high levels of illiteracy, while Russian training was basic and stressed obedience to authority.[11] Unlike more advanced European militaries, the Russian Army put little stress on developing an effective NCO class. And Russian equipment, while showing signs of improvement going into the war, was lacking in quantity and quality compared to that of more economically developed states. Russian command and control was extremely hierarchical – starting from the very top. Tsar Nicholas II was not only *de jure* commander-in-chief, he decided to play the role at the front during parts of the war – a job he was not able to handle. Russian logistics were also more primitive – the army had very few trucks (and would gain few during the war), and the Russian railway network was not as dense or well operated as the German. The result of all these deficiencies was slowness in mobilization and movement and – when the Russians met the more advanced German Army – disproportionately high casualties.

To see the gap between the two, we can jump ahead and look at the first large campaign that the Germans and Russians fought after the war started, during which the much smaller, but more cohesive and better-equipped, German Army soundly defeated a much larger Russian force that could not fight with nearly the same kind of effectiveness. This was the campaign that culminated in the famous Battle of Tannenberg in late August 1914, and it reveals just how little raw numbers matter in understanding military strength.

For the Russians, this campaign was the main focus of their operations. They had promised their French allies that they would invade Germany within fifteen days of the start of the war, which they did. However, with their logistical operations disorganized, instead of invading with 800,000 men, as promised, the Russian First and Second armies that crossed into Prussia had less than half that. Still, the Russians significantly outnumbered the German forces in the theatre by almost three to one: 485,000 Russian soldiers to 173,000 Germans.[12]

For the Germans, this was now a secondary theatre. The main effort was ongoing in France, where the bulk of the German Army, as part of the Schlieffen Plan, was aiming to quickly knock France out of the war. But even though they were greatly outnumbered in the east, through their better logistics, training, and command and control, the Germans were able to complete the complex and fast manoeuvres needed to pull off a stunning victory. The Russian forces were split into two wings that were too slow moving to meet up, and the Germans were able to concentrate on the Second Army, which they caught on its own just inside the German border. In the end, the Germans decimated the Russians, inflicting up to 90,000 casualties while losing fewer than 15,000 themselves. A whole Russian army had basically ceased to exist.[13]

In many ways, the story of Tannenberg is the story of military effectiveness on the Eastern Front in World War I. Though the Russians almost always had forces that were larger by far, when they went into battle against the numerically smaller – but more efficient, better trained, led and supplied – Germans, they usually emerged defeated. By 1917, the Russian Army had had enough, and it turned on its leadership and led the way to the Russian Revolution. A minority part of the German Army had brought the (numerically) largest army in the world to its knees.

If World War I shows that raw numbers can be deceiving, the preparations for World War II show how leadership preference – combined with society and structure, and economic/technological capacity – can create very different militaries with very different capabilities. Indeed, looking at the militaries of the main powers – the Germans and Japanese on one side, Britain and the US on the other, and the Soviet Union switching between the two – it's clear just how different each force was, and how a combination of leadership, society and structure accentuated these differences.

The German armed forces were very much created in the vision of Adolf Hitler, a World War I infantry soldier with first-hand knowledge of the trenches but almost nothing else. Hitler had come out of that war with a conviction that attacking the enemy's army was how wars were won, and the best way to do that was to focus on firepower and not mobility. As such, the Wehrmacht he constructed in the 1930s, and which he unleashed on the rest of Europe in 1939, was built to win battles – but not to win wars.

The Luftwaffe was one of the largest air forces in the world when the war started and its equipment and ethos very much reflected the leadership preferences of both Hitler and Hermann Göring, the Luftwaffe's commander-in-chief. However, the German air force also had a strictly limited utility, as it was only able to engage effectively in tactical attacks against the armed forces of another country (as opposed to strategic attacks against an enemy's economy). It had a range of aircraft with some strength but also some noticeable weaknesses that undermined the exercise of German air power. Its best fighter, the Messerschmitt Bf 109, was a nimble aircraft with excellent flying characteristics. And yet it had a very short range. Its fuel capacity was so small that after flying over the English Channel from France, the Bf 109 could only fight for about ten minutes over southern England before it had to return to base.[14]

The Luftwaffe's bombing force was made up of relatively light, two-engine aircraft that could actually only deliver a relatively small amount of ordnance. Its most famous aircraft at the start of the war, the dive-bombing Ju 87 Stuka, was a severely limited, drastically over-rated aircraft for precisely this reason. It was slow, single-engine, and capable of carrying a very small bombload. If undisturbed and allowed to attack when it wanted, a Stuka could deliver its ordnance with a high degree of accuracy. It was able to do this during the German conquest of France in 1940, when it gained its fearsome reputation. However, when the Germans turned to the strategic war against Brit-ain after the Fall of France, their military in general and the Stuka in particular failed spectacularly. The short range of the German fight-ers and the small bombloads of their bombers meant that their losses in aircraft became unsustainable, while their ability to damage Brit-ain's war-making capacity was minimal. While pictures and newsreels spread worldwide that seemed to show plucky, undermanned Britain fighting against a German aerial behemoth, in reality the Luftwaffe could do little to damage Britain's war-fighting potential. Lord Bea-verbrook, the Minister for Aircraft Production in Winston Churchill's government, wrote to a confidant during the height of the Battle of Britain that 'looked upon as a serious military operation', the effects of the German air attacks were 'small'. He went on to add: 'Production in the factories is affected more by the sirens than by the bombs and not much by either.'[15]

The situation of the Luftwaffe was repeated for the army and navy. Hitler decided before the war that the German Navy, even after the submarines had shown themselves to be very effective in World War I, should be based around heavy, expensive battleships with large guns. Interestingly, as chancellor, he had at first shied away from building many warships at all. Hitler had wanted, or so he said, peace with Brit-ain. During his first few years in power, he seemed to actively pursue an Anglo-German alliance, believing that Germany as a continen-tal land power should be a natural friend to Britain with its overseas empire and maritime concerns.[16] However, once Hitler understood that Britain was not going to be his ally, he decided to build a large fleet after all. And it was to be dominated by large surface vessels, par-ticularly battleships.

As a huge believer in the value of the heavy artillery he had seen in action in World War I, Hitler wanted his navy to be armed with the largest guns possible – and he got his wish. In February 1939, six months before the invasion of Poland, Hitler approved a building plan that would see Germany pour resources into the construction of eight super-large battleships (*Bismarck* and *Tirpitz* were the first of these) to be completed by 1944, to say nothing of the eight heavy cruisers to be completed by 1945.[17] It was a fleet that, in the end, would play little role in the war.

And finally, there was the German Army – the organization that most reflected Hitler's personal vision of war. With his experience of trench warfare, Hitler was convinced by firepower over mobility – and that is the army he created. It had a strong artillery force (and the aforementioned air support) but very few trucks with which to move forward. This meant that, throughout the war, much of the army was left having to advance (or later retreat) by foot – or, if they were lucky, horse. The German Army would thus fail logistically during some of its most famous campaigns, such as the invasion of the USSR in 1941.

Hitler's predilections also created a specific German military via his production policy. Worried about keeping the German people devoted to his rule, both in peace and war, he was actually very slow to expend resources to increase German military production until well after the war started. He continued to devote a huge amount of the economy to civilian goods, to make sure that people experienced as little deprivation as possible. The result was that Germany was an industrial laggard during the first few years of war. During the Battle of Britain, the British outproduced Germany by a factor of three when it came to aircraft. Moreover, when Hitler attacked the USSR, the Soviets were able to significantly outproduce the Germans in tanks, even with the dislocation to their heavy industry.

If Hitler is an extreme example of how an individual leader can create a specific military in his own image, his Japanese allies show how important political structure can be in creating a specific military. In the case of Japan, what stands out is the fact that the army and navy were basically self-governing and practically disconnected services – each free to construct the force they wanted without much regard for the other (or indeed for the wishes of Japan's civilian leadership).

For the navy, this structural independence led to the construction of some of the most extreme warships ever built – the *Yamato*-class battleships. Determined that they were to have a qualitative lead over any other fleet, the Japanese Navy decided to build even bigger battleships than Hitler. The result was *Yamato* and *Musashi*, each of which weighed about 70,000 tons and was armed with eighteen-inch guns. The large US-built *Iowa*-class battleships, which were laid down after *Yamato*, weighed fewer than 50,000 tons and sported sixteen-inch guns. It was an extreme gamble for the Japanese Navy – and one they lost. They ended up with the two largest battleships in the world just as the battleship was slipping into relative obsolescence in the face of the aircraft carrier. *Musashi* was sunk by US aircraft off the Philippines in 1944 and *Yamato* off Okinawa in 1945 – the latter going down without ever having sunk a US warship.

If the Japanese Navy's peculiarities led to the construction of these enormous white elephants, its societal impulses led it to do something just as self-defeating when it came to submarines. The Japanese had the makings of one of the most effective submarine forces in the world when they attacked Pearl Harbor and started World War II in the Pacific. They had excellent long-range boats and some of the best and most reliable torpedoes in the world. These submarines could have posed a massive challenge to US shipborne logistics, which had to sail supply vessels over many thousands of miles of ocean to reach American forces in the western Pacific. However, the Japanese warrior code, which prioritized attacking enemy military forces, meant that the Japanese Navy never did any such thing. It basically gave the US a free pass on logistics for much of the war – with disastrous results for Japan.

So, the militaries of both of the largest Axis powers were created and utilized with major flaws due to the peculiarities of their different leaderships, societies and structures. Japan's political structure led to particularly poor communication amongst the services. Hitler's personal preferences played an outsized role in determining what equipment and in what amounts it was provided to the German Army, while at the same time his desire not to make the German population feel the pain of war too much kept military production down for the first years of the war.

The same elements all interacted for the largest Allied power as well – the United States. The huge military machine that the US built and threw at the Germans and Japanese was very different from any other military in the world – and not just in scale. It also reflected

Franklin Roosevelt's view of what made for good politics and good war-making.

Roosevelt, a sea power obsessive his whole life, had long believed that the United States needed to control the seas to win wars. He later added aircraft to his understanding of strategic war when he saw their potential during World War I. He thought on the whole the US should avoid large land battles whenever possible – and when they were unavoidable, to keep casualties as low. He wanted them fought with machines first and foremost. In this way Roosevelt was the world's greatest practitioner of what might be called industrial/political warfare – using machines to control the movements of supplies and goods around the world, while using soldiers as little as possible. He even tried to educate the American people about his vision of war in his State of the Union address in January 1942 (just a few weeks after the Japanese attack on Pearl Harbor).[18] Don't get impatient, Roosevelt told the public:

> We know that modern methods of warfare make it a task, not only of shooting and fighting, but an even more urgent one of working and producing. Victory requires the actual weapons of war and the means of transporting them to a dozen points of combat.

Roosevelt's specific outlook was seen in his very lopsided military build-up in the late 1930s, as he was preparing the US for the eventuality of war. He understood early on that Hitler represented a particular threat to the US – the destabilization of the entire European balance of power. However, he was not convinced that most of the American population shared his concerns (and he was right). So, he started a major military build-up from 1937 onwards to get the country ready to fight, while politically claiming the US could stay out of European wars.

What Roosevelt did with this build-up was focus the large majority of his efforts on naval vessels and later aircraft. His first move was to push for the approval of what became known as the Two-Ocean Navy – a fleet large enough that the US could fight Germany and Italy in the Atlantic and Japan in the Pacific, all at the same time. Starting in 1937–38, and then accelerating greatly in 1940–41, Roosevelt deployed the industrial resources of the country to start churning out enough equipment for the US to control the world's seas alone – if it came to that. The plan was to build a navy powerful enough to defeat all the Axis powers and, after 1940, an air force with more aircraft than the German and Japanese air forces put together. Roosevelt was so determined to give the US superiority in the skies, that in 1940 he set a production target of 50,000 aircraft by 1942, a figure larger than the Germans and British could have produced at the same time.

While Roosevelt was pushing air and sea construction, the US Army's build-up was lagging behind. In 1940, when the armies of France, Britain, Germany, Japan, Italy and Russia each had more than a million soldiers, the US was fielding only 269,000.[19] Even many small European nations had armies of approximately half a million.

Once the US entered the war in December 1941, Roosevelt had to decide how to harness US resources at a time of full mobilization. What he and the country did was probably the most successful modern example of a full-spectrum power in action. The US had the world's greatest economic and technological base, and as a political leader Roosevelt had a sophisticated understanding of the best (and most beneficial) way to fight and win a modern war. US society was also happy to do its bit, in the knowledge that its government would be using the country's economic might to equip its armed forces to the highest degree possible. Finally, its political structure allowed the US to actually do what its population and political leadership wanted, and declare war.

The first and in many ways foundational question that Roosevelt faced was how to strike a balance between US personnel in the military and those kept in industrial production, and at the same time decide what resources would go to the army, navy and air force (then the USAAF, as it was structurally still part of the army though with its own officers). It was arguably the most important strategic process of the war, as it determined where, when and how the US could fight the Axis powers. In the end, often against the strongly expressed wishes of his most senior general, George Marshall, Roosevelt prioritized the building of aircraft and naval vessels, and maintaining production at home over sending industrial workers off to war. The result was that the US fought World War II with a relatively small army, and a very large navy and air force. That being said, what it really fought the war with in all three services was machines, machines and machines – as it used equipment in lavish amounts to reduce the number of military personnel.

The small size of the US Army in World War II is sometimes overlooked, as it is assumed that the US had numerically powerful forces. However, the reality was that the US fielded an army of approximately ninety divisions, which in relative terms to the size of the population was very small. In 1944, for instance, in what is often seen as the peak year for US mobilization, there were fewer than 8 million soldiers in its army, out of a population of just under 140 million.[20] At the same time, there were more than 7.1 million in the German Army (Heer) and Waffen-SS,[21] out of a population of approximately 80 million.

But while the US had a small number of soldiers, relatively speaking, it possessed enormous stores of equipment. You can see this in almost every metric, but aircraft production is the most striking. Aircraft were the most prioritized pieces of military equipment in the war. Germany, for instance, devoted about 50 per cent of its war economy to the building and equipping of aircraft — far more than any other category. The amount the Germans devoted to all tanks and armoured fighting vehicles was somewhere between 5 and 10 per cent.

The United States had a roughly similar percentage in its war economy devoted to aircraft — but what the Americans did with this was far more impressive. They built many times as many aircraft and, moreover, the most expensive and advanced aircraft in the world — making certain technological leaps that would have been beyond any other nation. The B-29 Superfortress bomber was mentioned earlier, but the overall US aircraft excellence can be seen again and again. For instance, the US went into World War II lagging behind Japan in the design and production of aircraft that could fly from aircraft carriers. The Japanese were deploying the fast, long-range and hard-hitting Mitsubishi Zero fighter, which outclassed anything the US could deploy in 1941 and early 1942. However, in very quick time the US gained the upper hand. With the construction of the Corsair fighter in 1942 and then the excellent Hellcat fighter in 1943, the US gained ascendancy over the Zero — part of its process of destroying the Japanese Navy in the Pacific.

The massive amounts of money the US spent on equipment and the relatively small army it fielded led the US to fight one of the most extraordinarily lopsided (in a good way) wars in human history. Even though the US was basically on the offensive for the entire war after 1941, and fought in every domain (land, air and sea) against all Axis countries, its armed forces suffered extraordinarily low casualties. The US suffered a total of 416,800 military deaths. The Germans suffered more than ten times this – 5,533,000 deaths – and the Japanese more than five times the US figure, at 2,120,000.[22] For the USSR the figure was so large that it is hard to know exactly, but would have been between 8 million and 10 million military deaths – twenty times (or more) the number for the US. The American figures for military deaths are so startlingly small that they were actually more like Yugoslavia's or Hungary's than all the other larger powers'. It was a loss rate that makes the US military effort arguably the most efficient per soldiers lost in combat in modern military history.

So, in the end, all the militaries that were built before and during World War II were different because of questions of leadership, society and structure. The difference was how these elements combined to take advantage of the economic and technological resources at their disposal.

After World War II: The Non-Military Powers that Could Have Been

Many powerful states have suffered catastrophic defeats in their history – and that includes modern history. France at the end of Napoleon's reign, and then when invaded by Hitler in 1940, was overrun by enemy forces. Germany in 1918 was forced to agree to a humiliating armistice, and disarm. And yet, in almost every case, such defeated nations have rebuilt their armed forces as soon as possible, often within years or at most a decade, and their leaderships have tried to re-establish them as significant strategic actors.

This did not happen to Germany (specifically West Germany) and Japan after World War II. In a spectacular development, both the Japanese and West German economies rebounded astoundingly quickly. Building on pre-existing networks and capabilities left over from the war, by 1950 both countries had put in place the necessary reforms to launch their economies as major forces in the world.[23] In the subsequent decades, Japan and Germany developed production facilities that rivalled and in some ways surpassed those in the US, to say nothing of the United Kingdom* and France, and started bringing to the market heavy equipment as well as some of the most technologically advanced goods in the world. Their domestic consumption went up markedly, but even more impressively, the two became arguably the most important international trading states in the world. These changes were so remarkable that a recent historian has labelled them 'miracles'.[24] And the economic charge lasted well into the 1990s – even compared to the US. Even as late as 1995, using GDP as a metric, the Japanese and German economies combined were actually larger than that of the US.[25]

What would normally have happened, if we lived in a world where all states wished to maximize their power in an unstable and chaotic world, would have been that Japan and West Germany would have tried to become major military powers and to extend their strategic sway. They both had the economic/technological power to do so, and both had powerful enemies right on their doorsteps – the USSR/Russia for West Germany (then Germany after 1990), and China for Japan. And yet nothing of the sort happened – arguably up until today, eight decades after the end of World War II.

In fact, as they were economically strengthening, the two states neither spent much on nor cared a great deal about their military capacities. In many ways, they were actively de-emphasizing military power. Certainly West Germany spent some money on defence during the Cold War, when the USSR had a massive army on Germany's border with the express aim of overrunning the country. But even then, starting from 1975, German defence spending began to fall considerably, from approximately 3.3 per cent of GDP to 2.6 per cent by 1988.[26] And with the end of the Cold War, German defence spending collapsed. By 2005, it was down to only 1.1 per cent of GDP, making Germany relatively the lowest spender of all the large economies in

---

* To help with the confusion between the British Empire, Britain and the United Kingdom, British Empire will be used when referring to the entire empire including Britain, Britain will be used regularly as shorthand for England, Scotland, Wales and Ireland/Northern Ireland in the world wars, while United Kingdom will be employed for the period after 1945.

Europe – with only Japan being lower amongst the large economies in the world.

The extraordinarily small amount that the Japanese spent on defence in the Cold War and afterwards is probably unique in the history of full-spectrum powers. Even though the Japanese constitution limited Japan's defence budget to only 2 per cent of GDP, Japan never approached even this small amount. For the last two decades of the Cold War, its defence spending averaged less than 1 per cent of GDP, and the end of the Cold War made no meaningful difference.[27] Even though the Chinese economy and later military grew in size and capability remarkably after 2000, Japan was still spending only 1.1 per cent of its GDP on defence in 2022. Germany, meanwhile, was only slightly higher, with a spend of 1.4 per cent in the same year (making Germany one of the lowest-percentage spenders in NATO). While both stated that they plan to spend more in the future, they seemed in no rush to fulfil plans to spend 2 per cent of their GDP on defence. Germany did not cross the 2 per cent threshold until 2024, two years after the Russian invasion of Ukraine.[28] Japan, on the other hand, is not scheduled to reach this threshold for all national security spending until 2027.[29]

The examples of Japan and Germany show how society and structure can make a huge difference in limiting the creation of military power. In both cases, the results of World War II seem to have created an entirely different societal paradigm through which to view defence. For Japan, which was even the second-largest economy in the world between 1968 and 2010, defence would be outsourced to another country (the United States). This was even more extreme than the basically cooperative relationship between the US and Britain during the last half of the nineteenth century, when they were the top two powers in the world. The Japanese were not even trying to be a strategic power. And what is remarkable is that this has continued long after any World War II hangover should have persisted. The war ended more than seventy-five years ago, long before most of Japan's current population was born. Clearly something societally changed in Japanese perceptions, and this has been maintained regardless of which party or leader is in power.

In many ways, the same situation has persisted in Germany – though interestingly it seemed to embed itself many decades after the war rather than immediately after. When the Cold War was over (indeed, starting a few years before it was over), the Germans basically outsourced their security as much as the Japanese. The slashed defence spending and reduced capabilities transformed it from the largest military power on the continent of Europe to a country with a decrepit, barely capable military.

And then the Germans went one step further. They basically decided to hugely augment one of their greatest continental security threats by making their own economy reliant on sources of fuel from this threat, which also required Germany to pump billions of dollars into that threat. Thus Germany chose to make its economy reliant on energy from Russia.

And Germany continued to do this even after Russia invaded Ukraine in 2014, seizing Crimea and parts of the Donbas. This illegal seizure prompted the placing of sanctions on the Russian economy – sanctions Germany ostensibly was following. However, that did not seem to stop the Germans from assembling a large economic stake in Russia between 2014 and 2022. Maybe most famously, this was exactly the time that Germany helped support the construction of the Nord Stream 2 pipeline, which runs from Russia, along the floor of the Baltic Sea, to Germany itself.[30] The pipeline was heralded as a cheap and efficient way of bringing Russian natural gas to Europe, and had it ever been put into operation, it would have made Germany almost entirely dependent on Russia for its energy.[31] The cost of Nord Stream 2 was $11 billion, with the Germans paying a large share.[32]

At the last minute, however, the Germans were saved from this energy vassalization not by their own actions, but by Putin's second invasion and US pressure. With the pipeline close to being finished, Putin launched the full-scale invasion of Ukraine, which led to a suspension of the whole project (and later an attack on the pipeline itself, which now sits broken at the bottom of the Baltic). In the end, the Germans were not saved by anything that they did; they were saved precisely because the power they were funding had constructed a military that, pound for pound, was one of the worst assembled in the history of military power. This brings us back to the start of the chapter. The army of Vladimir Putin was arguably the most overrated military force of the modern world, even more so than the military of Benito Mussolini in World War II, and the army of Tsar Nicholas II that the Germans handled so roughly at the start of World War I.

In fact, only one other mistake could rival the strategic overestimation of the Russian military by the analytical community. And that was the drastic underestimation of Ukrainian military power. If the Russians were considered militarily overwhelming, the Ukrainians were widely judged to be overmatched and seriously flawed. Their equipment was considered to be no match for the Russians technologically. However, what the Ukrainians lacked in equipment, they more than made up for with societal commitment. They fought back with intelligence and determination, and instead of lasting days they fought on for years, inflicting massive casualties and keeping the vast majority of their country free. Those, like President Biden, who assumed that Ukraine had no chance in its war, were soon changing their tune. As he said in a speech in Poland just a few weeks after the start of invasion: 'He, Putin, thought Ukrainians would roll over and not fight. Not much of a student of history. Instead, Russian forces have met their match with brave and stiff Ukrainian resistance. Rather than breaking Ukrainian resolve, Russia's brutal tactics strengthened that resolve.'[33] Three years in, the war had cost the Russians close to 1 million casualties.

What the Ukrainians showed in the power of their resistance was, once again, how looking at the outward manifestation of military power is deceiving. Even though the Ukrainians were supposed to be outgunned and facing a far more technologically advanced and capable enemy, they compensated for these deficits with a combination of better morale, better systems operations and better planning.

In some ways, of course, the lesson of the difficulty of judging militaries shown by the overestimation of the Russians and underestimation of the Ukrainians should have been no surprise (which makes the occurrence of these inaccuracies such a mystery). A military is so much more than the sum of its numerically countable parts. The largest and most powerful militaries, including that of a hegemonic United States, can be beaten in a war by a smaller, less powerful force. Technological advantages can be negated by simplicity; force can be countered by determination. Be it in Vietnam or Afghanistan, different forces can present such challenges to a larger military that the latter eventually decides the cost of fighting is not worth the benefit.

Ultimately, there is no one way to judge military power, but there is a guideline that should always be followed. Instead of looking at a military in and of itself — counting its equipment, reading its doctrine, discussing its weapons — look instead at the economy, leadership, society and structure that created it. Its strengths and its weaknesses will come from these.

Many of the most well-known full-spectrum powers have lost wars, sometimes spectacularly and comprehensively. Napoleon's France dominated Europe in a way that no power had since the Roman Empire. In 1812 he controlled a vast area that stretched from the west coast of Spain to the border with Russia, and south from the boot of Italy up to Scandinavia. But just three years later he had been vanquished twice by a coalition of European states that made a mockery of his vast empire. In the twentieth century, Germany was during the two world wars the dominant land power in Europe – and established control over much of the continent. And yet in both cases German dominance over Europe was incredibly short-lived. In fact, after its second attempt to control the continent, in World War II, the coalition of states that assembled to defeat it were so determined to end the individual threat posed by Germany that they cut the nation in two.

The strategic demises of Napoleon, Kaiser Wilhelm II, Adolf Hitler and later the USSR all came from the same basic element – their nations were overwhelmed by alliances of states that were collectively more powerful and determined. This reveals another one of the fundamental flaws in the great power view of international relations. The great power mindset divides up states between those who are supposedly so powerful they can do what they want, and those who are less powerful and must submit to their will. However, such a vision greatly inflates the individual strength of 'great' powers. Except in very rare cases of a hegemon so powerful that it can individually impose itself wherever it wants, states need allies and partners to achieve their strategic goals in both peace and war. In fact, one of the greatest tests of a power's abilities to harness its economic, leadership and societal strength is how it can translate all of these elements and use them to assemble and lead a larger coalition that can greatly amplify its security and influence. And failing in being able to create such an alliance can doom even the most powerful states.

Determining the First World War Before It Started

In 1914, Germany could have conquered any country (or two) on the European mainland – and probably had been capable of doing so for decades previously. After all, in the space of less than a year in 1870–71, Prussia – which was only *part* of Germany – had been able to invade and conquer France during the Franco-Prussian War. Since that time German power had only grown. Germany had become the second-largest industrial economy in the world (after the US) and deployed arguably the best army in the world.

Yet when Germany went to war in 1914, it was immediately in a very difficult position. It was surrounded by a much larger coalition of powers that included Britain, France and Russia. Moreover, Germany's own allies were rather limited in capabilities. Austria-Hungary, even though it had a large population, lacked the economic strength and societal cohesion to punch anything close to its weight. In the coming years it would at times be more a burden than an ally for Germany. Another of Germany's expected allies in 1914, Italy, looked at the state of the European coalitions and, at first, decided to stay out of the war altogether.

This revealed one area where Germany had constantly struggled since 1887 (when the Kaiser rashly abrogated the Three Emperors' League) and where Germany's strongest opponent in 1914, Great Britain, excelled – alliance-building. Indeed, it would not be unfair to say that the greatest difference between the two powers was that Britain before World War I was able to assemble a very powerful group of allies to support its strategic goals, while Germany had the support of a small number of strategic basket cases.

The success of Britain and the failure of Germany in alliance-building occurred for a number of reasons, one of which was that Britain had a greater understanding of how to appeal to the needs of its potential allies, while too often imperial Germany resorted to counterproductive strategies to try to get its way. British diplomacy in the decade before 1914 could be a textbook case of how a nation's leadership can properly diagnose its strengths and weaknesses and then pivot to work with other states – taking advantage of the former to make up for the latter. Thirty years before World War I, it was the

British who'd had an ally problem, and the Germans who were part of an excellent coalition that was looking after its interests.

The Three Emperors' League had tied Russia and Austria-Hungary into Germany's security, giving the Germans protection in the east and allowing them to keep their formidable armed forces aimed at France. Britain, on the other hand, had no allies of consequence on the European continent until after 1900 – with the exception of Portugal, with whom it had been allied by treaty since 1373.[1] However, Portugal was at this stage a small, relatively poor European state on the continent's periphery and had little ability to influence events in a great war. And not only did Britain lack allies, there was also growing enmity from much of the continent. France was its long-time rival for imperial power, and Russia was pressing down towards the British territories of India and in the Persian Gulf.

With the security of the Three Emperors' League, Germany looked at Britain with a form of strategic detachment. The Germans believed they had little to gain from establishing a strong security obligation with Britain, nor much to fear from British enmity. Otto von Bismarck, the legendary German chancellor who had helped create the league and was instrumental in humbling France in the Franco-Prussian War, reportedly said that if the British were foolish enough to send their army to invade, he would 'have the police arrest them'.[2]

For a while, however, the British did not believe it necessary to tie themselves to a continental army. Though the phrase 'splendid isolation' is sometimes used (incorrectly) to describe the period, until the end of the nineteenth century Britain did not consider making a serious pledge of mutual defence to a large European state. However, the outbreak of the Second Boer War in 1899, which came after a period of relative economic decline, made the hunt for allies take on a new edge. The British were a little surprised, and certainly concerned, to see how popular the Boers were amongst continental Europeans, understanding then how their imperial, naval and financial dominance had actually made them suspect in many minds.

To try to rectify Britain's strategic position, Germany was at first approached as a possible ally. When the attempt to reach an agreement with Germany failed, as much because of German reluctance as anything else, the British pivoted 180 degrees and started moving closer to Germany's two greatest European rivals – France and Russia.

It was a pivot that many, including the Germans, did not see coming. It had seemed for decades, indeed centuries, that Britain and France were mortal enemies – with a rivalry so fierce it would periodically erupt into wars so large they would result in the naming of new train stations or public squares. Only a few years before, the two had almost come to blows over control of the Nile basin, during the Fashoda Crisis of 1898. A pact settling their differences and launching them on the road to becoming allies would have seemed unlikely. However, in 1904, after the failure of alliance talks with Germany, the British swerved and agreed an entente with France – often called the Entente Cordiale.[3] This was no alliance at first, but a settlement of imperial differences (the French recognized British supremacy in Egypt and the British acknowledged French dominance in Morocco).[4] But what it did was set the ball rolling for closer and closer relations. Soon military talks were started between the two powers – talks that would culminate in them going to war together in 1914.

And an agreement between Russia and Britain might have seemed even more difficult to imagine. In fact, the Russians and British seemed perpetually on the verge of a major confrontation. Throughout the nineteenth century the two had crept inexorably nearer to each other as their empires expanded. The British moved their forces far into northern India, while the Russians progressively took more and more of Central Asia – often building railways that were financed with French money.[5] By the late nineteenth century they were almost touching – with Afghanistan being a borderland between these two expansionist, aggressive powers.

For Britain, this increasing proximity was particularly worrisome.[6] A railway from Russia to India would mean that the Russians could deploy a large army in the region – one that would be impervious to influence from the Royal Navy. The Russians were therefore a threat to the British 'Jewel in the Crown' in a much more serious way than any other power.[7]

The Germans were so convinced that Britain could never be friends with Russia and France that they first built up their new fleet specifically to hold the balance between these two blocs. They called it a 'risk' fleet, because they believed that neither Britain nor France/Russia would want to take the risk of Germany adding its fleet to the other side.[8] But then the British went ahead, and in a series of stunning diplomatic moves completely destroyed the German plans and upended the power coalitions of Europe. After negotiating the entente with France in 1904, which started the process of the two becoming full military allies in 1914, the British doubled down by signing an agreement with Russia three years later.

The agreement with Russia was particularly fascinating. The British, understanding that they had less ability to confront Russian forces heading towards India and also Persia (which was considered an important area of British interest), had started working strongly for a rapprochement with Russia from 1905 onwards. At first, this looked problematic, because Russia had just waged a war (unsuccessfully) against Japan – one of Britain's few allies. However, led by Sir Edward Grey, who believed that conflict with Germany was all but inevitable, the British government sent out lots of signals to the Russians that they were ready to make a deal.[9] The result was the 1907 Anglo-Russian Convention (sometimes also called an entente), which was not an alliance *de jure* but would evolve into an alliance *de facto*.[10] It was useful to Grey to use French words for his agreements with France and Russia, as that would help keep their ultimate meanings unclear. Though the Anglo-Russian agreement was far from an alliance (as was the Anglo-French entente), it meant that the British were now firmly ensconced with the French and Russians strategically. From then on, the military cooperation between the three countries would only grow.

Overall, the British move was one of the more successful and cynical diplomatic ploys of the pre-World War I era. By cosying up to Russia after first reaching an agreement with France, and also stoking tensions between Russia and Germany, Britain was able to provide some security for its empire and at the same time cement its growing friendship with Russia and France – while making Germany more of an enemy to both.[11] The agreements also seem to have led to an overall improvement in the Russian public's view of Britain.[12]

And so the British had taken their most problematic possible imperial enemy and turned it against their most worrying continental challenger. Through alliance politics, the British adjusted successfully to their relative economic decline and provided greater security and eventually the foundations of a winning coalition in World War I. But if the British were pulling off a masterclass in aligning alliance-building with protecting their empire and position, the Germans were a textbook case of how to destroy what could have been a winning European hand, through miscalculation and foolish bluster. The winning hand was clear: Germany had by far the best army in Europe (as it had demonstrated clearly in 1871), as well as the largest industrial economy from the late 1890s onwards. However, instead of using its power to consolidate its position at the centre of the continent and bring more states into its orbit, Germany frittered the moment away.[13]

It started in 1878 with the abrogation of the Three Emperors' League – a dangerous move in its own right. By leaving its alliance with Russia, Germany basically made the Franco-Russian Alliance possible – and practically inevitable. The military convention between France and Russia was duly signed in 1892. Germany was now sandwiched between possible enemies. However, that did not stop the Germans from antagonizing both of these powers further.

The antagonism of France and Russia by Germany often came with a healthy dose of embarrassment, which further cemented French and Russian hostility. The Germans, for instance, seemed to go out of their way to humiliate the French over Morocco almost immediately after the British recognized the French claim in 1904. In two North African crises, the first starting in 1905 and the second in 1911, the Germans challenged the French position in Morocco – behaving in a way that was frightening and yet also close to pointless. In 1905, for instance, during a Mediterranean cruise the Kaiser paid a visit to the Moroccan port of Tangier, which the French were claiming as part of their empire. Quite what the German government was trying to accomplish in challenging France in that way is hard to say; it might just have been an exercise of power for power's sake. As the Kaiser said at the time, 'You will have noticed that all Europe now does my will – in fear of me.'[14]

The move achieved very little except to drive the French closer to the British, something that was repeated in 1911. Then, a German gunboat appeared off Agadir, which was witnessing an uprising against French rule. It seems that the gunboat was part of an unplanned attempt to force the French to award Germany imperial concessions in other parts of Africa.[15] But it appeared an unthought-out gambit – unnecessarily threatening with no long-term plan behind it – and after a momentary diplomatic spat, nothing came of the incident.

When it came to the Russians, the Germans did a brilliant job of humiliating them in the Balkans. The whole story of the Balkan Wars before World War I shows the foolishness of building up weak allies while embarrassing stronger nations. The issue being faced was the rapid decline of the Ottoman Empire, which had ruled the southern Balkans for centuries. As Ottoman rule receded, many different ethnic groups in the Balkans, including the Serbs, Bosnians and Bulgarians, wanted their own countries. Of course, new, ethnically determined states would represent a threat to the Austro-Hungarian Empire, the most polyglot political construction of the age. Germany, having decided Austria-Hungary was its key ally, decided to support the Austrians as they tried to move in and take advantage of the Ottoman collapse.

Germany's devotion to Austria-Hungary was in some ways touching, considering how little power it brought to the table. The Austro-Hungarian Empire had a significant number of people, a relatively small economy and little societal cohesion. It was made up of a large number of different linguistic groups, many of whom retained long-standing historical animosities, including Germans, Hungarians, Czechs, Slovaks, Poles, Ukrainians, Italians, Slovenians, Romanians, Serbians, Croatians, Albanians and Ruthenians. However, what made Austria-Hungary an even more terrible ally was not just that it was relatively weak; it was also insecure. Fearing the rise of national identities, it was on the lookout to stamp out threats to its internal cohesion, and this made it expansive.

It was Austro-Hungarian weakness as much as anything else that caused World War I and brought Germany into conflict with three of the four largest powers in Europe (and eventually the US). Starting in 1907, Austria-Hungary started trying to incorporate many of the ethnic groups recently relieved of Ottoman rule.[16] It either took advantage of or precipitated a crisis which led it to annex Bosnia, a large piece of territory, populated by another ethnic group, which it had occupied since 1904. Germany ended up backing the move.

This ended up being deeply embarrassing for Russia, as it showed to the Slavic people of the area, including the Serbians, how weak Russia was if Germany chose sides. Russia styled itself the defender of the Slavic populations of the Balkans, a position that mattered a great deal to its reputation in Europe. Yet no matter how much Russia objected to Austria-Hungary's expansion into Bosnia, with Germany's support the Russians had to accept it. It was humiliating and embittering for Russia. It also meant that when in 1914 Austria-Hungary, taking advantage of the shooting of Archduke Franz Ferdinand by a Serbian terrorist, threatened to invade all of Serbia, Russia decided to risk war. Germany again backed its weak Austrian ally, and the war began.

So Germany was cementing itself with a weak ally in Austria, while embarrassing and frankly frightening the French and the Russians – and while all this was going on, the Germans decided to enter a naval race with the British. The history of this competition is one of the most famous arms race events in history. After the Entente Cordiale and the Anglo-Russian agreement, only the Germans were left to be a true naval competitor to the British. They promptly, and foolishly, took up the challenge. Starting in earnest in 1909, the two countries duelled for *future* naval dominance.

The building of HMS *Dreadnought* in 1906, discussed in chapter 1, had levelled the playing field when it came to naval power. By making all earlier battleships functionally obsolete, what the dreadnought did was give Germany, with its economic and technological power, an entirely new naval world in which to take on the British.[17] For the next three years, the two countries engaged in an acrimonious fight over who was building how many dreadnoughts, and how powerful they would be on the high seas in 5–10 years. It caused huge fear in the British government, particularly amongst those who were instinctively anti-German such as Edward Grey. This anti-Germanness was translated into massive British naval construction efforts from 1909 onwards, partly encapsulated by a famous phrase from that year: 'We want eight and we wont wait!' Eight was indeed the number of new dreadnoughts the British authorized in 1909 – a truly massive amount considering these were some of the most expensive constructions on earth. In the end, the British poured so many resources into the naval race that the Germans, who also had to fund a large army, were forced to relent.[18]

The comparative alliance positions of Britain and Germany in 1914 shows the difference between understanding the value of allies and not.*

---

* Germany's other large ally in Europe, Italy, actually abandoned it in 1914 and refused to join the war on its behalf. Italy would join the war in 1915, on the side of the Allies against Germany and Austria-Hungary, further confirmation of the failure of German alliance politics.

The British headed an alliance that was richer and had larger armies and larger navies. It had more committed populations, in the case of the British and French; financial systems, particularly in London, that were capable of raising far more in the way of funds; and combined industrial resources that could increase production more substantially. The Allies had a much better network of worldwide bases, based on global empires, and access to worldwide trade including that from the United States. The British also had an alliance with Japan, which provided further security for them in the Pacific. Germany, on the other hand, had Austria-Hungary and later the Ottoman Empire as allies, two states near the end of their existence.

As such, the most powerful army in Europe would have to get by on its own.

Alliances and the Outbreak of World War II

Adolf Hitler made one remarkably successful move for an alliance – one that immediately paid dividends. Of course, being Adolf Hitler he could not be satisfied with this one success and later blew everything up. The success was in negotiating the Nazi-Soviet Pact in 1939, making Stalin's USSR an ally in his plans for expansion. This alliance allowed him to take over most of continental Europe outside of the USSR in a very short period of time between 1939 and 1941 – before he could not help himself and ended it by invading his one-time ally.

Hitler actually thought a great deal about alliances. Long before taking power, in both *Mein Kampf* and his unpublished second book, he spoke of the need for Germany to ally with Britain. He believed that the two states represented no threat to each other – and indeed could help support the other in their very different aspirations. To him, Britain was global, imperial, maritime and part of a wide Anglo-American world. Germany meanwhile was continental, army-centric and industrial. Britain wanted to maintain its empire while Germany wanted to dominate the European continent, or so Hitler imagined it.

Once Hitler seized power in 1933, he was as good as his word (for a while). Hitler worked hard to convince the British that they could make a deal with him. In 1935, he negotiated a naval agreement limiting the German fleet to a tonnage no more than 35 per cent of the British fleet, partly to reinforce to the British that he would not be so foolish as to engage in a naval race with them as Kaiser Wilhelm's Germany had done before 1914. In 1936, Hitler told a visiting dignitary that he was keen to make a 'most generous' offer that if 'England gives us a free hand on the continent, we will not meddle in its affairs overseas'.[19]

And yet, no matter how many seductive glances Hitler cast at London, he could never convince the British to ask him to the dance. For no matter how unthreatening he tried to make Germany in maritime terms, his obviously threatening attitude towards his European neighbours made the idea of allying with him simply too extreme for the British governments of the time. What he failed to understand was that the British were never going to reconcile themselves to a German-dominated continent, any more than they would have a Napoleon-dominated continent or later a Soviet-dominated continent. Hitler's deal was one that, to too many British policymakers, did not guarantee the long-term continuation of the British Empire, but rather the beginning of the end of it. Thus in 1938 and 1939 Hitler became more and more estranged from the UK. After signing the Munich accord with Neville Chamberlain in 1938, which Chamberlain took seriously but Hitler did not, the Nazi dictator turned around and violated its spirit almost immediately. Instead of limiting his territorial wishes to just the Sudetenland, as he had promised Chamberlain, Hitler seized all he could of the Czech lands as well, including the capital, Prague. When afterwards Chamberlain stated that he would go to war to protect Poland, which was next on Hitler's list, the Führer finally realized that he had boxed himself in.

It was typical of Hitler in one way, as he never really understood other countries' motivations, strengths, weaknesses and perceptions. He could never accept to what degree they saw Germany – and in particular a Germany led by himself – as a threat to their security. Hitler instead trusted his own instincts, even when, as in the case of Britain, they were shown to be wrong. Once it was clear to him that there was to be no deal with Britain, he pivoted 180 degrees and started trying for a deal with Stalin and the USSR. As well as being outwardly anti-communist, Hitler always believed that Germany's future expansion would be to the east, through Poland and into the Soviet Union.

It was one of the reasons that before 1939 the idea of a Nazi-Soviet pact seemed inconceivable to almost everyone else in Europe.

Hitler, however, needed to do something to protect himself from a two-front war, and was willing to make major concessions to get Stalin's support. In one of the most cynical deals in diplomatic history, Hitler gave Stalin more than half of Poland, as well as the three Baltic states, in exchange for Soviet support for a German invasion of Poland. In the short term it was a strategic deal worth making – precisely because the British had forgotten one of the reasons for their success in World War I.

If Britain had gone into World War I as the leader of by far the larger and more powerful alliance structure, this was certainly not the case in 1939 – and much of the responsibility was down to Britain's own negotiating. In early 1938, the balance of alliances still greatly favoured the British, who had alliances or security guarantees with France, Belgium, Poland and Czechoslovakia. At the same time, they were arguably closer to the USSR than Hitler's Germany. However, the behaviour of the British government during the Czech crisis basically destroyed this advantageous position. In the end, Britain sacrificed an ally in an attempt to curry favour with Hitler (see the discussion of the issue at stake in chapter 2) and less than a year of extra preparation for war in case that failed.

Czechoslovakia had been created by the British government and the other signatories of the Versailles Treaty. Carved out of part of the old Austro-Hungarian Empire, it was made up mostly of Czechs and Slovaks, but it had a region, the Sudetenland, which bordered Germany and had a German-speaking majority. Parts of that German population, egged on by Hitler, started agitating for the right to leave Czechoslovakia and join Nazi Germany.

The British, led by Prime Minister Neville Chamberlain, could have sat at the top of an extremely powerful alliance opposing Hitler, but they lost their nerve. Chamberlain simply did not believe that helping Czechoslovakia was important enough for Britain to quarrel with Germany.[20] Some have defended the deal he made on the grounds that it gave the British an extra year to prepare for World War II. Others have questioned whether there was a politically acceptable alternative.[21] However, these arguments don't fully engage with the importance of allies. When Britain did go to war, for Poland eleven months later, the USSR was now allied with Hitler and Czechoslovakia no longer existed – as Hitler had simply seized the remainder of the Czech lands and Slovakia had become an independent (and pro-German) state. Even leaving out Mussolini, who was more pro-German in 1939 than 1938, the British had actively worsened their position through the Munich catastrophe.

This transformation in alliances between the start of World War I and World War II helps explain why the wars developed so differently in their early stages. In 1939, the Germans were able to concentrate all of their military force on France, whereas in 1914 they still had Russia to worry about to the east. Moreover, initially in World War II, the German economy and war industry were being greatly augmented by Soviet aid, whereas in World War I Germany had only Austria-Hungary to rely upon.

Of course, the British had the last laugh, as while they played the alliance game poorly in the run-up to World War II, Hitler would play it even worse during the war itself. He would throw away his alliance with Stalin, and declare war first against the US; his one significant European ally, Italy, was as much a drag as a support; and his most important global ally, Japan, was too distant to help the German war effort. His inability to play the alliance game would transform World War II in such a way that it led to his defeat and suicide.

Cold War Cooperation

The Cold War defined international relations for more than forty years and is often portrayed as a clash between the US and USSR, the two 'superpowers' of the post-World War II era. Each is seen as almost a sole actor, with a massive military and bristling with nuclear weapons. However, if looked at as two alliances in competition, the picture that emerges is one that is very different – and indeed one that helps explain why it ended as quickly, unexpectedly and decisively as it did.

Throughout the Cold War, the US had allies who possessed much greater economic and technological resources than the Soviet Union's. Starting with a foundation in Western Europe, including Britain, France, Italy and the by far wealthier and more populous part of Germany, the US was buttressed during the Cold War by economies that were some of the fastest-growing and most technologically advanced anywhere in the world. In Europe, the comparison between the American and Soviet allies was stark. The member states of the North Atlantic Treaty Organization (NATO), the US-led alliance first established in 1949, had the economic/technological resources almost equivalent to another 'superpower', while the Soviet allies who were signatories of the Warsaw Pact, established by the USSR in response in 1955, were more like a small group of oppressed prisoners. The US allies were a support for US goals, while the Soviet allies, in Europe at least, ended up being more of a problem than anything else.

The economic strength of the allies of the United States actually grew vis-à-vis the US between the end of World War II and 1980.[22] Not only did West Germany recover rapidly from World War II to become the third-largest economy in the world, the UK, France and Italy also showed the ability to rebound well from the economic dislocation, at least until the 1970s. Even less discussed allies such as the Netherlands, Norway and Denmark showed strong economic growth in these years. Much of the growth was in the important areas of sophisticated engineering and high-end (and high-tech) manufacturing.

The USSR, on the other hand, mostly because of its own doing, had reluctant and unsettled 'allies' on which it could not really rely. The states of the Warsaw Pact – Poland, East Germany, Czechoslovakia, Hungary, Romania and Bulgaria – all had communist governments imposed and kept in power primarily by the threat of Soviet power. Even then, there were notable periods of popular resistance to Soviet domination by Poland in the 1980s, Czechoslovakia in 1968 and Hungary in 1956. And this illustrates one of the most important attributes of allies – their willingness to be allies.

The states of Western Europe – though they often grumbled about US power and had segments of their populations that protested the presence of the US – consistently kept in power leaders that wanted to maintain the security link to the United States. They could have left at any time, as the French decision to opt in and out of the military command of NATO revealed. And yet, they did not. Indeed, NATO expanded regularly after its foundation in 1949, and kept expanding even after the Cold War was won.

Being under Soviet domination, in comparison, led Warsaw Pact states into relative economic decline. For a while there was talk of the good performance of Eastern European economies, including that of the USSR. However, recent work has shown that rising GDP figures in the eastern bloc at these times were almost certainly highly inflated (even if the policymakers themselves did not understand that).[23] Whereas places such as Czechoslovakia were some of the most developed parts of Europe in the 1930s, by the 1980s they were falling further and further behind the west.

Indeed, in the latter part of the Cold War, the differing ability of the two sides to manipulate technology for their strategic needs became clear. For instance, the Soviets were the first power to launch a satellite into space, in 1957. They followed this up by being the first country to launch a man into space in 1961. However, at that point their space programme went into a relative stall, and throughout the 1960s they fell further and further behind the US. They eventually watched as the US put the first man on the moon (a feat no other country has matched, to this day), and this kind of technological supremacy was put into weapons production, particularly in the 1980s, when the US showed the ability to produce weapons systems that the USSR could not match.[24]

The difference between the western allies of the US and the USSR's eastern ones was arguably more stark than that between the 'superpowers' themselves. Western European states of the Cold War era were, particularly in comparison to what has happened since, very well armed. Military spending remained high as a percentage of GDP throughout, and whole ranges of effective equipment were developed – from German Leopard tanks to British Tornado fighters. Some Western European equipment was (and is) so good that the US military adopted it for its own use. Even today, after a significant relative decline in European defence spending, the US is fielding Belgian small arms, Swedish anti-tank missiles and British mortars – to say nothing of a range of very advanced systems such as the F-35 fighter, which is being co-produced with European allies.

The Warsaw Pact provided no such support for the USSR. Even the basic reliability of its forces was called into question. If the USSR ever attacked West Germany – one of the most discussed possible war scenarios of the Cold War – Warsaw Pact forces were to be limited to secondary roles. The opposite was to be the case for NATO, which had West German and British forces assigned to holding arguably the most difficult parts of the front line – in northern Germany.

Not understanding the strengths and weaknesses of the different alliance groupings is one of the reasons much of the military analysis during the Cold War regularly overstated Soviet military capacity and often made dire predictions about the outcome of any war. The USSR was always greatly outmatched in the real capacities of warfare, economic/technological strength, leadership, governmental structure, societal commitment, and alliances. Its collapse at the end of the 1980s was the result of that basic and comprehensive inferiority.

If the balance of the alliances in Europe greatly favoured the US over the USSR, the situation in Asia also evolved in that direction – quite dramatically so from the 1970s onwards. In some ways, the basic story of what happened in Europe was repeated for two US allies throughout the Cold War – Japan and South Korea. These countries, which remained reliant on the US for security guarantees, were two of the fastest-growing states in the world throughout the period. In fact, Japanese growth was so spectacular that by the 1980s it seemed to be challenging the US itself.[25] Any such tension, however, masked the reality of the relationship. They remained allies throughout the Cold War, and in doing so provided a great deal of mutual support.

The final piece of the puzzle for the US and USSR in the alliance struggle of the Cold War was China – in many ways the poster child for how to lose a valuable ally and how to gain a strategic friend. When the Chinese Communists seized power after World War II, they looked up to the USSR and specifically Joseph Stalin as the leaders of world communism, and were loyal Soviet allies. But by the 1960s, the two powers were massing military forces on their border, and the relationship between them had moved from allies to potential enemies. It was an ideal situation for the US to interject itself.

The US had long thought of China as a possible strong ally – indeed that was the hope of President Roosevelt during World War II. He believed that the security of Asia, and through it the protection of American interests, would best be ensured if the US established a close working alliance with China. It was why he referred to the 'four policemen' controlling global affairs after the war (China was to be the fourth policeman, along with the US, USSR and UK). It is also why he invited the Chinese leader, Jiang Jieshi (better known to some as

Chiang Kai-shek), to the major international summit in Cairo at the end of 1943.

However, Roosevelt's plans all came to naught right after the war, when Jiang's Nationalist government was overthrown by the Chinese Communist Party led by Mao Zedong in 1949. For the next two decades this meant that China, instead of being a US ally, was very much in the USSR's orbit and hostile to US interests. It was during this time that the US had some of its most difficult moments in Asia. Not only was the Korean War a bloody and drawn-out affair, the US also ended up getting enmeshed in the Vietnam War, during which both the USSR and China provided the Communist Vietnamese government with aid.

And then China pivoted, and the whole situation in Asia changed. China's move towards the United States, if not as an ally then at least as a (temporary) strategic partner, was one of the most important developments of the Cold War. It happened first because of an internal struggle between the USSR and China over ideology.[26] When the USSR de-Stalinized under Nikita Khrushchev in the late 1950s, the Chinese Communists felt threatened. Having always favoured a Stalinist vision of power and party control, Mao started moving away from his erstwhile Soviet partners. Things became even more intense in 1971 when a pro-Soviet leader of the Chinese Communist Party, Lin Biao, fled to the USSR in murky circumstances, dying en route when his plane crashed in Mongolia. Mao accused Lin of trying to murder him and stage a coup.

The deterioration of relations between the USSR and China provided an opening for the US, and the administration of President Richard Nixon gratefully seized the opportunity. In 1972, after a series of quiet negotiations, a trip by Nixon to China was arranged, and it electrified much of the world, leading to a reset in US—Chinese relations that would last until the Cold War was over.[27] China was now more than happy to work with the US against the USSR, which transformed the US position in Asia and greatly complicated the Soviet one. Now massive Soviet armies had to be stationed on the border with China, and the two states became rivals for leadership in the Communist world.[28] Relations between the US and China even improved after Mao died and Deng Xiaoping rose to power. More pragmatic, and wanting to push forward Chinese economic development, Deng worked very comfortably with US presidents from Carter to Clinton, even after the Tiananmen Square massacre.

Overall, it was another sign of the failure of the USSR to operate alliance politics, and of the relative success of the US during the Cold War in doing so. It also illustrates the difference between allies and partners that are effective and those that are burdens. Much of the Cold War was presented as a period of relative Soviet success and expansion. The USSR added a number of states to its list of allies, scattered amongst the global south – from Cuba to Angola to Mozambique. However, these states provided little economic and strategic benefit, and in fact increased the economic burden on the USSR. Cuba, for instance, is often seen as a vital strategic ally for the USSR in the Cold War. That seems very debatable. It cost the USSR billions of dollars a year in the 1980s to keep the Cuban regime of Fidel Castro subsidized. This included transfers of oil, food and machinery. In exchange, the USSR received sugar – hardly a scarce commodity on the world market or one of great strategic value. And what did the USSR get beyond sugar? Actually, a defence burden, as Cuba was constantly seen by the US as a threat. This meant that the USSR had to provide military aid as well – in order to maintain a threatening position that further antagonized the United States. It was a lose-lose alliance for the USSR, though Castro did quite well out of it.

Though alliances rarely get the coverage of great powers, they have played an outsized role in determining international events in both war and peace. In peace, the key thing for a state – which is not always easy for a powerful nation to do – is to look at an ally as an asset from which it can benefit, not as a smaller state or a people it wants to rule. The desire to dominate ends up being counterproductive, turning possible allies into expensive burdens that may even rise up against that domination. It ceases to be an alliance and becomes an empire that is less than the sum of its parts. However, an alliance of states that work together, even if they are cognizant of the power differentials between them, can be mutually supportive and probably greater than the sum of its parts. Such alliances won World War I, World War II and the Cold War.

They might also decide the result of any war in the Indo-Pacific.

PART TWO

War

6.   Battles vs Wars

If ideas of power have become simplified and incoherent, the same is true of war. What I am aiming to do in the following five chapters is provide a more coherent process for assessing how a war might develop. Not so much for telling *how* a war will develop – but to provide an analytical framework through which to understand what matters.

One of the fundamental problems in the analysis of war is the focus on battles – time-limited military engagements in specified areas. Battles rarely cause but they usually reveal. What this means is that the result of a specific battle does not normally change the course of a war. Neither the level of losses incurred in a specific engagement nor the ground being fought over is strategically so important as to alter the direction of a war. Instead, in almost all cases, the results of a battle reveal how the two (or more) sides in a war are doing at that time in their continual struggle to create and deploy more of their own forces while they attempt to hamper their enemy from doing the same.

War is, in its essence, when the struggle over power moves from the perceived to the concrete. In its most aggressive form, that involves military forces from one state struggling to impose themselves on those of another. Carl von Clausewitz, the Prussian officer and military theorist who witnessed the Napoleonic Wars, is considered to be one of the most important thinkers on war and strategy in history. He famously stated that war is the extension of politics by other means. That is true, but it also makes the purpose of war seem far more sensible than it almost always is. War becomes an end in its own right. Wars usually mutate, and often expand, to become something very different than what was expected of them when they started, and as such the political goals that motivated a war's initiation rarely survive intact by its end. Indeed, sometimes just winning the war becomes the great end in and of itself, with the purpose underlying that goal of victory increasingly difficult to understand.

In such a dynamic, grotesque and unstable process, the role of any individual battle is usually of little importance in deciding the ultimate result. And that is a problem, in a popular culture that loves the idea of the decisive or dramatic battle, and in a professional culture that often relies on war games to try to describe the expected course of a war. Both of these attitudes stress the immediate over the long term and the ephemeral over the plodding. One of the most common misperceptions about any war, which depressingly seemed to get worse before the Russian invasion of Ukraine, is the idea that wars can be decided relatively quickly with military action involving the forces assembled for the initial battles, following plans that were developed before the war started.

This was certainly the view of many before the invasion of Ukraine in 2022. Most professional analysts even spoke about how long it would take Russia to conquer either parts or even all of Ukraine, with extraordinary specificity. In the most extreme cases, the war would be functionally decided in one day. A well-known analyst of the Russian military told NBC News that the Russian military 'could disorient the Ukrainian military and society so the conflict is basically over in a day or so'.[1] Professional military officers, including the most senior with access to the best intelligence, were also prone to strikingly specific statements. The Chairman of the Joint Chiefs of Staff, the US president's highest-ranking military adviser, reportedly told Congress in a closed-door session that the Russians would be able to conquer the Ukrainian capital Kyiv three days after the invasion happened.[2] It was the kind of assessment that was extraordinarily widespread, precisely because of the impact of the war-gaming view of conflict. Before February 2022, Russia was thought so strong that war games run by the US and others showed that not only could Russia conquer Ukraine, it would be able to overrun a number of NATO countries from a standing start (with little or no preparation). The most famous example of this is probably the war games run by the Rand Corporation in the years before 2022, which saw Russia overrun the Baltics in a matter of hours, with NATO flailing to try to stop them.[3]

It is not just the specificity of these 'short war' claims that is remarkable; it is also that they go against what we have seen repeatedly throughout the history of war, something that has been repeated constantly in the twentieth and twenty-first centuries. Rarely has a state, not even the United States at the height of its relative power in the 1990s, achieved its military objectives with ease and in such a short amount of time. In fact, when wars are over relatively quickly, it is normally because both sides have lost more equipment than they can regenerate quickly, such as in the 1973 Yom Kippur War. The US defeat of Saddam Hussein in the First Gulf War was a rare exception to the 'short war' illusion, but it was actually longer than people sometimes understand.[4] Overall, it was a campaign that needed more than forty days of constant air bombardment, and even then the US Army was never sent into the Iraqi capital Baghdad. The US campaign against Saddam Hussein in 2003, which did result in a relatively swift seizure of Baghdad, was fought against an army that had been operating under sanctions for more than a decade – and of course this battle did not end the Second Gulf War; it only ushered in a new phase that would last for many years. The idea that Russia therefore could win its war with Ukraine – having only the tenth-largest economy in the world, a system built on corruption, and a leadership prone to crushing dissent – made little sense.

The flawed thinking about a short and decisive war that would follow a predetermined script, which flourished widely during the run-up to the 2022 invasion of Ukraine, had many contributing factors. It was based on many assumptions that rarely prove true, and which affect a range of military operations from the basic to the most advanced. It assumed that Russian logistics would work efficiently, that supplies would be delivered in sufficient quantities and where needed, that equipment would function as advertised, and that command and control would work to oversee Russian forces throughout the operation. From a more advanced perspective, it assumed that the Russian military could operate complex systems not only in peacetime – but also under the pressure of war in a chaotic environment. It basically assumed that the Russian military would be able to win some battles at the start of hostilities – and through those battles be able to win the war. What was missing was any concern about the larger societal variables of corruption, or even basic motivation. Corruption was rarely discussed as mattering to the Russian military, and on one of the few occasions it was mentioned it was to say that any corruption issues had been greatly improved.[5]

As mentioned earlier in this book, the opposite assumptions were often made about Ukraine.[6] The Ukrainian military was portrayed as being so overmatched that it simply would not be able to respond effectively to Russian attacks. And where corruption was not seen as a major problem for the Russian military, it was seen as a major problem for Ukraine, hampering the Ukrainian state and making the country less attractive to support.[7]

This lack of consistency in assessing how a Russian invasion of Ukraine would develop, and what would matter when the two militaries clashed, points out one obvious weakness that has bedevilled much of strategic analysis since the foundation of the subject: the lack of shared methodology and agreement on what matters in war. If we have simplified our understanding of power with terms such as 'great power' and 'superpower', we have likewise simplified our understanding of war – or more precisely, our understanding of war is incoherent. What I am aiming to do in these five chapters is provide a more coherent framework for assessing how a war might develop. Not so much how to predict how a war will develop – but to provide an analytical framework through which to understand what matters.

The first step towards this is to construct an intellectual process for understanding war. As part of this, it is important to remember that pre-war plans and battles themselves usually play only the most limited role in determining the outcome of war. To try to understand how a war might develop, you need to move beyond what might happen when the two (or more) armies clash in the field in the opening stages – which in and of itself is almost always indecisive – and instead look at each military's ability to constantly generate new force (equipment and manpower) while eroding the generation of force on the other side. War in terms of militaries in action is basically a continual cycle of attrition and adaptation, which goes on until one side gains enough of an advantage that the other determines that the continuation of military operations is undesirable or even impossible, or the advantage is so strong that one side is completely conquered and the leader ends up shooting himself in a bunker.

Though this book focuses on more large-scale conventional warfare, this means of analysis applies equally to insurgency/counterinsurgency and smaller-war thinking. In the post-1945 world, for instance, some of the most impactful wars have occurred in the Middle East. Israel has fought a series of wars with its neighbours, and the US has engaged in a decades-long war to try to impose its vision of security on the region. Both will be discussed in these chapters.

One of the great failures of larger powers fighting such wars is their view that if they win the battles, they will win the war. The US military has arguably not lost a battle since 1942, or at the latest 1950 (the original Chinese large-scale intervention in the Korean War), and yet the US has lost many wars. From Vietnam through Afghanistan, the United States has not been defeated in direct engagement, but it has suffered defeat because, no matter how much force it has deployed – how much technological dominance it can exert – it could not stop its enemies from constantly generating enough new force to keep the war going. From the North Vietnamese coming back year after year with relatively large-scale forces, to the Taliban in Afghanistan constantly generating relatively small numbers of fighters, the US has been confronted by opponents it could always defeat on the battlefield but ultimately not in a war.

Of course this was not the case only for the US, and the relative lack of importance of individual battles can be seen by looking at the two largest conventional wars in human history: World War I and World War II.

The World Wars as Struggles of Force Generation and Destruction

World War I is one of the greatest examples of a war that quickly metastasized to become something very different than originally assumed. In 1914, when the war broke out, the large powers of Europe all had their different plans to try to win the war quickly through imposing themselves on their enemies by force.[8] The French had Plan XVII, a brave but dangerous scheme to take the war to Germany in a large offensive directly across the French border. The Russians had Mobilization Plan 19, which called for the concentration of their large army and an offensive either against Germany or Austria – depending on the situation at the start of hostilities.

Arguably the most famous was the famous German Schlieffen Plan, first developed almost a decade earlier by the German commander-in-chief, Alfred von Schlieffen. This was a scheme for Germany to rapidly win a war against its most likely foes – the combined forces of France and Russia. France was judged the most immediate threat and at the same time the one that could be more quickly defeated. Russia might be vast, with huge human resources, but the Germans calculated that it would take the Russians a significant amount of time to mobilize efficiently. Under the Schlieffen Plan, the Germans would use that time to overrun northern France and destroy its military.[9] The Germans planned to sweep through Belgium and come down behind the French Army, which they assumed would be massed on the Franco-German border. They would thus envelop Paris and trap French forces on two sides.

The strategic concept underlying the Schlieffen Plan was that, even though the French could mobilize more efficiently that the Russians, the Germans could overwhelm whatever the French could put in the field. The key, however, was for the Germans to do so quickly. Even if the Germans had to cede some territory in the east at first, it was assumed that the large but slow and ponderous Russian forces would take too long before they were a real threat. By that time France would have been dealt with, and the German Army would be streaming eastwards to deal with the Tsar's armies.

Of course, nothing like this happened. When the war started in August 1914, German plans failed.* Even after throwing the mass of their army against the French, the Germans lacked the resources to envelop Paris and crush the French Army.[10] Moreover, the German invasion through Belgium provided the pretext needed by the more hawkish members of the UK government, including Foreign Secretary Sir Edward Grey, to get Britain into the war on the side of France and Russia. The upshot of all this was that the Germans were stopped north of Paris during the Battle of the Marne – and soon found that they had no ability to drive France out of the war. Indeed, by the end of 1914 Germany found itself in what should have been a nightmare scenario, as its army was forced into hundreds of miles of trenches, stretching from the Swiss border to the English Channel – facing a combined Franco-British enemy that had access to superior resources. An entirely unexpected kind of war was about to be fought.

Even the fact that the Germans exceeded their pre-war expectations

---

* As did the original French, Russian, Austro-Hungarian and British plans, it should be noted. No one had a real idea of how the war would develop, even in its earliest stages.

in the east, where their smaller but more efficient army dealt a heavy blow to the Russians, the reality was that the original forces that all sides brought to World War I were consumed in a very short period. This exposed another common flaw in the understanding of what matters when it comes to the application of national power in times of war. Rarely is a war decided by the forces on hand when it starts (though these are often used to assume how a war will develop). Instead, the outcome of a war is usually determined by the total military force a state or states can generate and deploy during its course and, correspondingly, how that created military force can degrade the ability of their enemy/enemies to generate and deploy force in return.

As World War I would demonstrate. The different armies of the large European powers started creating large armies from 1914 onwards – far larger than they had believed they would need ahead of time. Arguably, the British had to recalibrate their expectations the most. In 1914, as hostilities were about to break out, their planners acted on the basis that a very small, six-division British army force would be enough to make a real difference in the land war between the French and Germans.[11] This force, which was just over 100,000 soldiers, was laughably small in the context of what followed. Soon the British introduced conscription and raised a large land army – to fight not only in France, but around the world. By the end of the war, there were more than 4 million men serving in the British Army.[12] And at its high point, there were more than 2 million British soldiers serving on the Western Front.

Other European states, which had larger armies than Britain to start with, also had to expand the size of their forces quickly. The number of military personnel mobilized by larger European states between 1914 and 1918 was sobering.[13] The Allies saw the British Empire and France mobilize about 7.5 million each, Italy 5.5 million, and Russia 12 million. The United States, which was only in the war for a year and a half, mobilized more than 4.25 million to add to the Allied total. Germany, in comparison, mobilized 11 million, Austria-Hungary 6.5 million, and Turkey 1.6 million.

Not only did these extreme figures show how much larger the Allies were in terms of personnel than the Central Powers (more on this in chapter 10), they led to extremely high casualties as armies grew and were equipped with ever-more powerful and deadly modern weaponry. The British, French, Italians and Russians suffered almost 20 million casualties between them (killed, wounded and captured);[14] the Central Powers lost more than 12 million. Combined, all these states suffered a number of casualties only a little less than the entire population of Italy in 1914. And considering the losses suffered by these armies, soldiers who served in them at the start made up only a small percentage of each force when the war ended. It has been calculated that a British soldier who enlisted in the infantry at the start of the war had an almost two-thirds chance of being killed or seriously wounded during the course of the conflict.[15]

However, just building up new forces was only part of the process of winning and losing World War I. It was also crucial to destroy the force that the enemy was putting into the field. In this way, the war quickly became a test of force attrition and force generation. Not surprisingly, it was a German commander who first started to do serious thinking about this – General Erich von Falkenhayn, the Prussian Minister of War and Chief of the Imperial German General Staff for much of the first half of the conflict. The Germans had hoped to win a quick war in 1914, but by the following year they found themselves facing a coalition with greater economic and technological resources. Moreover, it was also becoming clear that the military mobility expected by the Germans before the war – fast-moving ground forces that could manoeuvre around enemy forces – was almost impossible in this era of trench warfare and industrially designed and produced weapons. For Falkenhayn, the reality of the war was that defensive firepower – ranging from modern artillery to machine guns and even more effective standard-issue rifles – was so effective that advancing was always going to be hard. And once the two sides dug down, creating hundreds of miles of defensive fortifications, many of them deep, moving forward became even more difficult.

Falkenhayn, surveying the Western Front in 1915 and realizing how trench warfare and defensive power had changed the fundamentals of war at that time, decided to try to turn the reality of modern war to Germany's advantage. Advancing would be close to impossible, considering the advantages of entrenched defenders, so best not throw away troops in a fruitless effort to attack.[16] Instead, Falkenhayn decided to fight a grand attritional battle – to, in his own words, provoke France so that French forces would do the attacking and 'bleed to death'.[17] To bleed the French white, as it were, he would make an assault on the famous French town of Verdun – not specifically to take the town, but to compel the French to rush more and more forces to hold it. As Falkenhayn well knew, Verdun had a particular place in the French national psyche, being one of the places that had held off the Prussians for longest in the Franco-Prussian War of 1870–71. He figured, correctly, that if it looked like the Germans would take Verdun, the French would rush in soldiers and the Germans could kill them in great numbers.

He was half-right.

When Falkenhayn launched his campaign against Verdun in February 1915, the French behaved exactly as he expected. Under the overall command of Marshal Pétain (who would be installed as the pro-German dictator of Vichy France in 1940), French troops were rushed to Verdun with the stirring cry of 'They shall not pass!' (*Ils ne passeront pas!*). Doing exactly what Falkenhayn wanted, the French turned Verdun into arguably the most heavily defended place on the planet. It was soon almost entirely blasted, a sea of fortifications and mud, with hardly a tree left standing and all the buildings full of shell holes. And the Germans were able to inflict an extraordinary toll on all those French defenders packed into a very small and desolate area.

The problem with Falkenhayn's plan was that the Germans themselves suffered roughly equivalent casualties. It was so difficult for either side to move forward that when the armies clashed, they both died in masses. By early 1916, both armies were exhausted and their lines had shifted only a few miles in either direction – though the battle would meander on for almost the rest of the year. In the end, the total of casualties suffered was over 700,000 – almost equally split between the two sides.

The thing about Verdun is that it was only the start of what would be a series of increasingly bloody attritional battles stretching throughout 1916 and 1917, as the French, Germans and also British tried different stratagems to break the stalemate. By this point they were mobilizing more and more troops and building more and more weapons, in an attempt to gain the force needed to break through. Yet, whether it was a massive artillery barrage such as the British employed at the Battle of the Somme, or a rolling artillery barrage that was supposed to lead attacking troops forward (such as in the French Nivelle Offensive), or even assaults preceded by the heavy use of poison gas, advances were slow and casualties remained extremely high – and in most cases, as at Verdun, casualties were remarkably equally shared and the trench lines changed only marginally.

By the time the lines were eventually broken and one side made an advance, in 1918, the war had changed tremendously at sea as well as on land. By then Russia was out, the US was in, and aeroplanes, submarines and tanks were all being used in large numbers by the different combatants.

The war at sea diverged from its pre-war expectations as much if not more than the war on land. Before the war, as the Anglo-German naval race attested, it was widely imagined that the naval war would be decided by a duel between their competing forces of dreadnought battleships and battlecruisers – the largest and most powerful surface ships in existence. As it turned out, these capital ship forces barely fought during the entire war. The British had won the naval race over the Germans so decisively that the Germans avoided a major fleet action as a matter of course. In fact, there was only one pitched battle where the two main forces of the British Grand Fleet and the German High Seas Fleet met in action: the Battle of Jutland in 1916. And Jutland was actually a relatively quick affair as the Germans soon realized that they were facing a far too powerful British navy, and in an impressive act of seamanship they turned their big vessels on a dime and ran back to the safety of German ports.

However, if the battleship war ended up being a one-sided affair, the overall war at sea was anything but. Both sides realized that if there was not going to be a direct large fleet battle to decide things, there could easily be a decisive war over the control of commerce. For the British this meant instituting a blockade on Germany. Before the war there had been a major British debate about whether any blockade of Germany should be 'distant' (British warships kept around the British Isles stopping any trade from reaching Germany) or 'close' (sending British warships close to the German coast to throttle as much trade as possible, which would put the British ships at greater risk).[18] In the end, the close blockade was seen to be very risky, and the British mostly settled back and throttled German trade distantly, stopping and seizing vessels long before they came anywhere near the German coast. However, much to their surprise, while the British were blockading the Germans, they soon found themselves under a German counter-blockade, instituted by some of the cheapest and smallest warships of the time – submarines.

The British had won the naval race for control of the surface of the war's ocean so completely that building new surface ships had become a sideshow for the Germans, and Britain's greatest pre-war fears never came close to materializing. In the years before the war, the British Admiralty had worried a great deal that the Germans would convert merchant ships into surface raiders to attack British trade around the world.[19] This fear, however, was shown to be greatly overblown. However, the Germans quickly discovered that in the submarine they had a potentially devastating weapon against Britain's single most vulnerable point – its shipping lanes.

Britain could only exist as an independent power if it controlled shipping in the Atlantic. It could not feed itself with just its own domestic production, and it lacked the raw materials to keep all its factories working. Without trade, Britain would literally starve. No one before the war had quite understood how submarines could threaten that trade. They were considered primitive technology, and the Germans, for one, had very few ready for service. In September 1914, for instance, the German Navy had only nineteen U-Boats operational in North Sea ports (the ones that could threaten British trade), and another four deployed in the Baltic.[20] This was a risibly small number with which to try to cut British trade, as would be shown in 1917 and 1918.

Moreover, the submarine was expected to act within certain gentlemanly limits. Submarines were not supposed to sink merchant ships without warning, and were instead expected to surface near their civilian target and identify themselves so that the merchant seamen could safely leave the vessel before it was torpedoed. With such restrictions, no one, including First Lord of the Admiralty Winston Churchill, believed that submarines would figure decisively in the outcome of the war. He argued that the Germans would never resort to unrestricted submarine warfare, because it was 'uncivilized'.[21] Churchill – and almost everyone else – was wrong.

The Germans, with their ineffective dreadnought fleet, came to rely more and more on the submarine as the war went on. Almost all merchant vessels in the first years of World War I sailed singly on the high seas, without the protection of a convoy. This made them relatively easy prey – as long as the submarine could remain undetected. The

British actually tried to ambush German submarines by placing hidden armaments (illegally) on some of their merchant ships, with the aim of blasting away at any hapless German submarine that surfaced nearby to undertake its legal obligations. By 1915, the Germans had had enough of this gentlemanly form of warfare, and Britain's illegal attempts to circumvent it, and decided to allow their submarines to sink merchant ships without warning while remaining submerged. This kind of warfare, known as unrestricted submarine warfare, was both extremely effective and extremely contentious – and ended up having a huge impact on the course of the war. On the one hand, it gave Germany an unexpectedly effective weapon with which to strike at Britain. On the other hand, it ended up causing ever-increasing tension with the world's most powerful neutral nation – the United States.*

For the rest of the war, the German submarine would be the most effective weapon the British faced. In 1915, the British faced a crisis when the Germans first started their policy of unrestricted submarine warfare which, most famously, resulted in the sinking of the great ocean liner *Lusitania*, just off the coast of Ireland. However, this first phase of the policy ended abruptly when the US made threats and the Germans backed down. In late 1916, however, Germany decided to gamble on restarting unrestricted submarine warfare. The German government, in what seems an ill-thought-out manner, announced to the world in January 1917 that they were going to start sinking vessels without warning around the British Isles. It was part of an overall attempt to inflict a knockout blow on sea and land, and gain a decisive victory. The Germans were gambling that they could cut trade across the Atlantic, regardless of what the US did, driving Britain from the war. At the same time, they believed Russia was teetering, and a complete victory was in their grasp.

They would lose their gamble, though things seemed to go well at first. At sea, German submarines did a great deal of damage in early 1917, sinking record numbers of merchant ships on a trajectory that would have crippled the British. Yet, by the summer of that year, the German submarines were being countered by a growing British technological and productive effort in the building of escort vessels such as destroyers and corvettes. Once the British placed their merchant ships

* This will be discussed in detail in chapter 8.

in well-protected convoys, which they started doing in earnest in May 1917, the German submarine threat was relentlessly neutralized. It was a further sign of how war adapts and changes over time – a new technology/tactic was triumphing over a technology/tactic that itself had been mostly unthought of when the war began. In just a few years the war at sea had proceeded through at least two full adaptation cycles, so that submarine warfare, which had not been understood at the start of the conflict, was now being neutralized by developments that were even newer. The German gamble at sea had failed comprehensively.

Meanwhile, on land, the German Army had come up with a new plan to break the stalemate on the Western Front. After the Russian regime of Tsar Nicholas II fell under the pressure of the war – leading to the Russian Revolution – the Germans forced the new Bolshevik overlords of the USSR to agree to a harsh peace on German terms under the Brest-Litovsk Treaty in early 1918. This freed up about 1 million German troops to head west. At the same time, the Germans were faced with the prospect of British and French forces being reinforced by their newest partner – the United States.* Their way out of the puzzle was to try to break the stalemate on the Western Front using new stormtrooper tactics. Instead of relying on overwhelming firepower to blast the enemy into submission (a tactic that had repeatedly failed), the German plan was to take special troops and have them infiltrate and find gaps in the French and British lines. Only when this was done would an attack start, with a short, intense artillery barrage.

The tactic was a great success in one way. When the Germans started their 1918 offensive in late March, they quickly created large holes in the French and British positions and soon they were advancing swiftly. For the first time since 1914, it seemed like mobility had been restored on the battlefield, with the German Army pushing the British and French back for approximately thirty miles in places. It even seemed that Paris itself might be threatened. An obscure German corporal named Adolf Hitler, for one, was convinced that the German Army was on the verge of victory. In Britain, senior figures wondered if they were about to witness a military 'disaster' – maybe even a withdrawal of France from the war.[22]

---

* The United States refused to formally call itself an ally of Britain and France and preferred the phrase 'associated power'.

It was all a mirage. Hitler and others were looking at this as a battle, not part of a long attritional struggle. Even though the Germans were advancing, they were suffering unsustainable losses. Between March and July 1918, Germany lost 800,000 soldiers. It was a rate they could not sustain, and fewer than four months after the offensive started, the German attacks petered out.

Soon the balance of fighting moved inexorably against them. Hundreds of thousands of fresh American troops were shipped to France while the Germans were attacking, and British and French factories were together producing many times more aircraft, trucks and tanks than the Germans. The result was that when the German offensive stopped, the German Army was so weak and the Allied forces so much more advanced that the war began heading to its conclusion.

There were some strong signs of what would be seen on an even grander scale in World War II – combined arms warfare leading to fast advances. Masses of artillery with access to millions of shells were coordinated with attacking formations of hundreds of tanks, supported by clouds of aircraft both scouting ahead and launching ground attacks on German positions.[23] The result was mobility and firepower that could not be denied, and it was the Germans who found themselves in retreat. By October, the Germans had been pushed back more than 100 miles and the German Army cracked. In November, the Kaiser fled the country and the Germans sued for peace.

With World War I, the twentieth century started with an unmistakable lesson on the deficiencies of pre-war planning and how it is the process of producing and destroying military force that determines the outcome of a war – not the results of battles. It would not be the last. From World War II onwards, this would be a lesson that was repeated regularly.

World War Two: The Battle for Production

What was also seen in World War I was preparation for the massive competition in force generation that would decide World War II. This war saw all the major economies of the world straining to create weapons in unprecedented amounts, designing and adapting new technologies, and deploying them over thousands of miles in a relentless and constant struggle of relative destruction. And yet the famous battles by which the war is often defined played only a modest role in the destruction of that equipment – at times a shockingly modest one.

As with World War I, the plans with which the different states went into World War II bore little resemblance to how the war developed in reality. Hitler, who had moved from an insignificant German soldier at the front to the dictator of the German Reich, did not believe he was starting a general European war when he invaded Poland on 1 September 1939. He assumed that the Nazi-Soviet Pact he had signed with Stalin precluded such a general conflict. Yet while the early battles seemed far more decisive than they had at the start of World War I, they were quickly shown not to be. This was particularly the case in the event that very few people had expected – the Fall of France in May–June 1940. A German offensive in a few weeks did something that the German Army of World War I could never manage: it split the French Army, forced the British to withdraw almost all their forces from the continent (the British left one division behind in a sacrificial role), and then seized Paris and forced a French capitulation.

At the time, this caused many to assume that Germany had won the war, including Hitler. Germany now controlled almost all of Europe's resources and was allied to most of the rest – including those of the USSR. However, no matter how lopsided a battle the Battle of France turned out to be, the balance of world production – and thus the ability to generate new force, was not transformed by the results. Britain, a productive rival to Germany, stayed in the war, and in response to the Fall of France it would soon receive far increased aid from the United States. Hitler would be left thwarted by British air and sea forces for the rest of the year, losing more equipment than Germany was able to build and leaving him with no actual way to bring the war to a successful conclusion (from his point of view). Even the Fall of France did not change the basic fact that, until the Germans could start generating considerably more force than the British, while attriting British equipment more quickly, they would be stuck.

When this reality hit home for Hitler, he decided his only way out of the conundrum was to try to change the balance of power more in his favour by invading the USSR. This invasion, which commenced on 22 June 1941, is often seen as leading to the greatest land battles in human history. The clash of German and Soviet armies, each with millions of soldiers and thousands of tanks and aircraft, led to superlatives about the size of the campaign and the greatness of the battles that they fought. Yet what is striking about these great battles on the Eastern Front is the small amount of equipment they destroyed compared to the amount that was produced (and destroyed in other parts of the production and logistics system). Maybe the best way to see this is to look at two battles that are often seen as decisive or the largest battles of the war – those of Stalingrad and Kursk.

The Battle of Stalingrad, which started in the summer of 1942, emerged once again out of what seemed to be a successful battle – or at least campaign – for the Germans. In late June 1942, they launched a great offensive against the USSR, with the aim of driving deep into the Caucasus and seizing control of the Soviet Union's most important source of oil. The German 6th Army was to provide cover on the offensive's north flank, driving towards the Russian city of Stalingrad – strategically placed on the Volga River – to protect the main force that was plunging to the south-east.

At first the campaign went very well for the Germans, and the 6th Army raced ahead for hundreds of miles, reaching the outskirts of Stalingrad by late August.[24] However, its progress then slowed markedly. The Red Army engaged in an effective urban warfare campaign which drew the Germans into the city. A few months later, a catastrophe unfolded for the 6th Army. With most of its forces fighting for Stalingrad itself, the Russians attacked the weaker forces protecting its flanks to the north and south, trapping the Germans in the city. There they would linger for months, until, having exhausted their supplies, the entire 6th Army surrendered by 2 February 1943.

German losses have been portrayed as staggering at Stalingrad, but in equipment terms that is grossly exaggerated. At the high point of the battle, for instance, Germany made a concerted effort to exert air power to help the surrounded 6th Army. They began the largest air-supply effort that they would try in the war, and devoted a great deal of other aircraft to combat patrols. Even flying in the often terrible winter weather, the German aircraft losses were limited. On the entire Eastern Front from 19 November 1942 to 31 January 1943, when the Luftwaffe effort was at its height, the total number of German aircraft lost was 900.[25] In comparison, during that time Germany built somewhere between 3,000 and 4,000 aircraft.[26] So, the Stalingrad losses, while not small, were hardly crippling, and represented less than one month's worth of construction. During the Battle of Britain alone, the Luftwaffe lost more than twice as many aircraft (1,887) as they lost on the whole Eastern Front during the last two and a half months of the Battle of Stalingrad.[27] And German aircraft production in 1940 was much smaller than it was in late 1942 and early 1943.

The Battle of Kursk, which happened six months after the Battle of Stalingrad ended, reveals a similar story, this time for tanks. Kursk, or Operation Citadel, was the last great German offensive on the Eastern Front and has often been called the largest battle of the war. By the summer of 1943, the Germans and the Soviets had both built up large armies around a salient that stuck out into the German lines, centred on the city of Kursk. The offensive was an attempt by the Germans to collapse this salient with attacks from the north and the south.

When the offensive started, it did represent a very large armoured battle, as the Germans had just under 3,000 tanks in the area and the Russians had approximately 5,000. The Germans also deployed 2,000 aircraft and the Russians more than 3,000 – so there was a decent amount of aircraft (though it would not qualify as the largest air campaign of the year by a long way). The Germans began Operation Citadel on 5 July, but by 12 July it was clear that, for all the fighting, the Germans were not going to be able to break though Soviet lines. When news came in that the British and Americans were landing in Sicily, Hitler called off the attack and had the Germans take up a defensive position.

Until recently, most of what has been written about Kursk, and particularly the German losses, was fantasy. For decades there was talk of a disastrous German rebuff in an engagement at Prokhorovka.[28] It was said that this was one of the largest tank battles of the war, when hundreds of German tanks faced off against hundreds of Russian tanks, fighting so close that they even collided. The Germans were said to have lost hundreds of tanks in the carnage, including some of the most advanced Tigers and Panthers that they possessed. German casualties were also said to be extreme. During the height of the Cold War, Soviet historians liked to boast that the Red Army killed '150,000' Germans at Prokhorovka, to bolster their claim that the USSR had won World War II in Europe.*[29] It was all nonsense, made up by a Soviet commander to try to salvage his reputation after a disastrous loss of equipment by the forces under his command. The Germans overall seem to have lost about three tanks during the fighting at Prokhorovka, and the main unit doing the fighting actually reported more units operational a few days after the battle than before.[30] The Red Army, on the other hand, lost well over 200 tanks.

This was a sign of the light losses the Germans suffered overall during Kursk. When the dust settled, German losses during the ten days at the start of the battle, when they were on the offensive (and including at Prokhorovka), would have been around 300. This is a tiny figure in comparison to Germany's 1943 annual output of AFVs (armoured fighting vehicles), which was around 11,000. As such, the losses at Kursk would have been less than two weeks' worth of German AFV production.[31]

What has happened is that the need to insert drama and hyperbole into a description of battles has led them to be described as producing 'devastating losses' or being 'crippling blows', when nothing of the sort is true. Far more equipment was destroyed outside these battles than in them, and moreover it was destroyed in many different ways – from direct engagements to long before it could be used in combat. In the Pacific, for instance, the Japanese lost huge amounts of aircraft just trying to fly them from the factories in Japan to the forward areas thousands of miles away where they were supposed to fight. Aircraft broke down along the way, got caught in terrible storms, or pilots simply got lost and ran out of fuel over the vast emptiness of the Pacific. The fact that the Japanese had to start rushing their pilots through training to be able to keep generating the force needed to fight the US made things worse, as less well-trained pilots might not just get lost, they might also crash on landing, damaging their aircraft in ways that would be impossible to repair at the forward bases.

In 1943, such non-combat losses of Japanese aircraft were considerably higher than their losses in battle. And this illustrates another of

* These Soviet claims were rarely challenged by western historians during the Cold War – even though they were patently absurd. If the Soviets had killed 150,000 Germans at Prokhorovka (a short engagement) they would have killed approximately six times as many Germans as died in the entire invasion of France in 1940.

the problems of believing that wars are determined by battles. You can actually engage and cause the destruction of enemy forces long before they get to the battlefield – indeed that is preferable. If you only destroy enemy forces through direct action, they can be used against you. If you destroy them before they can be used – or even prevent them ever being built – this is exponentially more powerful.

So, looking at both world wars, the battle-centric view of war being decided by time-limited engagements over pieces of ground seems more and more inadequate. This is why when trying to analyse how a war might develop, it is important to broaden the means of analysis from trying to guess what will happen when the armies originally clash, to looking at deeper indicators of how those armies can continue to operate, be equipped and regenerate.

7.   Weapons vs Complex Operations

Recently, there has been some discussion about how the future of war will be a contest between the operations of systems – be they complex, complicated or even chaotic.[1] In each case, it's the linking together of a range of weapons, sensors and decision-making processes that ultimately makes the difference between success and failure. Examining the capabilities of individual weapons, from this systemic point of view, is mostly pointless. It is having the ability to get the most out of a weapons system – by protecting it, providing it with the best targeting data, and operating it with the greatest speed – that separates a successful military from a ponderous one.

In World War II, it was a lesson that the Allies used to their advantage regularly to defeat Germany in 1944 and 1945. Even in that late phase of the war, the Germans were building some of the best individual weapons in the world – from the excellent hand-held anti-tank Panzerfaust to the most advanced, combat-ready jet aircraft such as the Messerschmitt Me 262. Perhaps most famously, they were producing the most powerful individual tanks – from the fast medium tank Panther (Panzer V) to the super-heavy, powerfully armed Tiger (Panzer VI). If an individual US Sherman or British Churchill tank came across one of these German machines and had to fight a one-on-one battle, the American or British vehicle would have been in trouble.

How the Allies compensated was by integrating their less effective tanks into more powerful forces capable of combined arms operations. They provided their armour with heavy, regular artillery fire, for one. However, even more important was the way the Allies integrated air power with their tanks. They used aircraft to scout ahead and examine German defences, and then, if needed, attack those defences before their tanks arrived. On top of that, the Allies kept their tanks better supplied. They had, for instance, fleets of trucks able to carry fuel to forward-moving forces, allowing them to better exploit openings when chances arose. In other words, Allied systems triumphed over excellent German weapons.

If anything, today the importance of being able to undertake complex operations is even more important. New technologies such as artificial intelligence (AI) seem poised to speed up and even autonomize the decision-making process of weapons systems considerably. We could potentially see the human being removed from the decision-making process altogether. That might seem like a revolution in military affairs, but it is more a culmination of what has been happening for centuries.

In just the last century and a half, the technologies of war have transformed how, when and what can be engaged. In the mid-nineteenth century, many of the aspects of war retained similarities to centuries past. Naval vessels were powered primarily by sail, stayed on the ocean surface and engaged targets within visual range. Soldiers still fought primarily with arms that were effective only over short distances and required muzzle loading, a process that strictly limits the number of shots that can be fired. Air power, if it could even be said to be in existence, would have been by hot-air balloon.

In the coming decades, the technological changes in warfare exponentially changed the speed, range, accuracy and possibilities of kinetic engagements. A combination of precision heavy engineering started producing artillery pieces in large numbers which could fire projectiles for miles with reasonable accuracy. The same factories also churned out machine guns – small arms capable of firing hundreds of rounds a minute – which could single-handedly stop a large group of attacking infantry. Then the combustion engine entered the mix, transforming how vehicles were propelled on land, at sea and in the air. In World War I, these changes culminated in battleships that were the most complex machines heretofore built by human beings, as well as masses of tanks fighting on the battlefields and fleets of trucks ferrying supplies to the front lines. It also heralded the introduction of the aircraft as a military weapon – something that would further expand the area and possibilities of fighting.

During the interwar period, aircraft became longer-ranged and more robust and could carry much heavier loads of ordnance. This meant that when World War II broke out, the possible area of battle had expanded far beyond the front lines, to hundreds of miles from the point where an aircraft could take off.

Since then, the ability to engage has extended even more – to thousands of miles away, with extraordinary precision. The appearance of computer technology, added to advances in efficient propulsion, has meant that targets can now be identified, prioritized and then fired upon by someone a continent away. Moreover, the growth in technological capabilities has meant that it is never a single weapon that matters; rather, the ability to integrate many weapons and even systems within a fast, complex operation is what separates an efficient military from a plodding one. In other words, it's not about the number of tanks, aircraft or artillery pieces. It's whether you can integrate the actions of all of these, in different combinations, that becomes one of the ultimate tests of an advanced power at war.

The Aircraft Carrier Task Force

In World War II, it was the integration of air and sea power that posed maybe the most challenging questions when it came to complex operations. And in the aircraft carrier task force, this challenge reached its most complex stage. Aircraft carrier task forces were used by the United States to dominate the war in the Pacific. They were basically the largest floating airfields in the world – capable of carrying, supplying, launching and even repairing a force of aircraft that was more powerful than almost all national air forces. They were also the ultimate example of how to combine technological adaptations, excellence, mass production and training in a large, very complex operation. To give one example of this process, the US changed its carrier aircraft almost entirely in World War II. When the war started, it was decided to press on with building a new generation of heavier, longer-range aircraft to be able to overwhelm Japanese carrier task forces.[2] However, in making the aircraft heavier, they were confronted with the fact that launching them off aircraft carrier decks was becoming more difficult. So, an effective aircraft carrier launch catapult needed to be built and put on each carrier.

To operate, such a force needed unprecedently large logistical support systems and command and control capabilities. The logistics support required so many cargo vessels that they were even nicknamed the 'fleet train'. This was a logistics service that eventually reached over 300 vessels, whose job it was to keep the carrier battlegroups at sea for what would have been periods of time that would have been unimaginable before the war. The logistics vessels carried every supply imaginable, including 'fuel oils, food, ammunition, airplanes, clothing, general stores, personnel, and towing and limited salvage detergents'.[3] This extraordinary weight and variety of supply were needed not just to keep the aircraft carrier task force moving, but to support continual military operations. During the Okinawa campaign in 1945, for instance, the fleet train delivered more than 10 million barrels of fuel oil, more than 320,000 barrels of diesel, and over 25 million gallons of aviation fuel.[4] The fleet train was a full-service floating naval base.

And this was not just a case of loading up lots of ships and dispatching them to the fleet. Resupplying vessels out of port required excellent seamanship and the ability to command and control large numbers of vessels while closely coordinating timings. All the ships in the fleet needed to have their supply situations monitored and controlled, so that it could be decided which ships were available to be sent for resupply and which had to wait. Generally, the larger warships, such as battleships, cruisers and some carriers, submitted their needs the evening before getting resupply.[5] As they headed overnight to rendezvous with the fleet, the supply ships had to go through their mountain of supplies and make sure they had everything needed for the specific vessel they would be meeting. Then when that warship appeared, usually the next morning, the agreed-upon supplies had to be transferred, over water, into the warships as quickly as possible, so that they could get back into action. Of course, that wasn't all – throughout this, the weather and seas needed to be closely monitored so that the resupply could be effected as efficiently as possible.

Not only was this force technologically and industrially a massive leap, its command and control (C2) system represented something entirely new in terms of sensors and computing technologies. A US aircraft carrier by 1945 was basically being controlled by the information received and processed by what was called a combat information center (CIC). What made the CIC so novel was that hardly any of the data being collected on a range of enemy threats (and many other variables) came from human eyes or ears.[6] The information was instead collected by a range of different detection devices, from radar scouting out Japanese aircraft and naval vessels, to sonar watching out for Japanese submarines. There were also sensors collecting information about the US forces. The aircraft carrier's planes had to be monitored while in the air, and other US ships in the task force had to have their courses checked so all vessels could manoeuvre safely in the water. And, as always, information about the weather and seas needed to be tracked so that the task force could chart out a safe sailing course moving forward. Finally, there were sources just listening out for radio chatter, in case an important stray piece of intel came in.

All this information was handled by the nine officers and forty men who worked in a typical CIC, processing thousands of pieces of information from a mass of sensors, and then feeding what they considered important or necessary to the bridge. This was all so those in command of the vessel could order course changes, launch aircraft, recover aircraft and the like, making that carrier both devastatingly effective in attacking Japanese targets while at the same time keeping other US carriers remarkably safe. After the CIC went into full operation in 1943, the US never lost a fleet carrier for the rest of the war.

Added together, the logistical and C2 systems used by aircraft carrier task forces were a huge force multiplier for the United States. They could keep their carrier groups on operations for very long periods without having to head back to port – so much so that when the British sent a carrier task force to work with the Americans in 1945, they were overwhelmed by the systems they saw in action. The commander of the British naval forces in the Pacific, Admiral Fraser, reported back to London that 'with easy grace' the US Navy was 'striking here one day, and there the next, replenishing at sea and returning to harbour as the situation demands'.[7] The British – the second-largest sea power in the world at the time, with a fleet arguably more powerful than that of the rest of the world combined (other than the US) – had to struggle to keep up.

The truth of the matter was that the United States was the only country on earth that could have carried off such complex operations on such a grand scale. The first reason for this is that it required masses of specialized vessels. The American force that invaded Okinawa in 1945, for instance, was made up of more than 1,200 vessels.[8]

The Okinawa Expeditionary Force, April 1945

Ships allocated

Battleships	10	Transports	134
Heavy cruisers	8	High speed destroyer transports	36
Light cruisers	4	Cargo ships	65
Escort carriers	18	Repair ships	5
Destroyers	82	Tugs	8
Destroyers escorts	54	Salvage vessels	1
Minelayers	17	Landing ships	303
High speed minesweepers	13	Landing ships dock	6
Minesweepers	42	Landing craft (all types)	294
Motor minesweepers	40	Netlayers	12
Patrol and scout craft	79	Unclassified	1
Seaplane tenders	10		
HQ ships	8	**Total**	**1,250**

And this massive force was on top of the large carrier strike forces that were sent out to protect the landings and attack Japanese targets.

However, mass was not enough. These vessels had the best technology, and were crewed by members of a society that was conversant in advanced logistics and had lots and lots of money. This also highlighted how technological growth had made war a competition of complex operations, not individual weapons or groups of soldiers. It was the interaction of many different systems that effectively afforded the really advanced military powers a huge advantage over the lesser. And after World War II, the pressure to be able to undertake complex operations only grew. With the technological expansion of computing, nuclear weapons, and arguably today AI, the ability to combine lots of different technologies has become a task of the highest importance, and the greatest challenge.

Perhaps the best way to illustrate this growth in importance is to look at two complex operations that came together in the fast carrier task force – air power and logistics.

SEAD: Suppression of Enemy Air Defences

Since the advent of the aircraft, air power has transformed the possibilities of attack. It has allowed the side in a war that can grasp air superiority or even air supremacy the ability to target the enemy in a way that before aircraft was impossible to imagine. Even with its own army hundreds or thousands of miles away, with air superiority a military force can attack the political nerve centres, places of production, transport infrastructure, and power generation sources that create and control an enemy's armed forces. At the same time, air power has enabled the most effective attacks on the enemy armies themselves. Starting from the end of World War I, when aircraft first appeared in mass over the battlefields of the Western Front, air power added an element of flexibility, identification, range, and eventually targeting accuracy that was not available before.

The foundation of the air power advantage, at least until the last few years, was human-piloted, fixed-wing aircraft.* Such aircraft had multiple roles and could themselves carry multiple systems of attack, from cruise missiles capable of hitting targets a thousand miles away (such as Tomahawk missiles) to armour-busting Gatling guns that could scythe through a column of AFVs at closer range. The problem facing the fixed-wing aircraft was always whether they were able to fly with enough freedom of action and survivability to launch their systems effectively. This ended up being a much harder task than the first air power thinkers imagined. Though there was the idea in the inter-war period that 'the bomber will always get through', it was regularly shown that aircraft were quite vulnerable to a range of anti-air systems. These could be anything from land-based artillery (often called flak) to fighter aircraft sent out to destroy bombers, such as in World War II. Since then the systems devised to shoot down aircraft have broadened to include a growing range of very powerful anti-air missiles, from smaller handheld systems to larger systems capable of firing multiple missiles in short order. We might see a whole new generation of anti-air UAVs deployed in the near future.

---

* There is a major debate going on about whether the unpiloted UAV is replacing the fixed-wing piloted aircraft, a debate that will probably swirl until the next war.

With so many threats to an aircraft's survival, let alone functionality, suppressing enemy air defence (sometimes known by the acronym SEAD) has become the prerequisite to any successful air power campaign.[9] In World War II, for instance, being able to execute SEAD or not played a large role in determining the success or failure of an air campaign. Perhaps the greatest failure occurred in one of the most famous air battles of all time: the Battle of Britain.

After the Fall of France in May–June 1940, Hitler turned to try to knock Britain out of the war and cement his hold on Europe. The issue he faced was that he could not control the seas, as the German Navy was too small, so if he was going to attack Britain – either directly through invasion or through strategic air power – he would have to establish air superiority over areas of southern England and the English Channel for considerable periods of time. This would be the first task of the German Air Force (Luftwaffe) when the Battle of Britain commenced in July 1940.

Hitler, and the head of the Luftwaffe, Hermann Göring, believed it would be possible to use air power to subjugate Britain, as the Luftwaffe had played a key role in overwhelming French resistance days previously. However, in attacking the British, the Luftwaffe was faced by an enemy that had the most technologically advanced and well-conceived air defence system in the world. In particular, the British had pioneered the creation of radar systems as a front line of defence. By sending out electromagnetic pulses and charting their return, radar could locate aircraft far beyond visual range. Starting before Hitler invaded Poland, the British had constructed an integrated system of radar stations across the south and east of England, which was given the name Chain Home – a system that they continued to upgrade throughout the war. By the time the Battle of Britain started, Chain Home could pick up Luftwaffe aircraft eighty miles away – often just after the Germans had taken off from their bases in France.[10]

But radar was not all. The British had also instituted a superb system of command and control to take advantage of the information that Chain Home provided. This was nicknamed the Dowding System after RAF Air Chief Marshal Hugh Dowding, the head of Fighter Command. It brought the information from Chain Home and other spotting systems together into Fighter Command, where a counter was decided upon, and then the orders went out to the different geographical commands so that the right aircraft in the right places could be dispatched to meet the German threat. The Dowding System was also a fully integrated operation, combining aircraft with anti-air artillery, searchlights and even barrage balloons in one command structure.[11]

These operational advantages gave the British an unsurmountable advantage in the Battle of Britain. They could 'see' German aircraft long before German aircraft could see them, and British command and control could react efficiently and quickly to dispatch British interception aircraft — most famously the Spitfire and Hurricane fighters — to shoot down the attacking Germans.

The results of the British excellence in anti-air systems, and the German inability to execute a competent SEAD against them, made the Battle of Britain a decisive victory for the RAF. At first the Germans did not even know what the British radar stations were, and risked sending over some of their slowest and most vulnerable aircraft — the famous Ju 87 Stuka dive bombers — to attack coastal targets. These aircraft were massacred. On 18 August 1940, 109 Stukas were sent to attack British targets in southern England, 21 per cent of which were shot down.[12] From that point on, Stukas were rarely used against Britain.

Still, the Germans tried various tactics to contend with British air defence, from mass attacks with bombers and fighters to changing the times and methods of attack. The results were all basically the same, however. No matter what the Germans tried, even if they seemed to have a day or two of success, British systemic excellence meant that German losses became unsustainable. By the end of September, the Luftwaffe threw in the towel. They stopped trying to hit specific targets by flying by day (when it was too dangerous) and instead switched to higher-altitude night-time bombing. This was much safer for the bombers, but it was highly inaccurate, making it impossible for the Germans to hit anything with confidence beyond a city-sized target. Though it was dramatic and extensively covered by the press, this period of the Battle of Britain — called the Blitz because the Germans attacked London at night, often causing impressive fires — was actually a sign of Germany's complete failure in SEAD. It was the moment when Hitler confirmed that he could not drive Britain out of the war, and so would turn to invade the USSR in 1941, to deprive the British of a possible ally in the future. In that way, the failure of German

SEAD in 1940 contributed directly to the defeat of Germany in the coming years.

When in 1943 Britain and the United States turned the tables on Germany and started their own mass bombing campaign, known as the Combined Bomber Offensive (CBO), they too were presented with a major challenge in overcoming anti-air defences. By this point the Germans had their own radar, were building masses of anti-air guns and, most problematically for the Allies, were devoting the vast majority of their fighter aircraft to the job of shooting down British and American bombers. In the second half of the year, for instance, the Germans devoted far more aircraft to defending Germany than they did to the Eastern Front (which many historians argue wrongly was the key theatre for the Germans). In production terms, the anti-air war was the most expensive and technologically advanced war Germany was fighting.

In 1943 the Germans in many ways had the upper hand, because of their massive expenditure on effective anti-air resources. The British, not believing that their Lancaster bomber, the backbone of their fleet, could survive in daylight against German defences, had switched most of their efforts to the night-time bombing of German cities. Like the Blitz, but on a far grander scale, the British did immense damage to places such as Hamburg, but their lack of accuracy meant that the long-term toll of their raids was more questionable. The German population proved relatively resilient, and economically the Germans were able to get production back up and running more quickly than originally expected.

The US experience was quite different. The US Army Air Force (USAAF) – the precursor to today's US Air Force (USAF) – always favoured daylight attacks on particular targets of economic importance. Rather optimistically nicknamed 'precision' bombing, by 1943 the US plan, which had been developed in great detail after studies written by a large team of leading business figures, was to destroy certain key production areas in the German economy, and through that bring German war production to its knees.

Maybe the most famous of these targets was German ball-bearing production, resulting in two major raids in the second half of 1943 in the cities of Schweinfurt and Regensburg. The first, which was in August, was a moderate success for the Americans in that they damaged some ball-bearing production. However, the loss rate for US bombers, which reached 20 per cent for the units involved, was unsustainable and no raids were attempted again until October.[13] When the USAAF returned, however, their ability to suppress German air defences was no better. The attacking bombers were shot down by a relentless combination of German fighter aircraft and the masses of flak protecting the targets. Of the 291 bombers sent against Schweinfurt and Regensburg on 14 October 1943, 60 were shot down, a further 21 crashed in England on their way back to base, and 121 needed repairs.[14] The American losses were so extreme that it was nicknamed Black Thursday.

This loss rate meant that the USAAF called for a halt to any long-range raids into Germany until German defences could better be neutralized. One major change was that the US was able to develop, build and deploy enough long-range fighter escorts to suppress German fighters trying to get to the American bombers. The most famous of these long-range fighters was the P-51 Mustang. With disposable drop tanks carrying extra fuel, a Mustang could fly a roundtrip of approximately 1,400 miles. This meant that it could fly with heavy US bombers deep into Germany and back, providing them with protection against any German fighters trying to shoot them down. The results of these SEAD efforts were that US bombers in 1944 had a much higher-percentage chance of attacking their target, and the results of this were devastating for the Germans. Within a few months, the German fuel oils industry had been brought to its knees, severely crippling both the military and the economy.

In the coming decades, the complexity of SEAD grew as anti-air technologies improved. In particular, ground-based anti-air systems proliferated and became capable of firing ammunition such as surface-to-air missiles (SAMs), which had the ability to lock on to the target and fly without human guidance. In 1991, the Iraqi armed forces had what was thought to be one of the most advanced anti-air systems in the world.[15] It possessed a force of thousands of SAMs, as well as 10,000 anti-air guns and even some advanced jet fighters. At the same time, the Iraqis had a number of advanced French and Chinese detection systems, both passive and active, that were capable of scanning the skies looking for threats. These systems were linked together by a French-made computer network, nicknamed Kari, which fed all the information to a centralized air defence headquarters in Baghdad.[16]

The US Air Force, therefore, as its first task in the war to liberate Kuwait, had to deconstruct this anti-air system, and to do this they put in place arguably the most successful SEAD campaign in history. The US-led coalition was able to collect intelligence on the range of Iraqi anti-air capabilities, and then act on it ruthlessly and quickly to destroy the selected targets. Combining 'centralized control' with 'decentralized execution', the coalition air forces were able to use a wide range of airborne systems to strike Iraqi targets rapidly – sometimes before the Iraqis had any idea that they were being targeted.[17] The result was that the US had not just air superiority, but actual air supremacy for much of the campaign.

Since Desert Storm, undertaking SEAD has become even more complex. The broadening of anti-air technologies, and improvements in their accuracy and effectiveness, means that the process of neutralizing enemy anti-air capabilities requires many different systems working together with extraordinary precision. For the most advanced air forces, such as the USAF or the top-line NATO services, SEAD proceeds along the following lines. First, the enemy's air-defence capabilities (often referred to as their integrated air defence system, or IADS) must be understood and broken down into their component parts. Once that is done, what would normally be targeted is a combination of the enemy's command and control (C2) system and its long-range warning radars. Having at least partially 'blinded' the enemy's vision, the next step is to go after the anti-air systems themselves, starting with the most advanced SAMs – which represent the greatest threat to the attacking force's most high-value air assets. If this can be accomplished, then a larger number of air assets can be used against smaller SAMs, progressively reducing the threats that the enemy can pose. Then there is the need to maintain a constant cycle of Find, Fix, Finish (find new anti-air assets, fix their exact location, and finish them off) to keep the attacking force's own aircraft as safe and operable as possible.

Only once a SEAD campaign is successfully implemented can air power actually be used effectively. Even then, SEAD remains a primary concern of the best air forces, as the enemy can always bring in new systems to try to contest the air. Needless to say, to run such a campaign requires the ability to run layered systems in response, and extraordinary skill. Command and control must link a larger ground-based Combined Air Operations Centre with airborne warning and control aircraft (AWAC). Indeed, a SEAD campaign is constantly being adjusted in order to operate as part of an overall composite air operations (COMAO) plan. This underlying plan integrates the operations of aircraft – sometimes from many countries, such as in NATO operations – so that they can all be effective in achieving the mission's objectives.

For such a thought-through plan to be effective not only requires excellent, well-maintained equipment; it also requires extremely skilled staff who have been constantly drilled in their different tasks and who can work together as efficiently as possible as a team. It is one of the highest tests of systemic warfare, and allows multiple pieces of equipment to be used together to create something far more effective than the individual elements in action.

Logistics, Logistics, Logistics

Armies have always needed supplies, usually lots of them. Getting those supplies from the places of their production to the armies in the field – often hundreds or even thousands of miles away – is a process that has regularly made or broken military campaigns. Going back to the great invasion of Greece by the Persian emperor Xerxes in 480 BCE (sometimes referred to as his second invasion), it can be seen how the largest and most powerful military forces can be crippled by the lack of supply. Though movies might make it seem that Xerxes was stopped on land, he won every land battle he fought during the invasion, including the Battle of Thermopylae. The invasion failed when the Greeks cut off his maritime supply routes after the naval battle of Salamis. After Salamis, Xerxes personally retreated to his empire, leaving behind a much smaller military force, which the Greeks dealt with the following year.

So, logistics has always mattered. However, in the twentieth and twenty-first centuries it has become an increasingly complex operation, as the different means of supply have grown and the different components that need to be supplied have exploded in number. Logistics as a process could be said to be exponentially more complex now than in the nineteenth century.

The change in delivery systems has come from the growth first of the railroad, then land vehicles, then aircraft – all going hand in hand with the significant enhancement of naval vessels in terms of size and speed. In 1850, for instance, it would have taken a military force months to reach the Pacific from Europe. Today, the vanguard of a military force, complete with some vehicles and elements of air support, can be deployed a similar distance in less than a day.

The importance of the interconnectedness of rail and road (and sea) helped determine the course of World War I. On the Western Front, both sides had to deal with the fact that modern armies required huge amounts of supplies to function. In previous wars, feeding the soldiers (and the animals bringing the supplies – mostly horses) was the primary concern of logistics. During World War I, however, it was feeding the needs of machines that came to dominate.[18]

Indeed, during the war the logistical differences between the western Allies and the Germans eventually became stark. Throughout the conflict the German Army remained reliant on the horse as a vital means of transport, to bring supplies from the rail heads to the depots and from the depots to the front line. The reliance on horses meant the further the German Army strayed from working rail lines, the less effective it would become.[19] Even in 1918, the army's advance was mostly supported by horse-drawn transport.[20] This logistical deficiency helped limit their advances once they broke through British and French lines during their offensive in spring 1918. This remains one of the best examples of how a great tactical advantage can be thrown away by a military that can't operate an effective logistical system.

Meanwhile the western Allies, particularly the British, grew to rely increasingly on the truck, especially once horse-drawn transport revealed its limitations. At the start of the war, the British, like the Germans, had very few trucks or cars in their army.[21] By 1918, however, the truck situation had been transformed. By the war's end, the British Army was operating 26,809 trucks, which worked out to 450 for every mile of the front that the British covered.[22]

What the truck did was expand the supply loads that could be carried, though the British still used horses in large numbers as well. That being said, it was a hard learning process, as getting logistics right with any new technology was a constant struggle. In fact, in the first part of 1916, when British industry was beginning to produce a record number of shells, the problem the British Army faced was creating an efficient depot system to get those shells distributed to the troops who needed them.[23] Only when this was at least partially corrected, in the late spring and early summer of 1916, did the British assemble the fire-power needed to launch the Battle of the Somme. Even then, once the battle started in July, the process of delivering the shells to the front in the mass quantities needed to maintain the planned-for heavy fire first strained and then led to a collapse of the British transportation system.

It was not until late 1916, with the appointment of Sir Eric Geddes, a transportation expert, to attack the problem, that a more modern logistics system was put into operation. Geddes broke down the British Army's logistics into five categories, based on the means of transport used: docks, railways, canals, light railways, and roads.[24] Working with specialists in all these categories, he made sure that the British had the physical vehicles needed for each means of transport, but also that each had sufficient workforces to keep functioning at high efficiency. Geddes's system not only made sure the British Army was arguably the best supplied for the rest of the war; it also freed up a large number of soldiers, who had been previously doing supply work, to man the front lines.[25] Adolf Hitler, serving on the Western Front in 1918, was astounded to see the vast amount of supplies that the British were able to bring to their soldiers at this time.[26] This mass of equipment was important in stopping the German offensives in 1918 and then driving the German Army back relentlessly in the last few months of the war.[27]

World War II was also to a large degree determined by which side could maintain the logistical flow of supplies to its armies and which could not. In the Pacific, for instance, supply was always Japan's Achilles heel. On the map, the Japanese had set up a very impressive defensive position by the summer of 1942. They controlled an area stretching from a number of island chains out in the central Pacific, down to the south Pacific and through New Guinea and the Dutch East Indies (present-day Indonesia), before reaching the Asian main-land at Singapore and along the coast through Malaya, Thailand and Burma. It was one of the largest empires that has ever been assembled, and was protected by a series of major air-sea bases throughout.

However its very size also presented the Japanese with one of the greatest logistical challenges any power has ever faced. It was many times the size of Hitler's empire, for instance, and the Japanese had to be able to support forces that were almost 10,000 miles apart at the extremes. For aircraft deployment and supply, this was a nightmare, particularly once the original preferred method of logistical support – the aircraft carrier – was no longer available. Early in the war, Japan would often use aircraft carriers to ferry its aircraft to their forward places of deployment. However, after the carrier losses suffered at the Battle of Midway in June 1942, the Japanese increasingly had to switch to flying their aircraft out, which led to a spike in aircraft and pilot losses and set up a logistical catastrophe.

Flying over the vast distances of the Pacific was an extremely diffi-cult task for the most skilled of pilots, let alone those who were newly trained. The vastness of the ocean, the unpredictability of the weather and the long distances between bases led to a spiralling rise in Japanese losses in 1943 and 1944. And this was only one of the great logistical challenges facing Japanese aircraft. Even those that reached their distant bases might find that there were no spare parts for repair. Aircraft were made up of a huge number of specialized components, from tyres to propeller blades, which needed to be of particularly high quality. If an aircraft was damaged on landing, it could be out of commission for long periods unless spares were available.

The US compounded this logistical vulnerability by deliberately bypassing many of the largest Japanese bases where supply was concen-trated in a campaign known as 'island-hopping'. This strategy basically left masses of Japanese troops sitting in facilities such as Rabaul or Truk without supplies, and the US did not need to attack them for that very reason. A large base was not particularly threatening if the Japanese forces there lacked the logistics to keep their equipment running.

Since World War II, the ability to operate logistics systems at a long-distance scale has continued to grow more complex. It has also continued to determine success in military operations, and has her-alded important milestones in strategic history. The first time a large western military force was defeated outright in a war as part of an end-of-empire struggle was when the French were defeated by the Vietnamese at Dien Bien Phu. It was a logistical defeat that spelled the beginning of the end of the French empire in South East Asia.

The French had decided to lay what they believed was a trap for Vietnamese insurgency forces. In March 1954, they deployed a large, modernized army in a remote part of north-west Vietnam, hoping to draw the Vietnamese into attacking – and thus destroy them with advanced firepower. The Vietnamese, however, took advantage of the remote location and went right after the main French vulnerability – their tenuous supply line. To keep their modern force supplied, the French needed to fly in large quantities of goods, as there was neither a working road nor railway in the area. To cut them off logistically, the Vietnamese dragged heavy artillery through the jungle and placed it on higher ground surrounding the French airstrip. The clever positioning made it almost impossible for the French to hit the Vietnamese artillery, but left the French in the valley below sitting ducks. When the Vietnamese zeroed in on the French airstrip, it became almost impossible for the French to receive supplies. They had effectively been neutered. The Vietnamese then strangled the French forces, coming down from the hills. On 7 May 1954, less than two months after the battle started, the entire French position at Dien Bien Phu had been overrun.[28]

The French logistical experience at Dien Bien Phu showed that while aircraft increased the range of supply possibilities, they also required huge economic and technological capabilities to make them work. Indeed, it is arguable that only the US has the ability to provide efficient, long-term logistical support by air – and it has stretched even US resources at times.

In World War II, when the United States first opted to try supplying its major military forces by air, it undertook one of the most extraordinary logistical operations in history – requiring massive effort and coordination to pull it off. This was to enable the deployment of the most expensive fleet of aircraft heretofore constructed – the B-29 bomber, deployed in China in 1943 to start a strategic air campaign against Japan.

The B-29 had emerged from the single-most expensive weapons programme of the war, the Very Long Range (VLR) bomber programme that was first kicked into action when the US government became worried that they might have to fight Nazi Germany and Japan alone. A VLR bomber needed to be capable of bombing Nazi Germany from Iceland (and flying back), requiring an aircraft of far greater capabilities than anyone had designed to that point. It needed to have a pressurized cabin, high fuel capacity, powerful engines and be able to carry a massive bombload. The deployment of such an aircraft would also require a massive logistical support network.

The B-29 was the most successful design to emerge from the VLR programme and was the bomber eventually put into full production. Once it started emerging in significant numbers, it was decided that it was not needed to bomb Germany but should be used to bomb Japan – from bases in mainland China (codenamed Operation Matterhorn). The only problem was that reaching these bases from the US was one of the most difficult transportation challenges on the globe. There was no way to ship all the heavy equipment needed to keep these brutally expensive aircraft operating, so not only did the aircraft have to fly in, almost all their supplies had to be sent in by aircraft as well.

This turned into arguably the most difficult logistics operation of the war. Deploying the B-29s to India, their last stop before being flown into China, took a flight plan with five legs totalling more than 11,500 miles.[29] The aircraft started from their dispatch point in Kansas, and flew to Newfoundland, then Marrakech, then Cairo, then Karachi, before finally reaching Calcutta. And this long journey had to be done not only by the B-29s, but by aircraft carrying supplies to keep the B-29s in action. The amount of supplies that these aircraft demanded could have equipped many large armies fighting on the European continent. When the plans were first put together, the US Army Air Force estimated that to keep executing Matterhorn into 1945 would require an airlift capacity of 103,000 tons a month.[30] To put that into perspective, it was eleven times as much weight as the Germans estimated they needed to supply their entire 6th Army when it was surrounded in Stalingrad.*

After World War II, the US continued to maintain the most advanced air-delivered logistical systems in the world, allowing them to deploy forces around the world in extreme ways. The Vietnam War was only possible for the United States because of the enormous efforts that were put into the airlift to get American forces and supplies into the theatre. The US had to use a wide range of support aircraft, from the workhorse Douglas C-47 at the start of the war, to the large Lockheed C-130 that could carry fifteen tons of supplies, to the De Havilland C-7, designed to land on shorter runways in the jungle. This

---

* It should be noted that the Germans never were able to deliver such an amount.

force ended up ferrying a massive 7 million tons of passengers and supplies between 1965 and 1973.[31]

However, airlift remains only one part of a complex logistics operation. For truly heavy warfare, air logistics will never be able to carry enough supplies, as the amount that can be put in an aircraft cannot meet the voracious needs of a large combat force for long enough. Both the First and Second Gulf Wars seemed fast – but that was only the combat parts. The logistical efforts took far more time than the battles. The deployment of heavy US ground forces, mostly by ship, was started months before the forces involved could go into action. Though the land campaign part of the First Gulf War lasted a mere four days, the US had been unable to launch the operation for almost six months after Saddam Hussein invaded Kuwait. Likewise, the Second Gulf War – which saw the US streak from the Iraqi border to Baghdad in just a few days – was launched in March 2003, eighteen months after 9/11, which had been the trigger event behind it. If both these campaigns seemed lighting quick, it was only because painstaking months of logistical efforts had preceded them.

Air Power and Logistics in Ukraine

The inability of the Russian military to competently operate complex systems such as SEAD at the start of the invasion of Ukraine in February 2022 was one of the reasons the initial invasion failed. When it came to air power, even though the Russians had by far the more advanced systems, they could not coordinate their command and control with their data collection and their attacking forces to neutralize Ukrainian anti-air forces. Indeed, after a few days of surprisingly high aviation losses, the Russians stopped undertaking the kind of combat air patrols that would be a huge part of US or NATO air planning. We were then confronted by the rather remarkable sight of Ukrainian forces operating in broad daylight on open roads, which was a key element in their ability to respond effectively to the Russian invasion.

If the Russian struggled with SEAD, they also showed a serious limitation in handling logistics. They seemed to opt for the simplest option possible, loading up their trucks and sending them down the open road to Kyiv. When the line of trucks stopped moving forward, the trucks had nowhere to go for days, and the world was left with the ludicrous spectacle of the miles-long columns of inert vehicles. Eventually the Russians had to pull their forces out of all the areas of northern Ukraine that they had moved into at the start of the invasion.

And of course, these two complex systems were only some of the systemic failures of the Russian military at the start of the war. There was a combined arms failure to coordinate land and air forces, command and control failures, maritime failures, etc. Yet few of these problems had been anticipated before the invasion commenced. Then, there had been a widely shared assumption that the Russian military could operate its systems in complex operations when in fact they had no comparable real-world experience of doing so.

For instance, the idea that Russia could operate its air power effectively was almost always based on the Russian use of air power in Syria in support of the Assad regime.[32] However, Russian planes – the technical characteristics of which many analysts loved to trumpet – did not have to worry about SEAD in Syria, as they were attacking forces without modern anti-air capabilities, or even spending their time bombing helpless civilians. In such conditions, dropping bombs is not particularly difficult. In fact, the Syria experience is arguably one that, if anything, made Russian air power worse. It dumbed down a complex operation into something much simpler – but unfortunately people looked at that simple process and assumed that was enough, when it never was and never could be.

Understanding how a military can operate its systems will tell you more about how it will perform than drooling over its supposed weapons.

If a military requires the ability to effectively manipulate systems in complex operations to achieve its goals in any war, that is not something impersonal. Even in an era with growing AI – which will, inevitably, end up making a large number of decisions – it is the human element (for now) that will do the training, plan and develop the complex operations, and decide when and where it goes into action. And yet, to assess how this human element will affect war, we are faced with a terribly difficult task – one akin to trying to assess the workings of the human mind itself.

Germany in World War II might be the most famous case study of how all these human factors interact. There was the basic nature of Hitler's personal leadership and dictatorial rule, which determined where and how Germany would fight the war. Not only did he push the construction of a Germany military with distinct strengths and weaknesses, he also decided when he would use it to attack his neighbours. From the very moment he decided to order his army into Poland on 1 September 1939 (a completely personal choice) to his decision to invade the USSR in June 1941 and his declaration of war on the United States in December 1941 (before the US had declared war on him), Hitler personally decided the timing and number of Germany's major enemies.

Moreover, he ended up playing a personal role in many other questions of the war, both tactical and in terms of production. He favoured heavy tanks, for instance, and this meant that Germany built the super-heavy Tigers and King Tigers. While both seemed impressive, they were impractical in many ways, and needed huge amounts of fuel. They were also so over-engineered and complex that Germany could only build a relatively small number compared to Soviet or US tanks.

Hitler also believed that anti-air artillery (flak) was the best way to defend German cities from Allied bombers, and as such Germany invested massive amounts in building anti-air guns and massive quantities of shells that could be fired from them. He even involved himself in aircraft design. When Germany started putting together the plans for its first combat-worthy jet-engine aircraft, the Me 262, Hitler decided, thankfully for the Allies, that he wanted it to be a dive bomber and not a fighter. He forced designers to spend months trying to make the aircraft suitable for a role that did not match its capabilities, and one which could not have helped the German war effort. Only after it became clear that a dive-bombing design was not practical, and that Germany desperately needed to do everything possible to fight the British and American bombers, did Hitler allow the Luftwaffe to press ahead with the Me 262 as a fighter. However, by the time the Germans came up with an effective jet-fighter design for the Me 262, it was far too late in the war for it to make any difference.

Now, if Hitler could help determine when and where the German armed forces would fight, the people in the armed forces themselves played an enormous role in their effectiveness (or not). This can be seen in a range of other human factors, from morale to training. The morale of the German soldier and civilian remained surprisingly high throughout much of the war – higher indeed than Hitler had expected. This was not because of the ideological impact of Nazism, however, but rather a series of different factors, some material, some psychological, that kept German society supporting the war effort.

For instance, the German population enjoyed a relatively high living standard throughout much of the war. Hitler believed that he needed to keep his people motivated in support of the war he had started, and so tried to limit the impact of the war on their lives to make sure that they did not lose their desire to fight. He was haunted by what he believed was the German loss of faith in 1918, which he blamed on the Jews, seeing it as crucial in having transformed World War I from a conflict that Germany was about to win into a humiliating defeat.

The result was that, particularly for the first few years of the war, the German population was as protected by Hitler as possible. Unlike the British, he did not resort early in the war to the mass mobilization of the population for war production, and he kept the food allowance extremely generous in comparison to any other country at war in Europe. With the war going well for the first two years, Hitler even 'shelved' pre-war plans for economic mobilization and maintained the production of consumer goods at a very high level.[1] It was not until 1942, when the war started to turn against Germany, that real cuts were made in the amount of consumer goods on offer.

With food, the situation remained remarkably stable for even longer. In 1943, the average German consumer would have had a daily allocation of approximately 2,400 calories of food, with soldiers and those in heavy industry getting 3,000.[2] This was more than double that of the Italian ration.[3] Admittedly, the German food might have become more dull as the war progressed – as meat supplies would have declined and vegetable and potato consumption risen – but that might even have made the population healthier.

Hitler's focus on keeping the German population relatively sated and happy was one of the reasons that German war production did not rise as steeply at first as that of Britain. During the Battle of Britain – in which the plucky Brits were fighting off the supposedly mighty Luftwaffe – British aircraft production was approximately twice as large as Germany's.

But Hitler might actually have underestimated the German population's willingness to suffer. As the war went on, the Germans remained remarkably willing to fight and die in large numbers, even as their cities were being devastated by Allied bombers. Though the hope of British strategic bombers (and the fear of Hitler) was that this bombardment would lead to a collapse in the population's inclination to support the war, in the end there was little evidence to support that hope. The German population, much like the German soldier, ended up supporting (or at least not opposing) the Nazi regime until the bitter end. Indeed, the loyalty of the German people towards Hitler and the Nazis was so strong that it has since caused a great deal of soul searching.[4]

Quantifying any of the different ways that human qualities shaped the course of a war is almost impossible. However, to try to understand how a war will develop they must be taken into consideration. In terms of categorization, it might be best to say that the human elements most impact the conduct of war through leadership, training and morale, and societal commitment – and the way that all three interact.

Leadership

If the leadership of a state plays a major role in determining how it accumulates and creates its power, the impact of that leadership is arguably heightened during war. The demands of war leadership usually see political leadership making decisions on a vast array of questions from the strategic and economic to the technological. As the case of Hitler shows, this decision-making affects every element of the war-fighting structure. This is true in democratic as well as autocratic and totalitarian states.

Germany in World War I is another powerful example of how leadership can make transformative choices in war – even changing a potentially war-winning situation to one of total defeat. In late 1916, Germany was in a situation of some advantage in the European war. During that year it had remained on the defensive on the Western Front and repelled British and French offensives. At the same time, in the east, Germany was starting to put great pressure on the Russian state of Tsar Nicholas II. In 1916, the Russian Army suffered massive losses, even when winning some battles as part of the Brusilov Offensive.[5]

The German leadership in World War I was very different from Hitler's dictatorial rule, and that partly enabled the disastrous choice it made. Germany from 1914 until 1918 was led by a combination of civilian politicians, the military and the Kaiser, with the military increasingly dominating as the war went on. In late 1916, the German leadership had to determine the priorities for the coming year. They could have chosen to focus their forces on the weakening Russians (who would soon basically collapse as a fighting force anyway). However, looking at the war, they made the rashest decision possible – and it was one that was in no way forced upon them. They decided to provoke the greatest economic/technological power in the world, the United States, into joining the war against them.

The German decision to restart unrestricted submarine warfare in early 1917 is one of the most catastrophic choices in strategic history. As mentioned earlier, the Germans had tried unrestricted submarine warfare around the British Isles in 1915. However, this ended up leading to a crisis with the US and by early 1916 they had pulled back under the threat of a breakdown in relations with America. At the end of 1916, however, there were calls to restart the campaign.

By this time in the war, it was not the German political leadership that wanted to return to unrestricted submarine warfare. The civilian chancellor, Theobald von Bethmann Hollweg, was actually deeply worried about the idea, knowing that it risked the possibility of bringing the US into the war.[6] The Kaiser, now becoming more of a marginal figure, was also of two minds. However, senior officers in the German Navy, including Admiral Henning von Holtzendorff, were determined to get back to the submarine war. Relying on what only can be called the most optimistic of projections, they produced a memorandum in December 1916 arguing for a return to unrestricted submarine warfare.[7] They believed that with just over 100 submarines, if they were allowed to attack merchant shipping without warning, Germany would be able to cut off Britain from the run of the seas and keep all US power in North America.[8] The navy next got the army high command on side, and then was able to convince the Kaiser (making perhaps his last destructive decision as national leader) to support the plan. In the end, even a reluctant Hollweg could no longer resist. The German chancellor made one final attempt to start peace negotiations, but when his effort failed, he went along with the rest of the German leadership.

On 9 January 1917, the German leadership met and agreed to go back to unrestricted submarine warfare. In a rather mundane meeting, during which they focused on trivialities and showed not the slightest awareness of what they were doing, Germany's leaders committed strategic suicide.[9] It is as good an example as any of how system and personality can meet and cause a catastrophe in war.

The United States duly went to war with Germany in April 1917, and the German submarine threat was eventually controlled by the introduction of convoys. Eventually, huge numbers of goods, soldiers and raw materials were crossing the Atlantic – all to crush the life out of Germany. In the second half of 1918, Germany was defeated by overwhelming Allied force. And so, by a decision of its own leadership, Germany had laid the seeds of its own destruction.

Mussolini in World War II did something very similar, though being Mussolini it was even grubbier. Interestingly, when Hitler decided to invade Poland in August 1939, and asked the Italian dictator for his support, Mussolini showed some sense and demurred.[10] Mussolini did not believe his armed forces were ready for a major European war and saw little benefit in taking on the French and British navies in the Mediterranean to help Hitler. To forestall Italy having to join with Hitler, Mussolini asked for so much military support from Germany that the Nazi dictator had no option but to refuse.

However, his good sense did not last. In May 1940, after Hitler had attacked France and had the French Army on the ropes, Mussolini could not help himself.[11] The idea of missing out on the booty he would get by going to war – and the personal need he had to be a conqueror – drove him to enter the war on Hitler's side, precisely when the German dictator had no need for Italian help.[12] Indeed, when Mussolini declared war on 10 June 1940 and sent his army into France, Hitler was not particularly impressed. It turned out that Mussolini's army was definitely not ready for war, and it performed appallingly in its invasion. It was stopped almost immediately by a much smaller force of French soldiers, and the Italian Army showed fundamental weaknesses in systems operations such as logistics (discussed in chapter 7), as well as the human elements of command and control and also training and morale. Embarrassed, Mussolini asked the Germans for help to get Italian forces further into France before the French surrendered. They refused, and when the armistice did come into effect in June 1940, Hitler made sure Italy only ended up with a tiny slice of French territory instead of the large chunk the Italian coveted.

One might say that any self-respecting dictator would have acted as Mussolini did – joining the war when Hitler was in the ascendant. However, that is not true. The Spanish dictator Francisco Franco, only a few months later, ignored Hitler's blandishments and refused to have Spain join the war on Germany's behalf. Like Mussolini in 1939, he asked Hitler for so much support for the Spanish war effort that Hitler blanched. And from that point, Franco was able to stay out of the war. While Mussolini ended up being gunned down on a nondescript Italian street corner in 1945, Franco died in his bed thirty years later.

So, leadership can determine how wars are started – and it makes massive differences in how they are fought. This has been the case even in leaderships that are very different from one-man dictatorships. Maybe the greatest example of this is Hitler and Mussolini's greatest ally in World War II – Imperial Japan.

Japan at this time had one of the most remarkable war leadership structures in modern history. The army and navy were basically self-governing entities, each of which had high representation in the Japanese government. Though the government also had a prime minister, the ability of that person to give orders to the army and navy was limited. For the government to take coordinated action, therefore, the army and navy had to be in agreement. Even then, once the decision was made to go to war, the military were to a large degree free to prosecute the war in whichever way each service wanted.

The result was that, when it came to World War II, for much of the time the Japanese Army fought one war and the Japanese Navy another – with neither service able to do much to influence the other, or even, as it turned out, to find out basic information from the other. It ended up being a recipe for disaster.

The Japanese Army, for instance, precipitated World War II in Asia by launching, without the knowledge of the navy, the invasion of China in 1937. From that point on Japan's Kwantung Army made most of the decisions for itself about how and to what depth the war against China would be pursued. Eventually, somewhat to the dismay of the Japanese government, the army ended up involved with an invasion that covered thousands of miles of China, and one that stretched Japanese resources to the utmost.

And if the army didn't listen to the navy – or anyone else really – when it came to the prosecution of the war, the navy was little better. After the Japanese attack on Pearl Harbor had started the war with the United States, the navy was allowed a great deal of latitude to prosecute the war in the Pacific against the Americans. The result was that the Japanese Navy decided on the very risky Midway campaign in late spring 1942. Looking to draw out the US fleet, Japan sent its most valuable warships – its aircraft carrier strike force – thousands of miles into the central Pacific to fight the United States close to American facilities in Hawaii.

This led to one of the most famous defeats in World War II. The Japanese fleet of four carriers was met by a US fleet with only three, but one which was operating with the advantage of its command being able to decipher Japanese codes and knowing the Japanese were on the way. The American fleet was thus perfectly placed to intercept the Japanese when the latter were at their most vulnerable. The eventual result was the sinking of all four of the Japanese carriers and only one of the American. It was a heavy blow, which the Japanese Navy had brought upon itself. However, in a further sign of the basically chaotic way in which the Japanese leadership system fought the war, the naval leaders covered up the scale of the losses, and claimed to the Japanese public that they had won a smashing victory.[13] Even the army, which had an idea that the battle had not gone exactly according to plan, had no idea of the true scale of the losses the navy had suffered.

If human leadership and governmental structures played a great role in determining the outcome of World War II, after the war the reality was no different even for the greatest global power in world history – the United States of America. The US in its great period of dominance saw significant oscillations in its application and usage of military force, depending on who was president. Maybe the most fascinating is the contrast between George H. Bush (president 1989–93) and his son George W. Bush (president 2001–9). Both Bush presidents would be war leaders for the United States, though each went down a very different path.*

Under George H. Bush, the United States found itself at war with Iraq after the Iraqi dictator, Saddam Hussein, ordered his army to undertake a wholly unnecessary invasion of Kuwait, Iraq's neighbour, in 1991. In reaction, GHB put together a large and in many ways unprecedented coalition and assembled an overwhelming force which ejected Iraqi forces from Kuwait after a forty-day air campaign and a four-day offensive. At that point, GHB could have continued on to reach Baghdad and overthrow Saddam Hussein. The Iraqi Army had basically been rendered inoperable by US forces, and there was practically nothing they could have done to stop the military behemoth the US had assembled. GHB, however, paused and then stopped. He chose to limit his military victory to the restrained goals of returning the Kuwaiti government to power – and had no desire to use US forces in a state-building role in the Middle East. He certainly was no fan of Saddam Hussein, but he was also aware of the risks, political and otherwise, that the US would be running if it invaded and occupied Iraq.

---

* The contrast between the policies of the Bushes will be discussed also in chapter 10, which focuses on the importance of alliances in winning wars.

GWB acted very differently a decade later. After the 11 September 2001 terrorist attacks on the World Trade Center in New York City and the Pentagon in Washington, DC – which left almost 3,000 Americans dead – GWB decided to support a radical policy of remaking the Middle East through military force. The speech he gave to a joint session of Congress on 20 September divided the world in the starkest terms, and proclaimed a long-term struggle between the US and those that supported terrorism.[14]

> Americans should not expect one battle, but a lengthy campaign, unlike any other we have ever seen. It may include dramatic strikes, visible on TV, and covert operations, secret even in success. We will starve terrorists of funding, turn them one against another, drive them from place to place, until there is no refuge or no rest. And we will pursue nations that provide aid or safe haven to terrorism. Every nation, in every region, now has a decision to make. Either you are with us, or you are with the terrorists . . . From this day forward, any nation that continues to harbor or support terrorism will be regarded by the United States as a hostile regime.

Even though Saddam Hussein (still in power) had absolutely nothing to do with the 9/11 attacks, GWB cobbled together a much less impressive military alliance and sent US armed forces into Iraq specifically to bring about regime change. The result was a long, brutally expensive, ultimately self-defeating, catastrophic war. Though Baghdad fell quickly and the Iraqi Army melted away, the US found itself occupying a country it had no idea how to run. The result was years of war, as GWB had to keep sending military force into Iraq to try to quell a rebellious and unreconciled Iraqi population. Indeed, in 2007, when it seemed that the US population was turning decisively against this war, GWB opted for a major escalation in the fighting and the deployment of many more US forces, known as the 'surge'.

Was there any consistency in the war leadership decisions demonstrated in this period? There does not seem to have been – and that's the point. When trying to assess how a nation or power will behave in war, you need to take into consideration its human leadership – and the challenge is in trying to determine how that leadership will work.

Training and Morale

The effectiveness of an armed force in the field is as much, if not more, down to the training and morale of the soldiers operating the equipment than it is the equipment itself. Throughout the twentieth and twenty-first centuries, armed forces with better training and morale have regularly outperformed those that are larger or have more and/ or better equipment – if the latter forces are not as committed or well prepared to fight.

This was evident even before World War I. When the Russian and Japanese navies squared off during the Russo-Japanese War of 1904–5, it was widely thought in European circles that the Russian fleet would triumph over the Japanese. After all, the Russians had more modern warships, and the Russians were European. The naval war between the two, however, ended up with a lopsided victory for the smaller Japanese fleet, with much of the difference coming down to greater training, preparation, and aggression at sea.

The Japanese Navy was one of the most efficient naval forces in the world in 1905.[15] They had based much of their naval structure and shipbuilding on the British, and had put together a force that had excellent materiel, but also seamen who were well trained. When British observers saw the Japanese fleet not long before the war started, they were wowed by the 'very remarkable state of efficiency' being demonstrated by the Japanese.[16] The Russian Navy, on the other hand, was deeply flawed – corrupt, and ponderous.[17] However, that did not stop it from having a confident outlook on any war with the Japanese in the Far East.[18]

The basic differences in training and efficiency showed in the greatest naval battle of the war – the Battle of Tsushima, fought in May 1905. Tsushima was a quick and lopsided affair and witnessed the destruction of almost all the major warships of the Russian fleet. This fleet had cruised thousands of miles around the globe, and its very state spoke of shortcomings. Instead of being an efficient and impressive force, many of those who saw it steam by – or even rest and refit in friendly ports – spoke of the dilapidated and disorganized nature of its warships.

The Japanese fleet, led by Admiral Togo, was well drilled and ready for action. When the fleets met, the Japanese had a properly thought-out plan, as well as the ships and men to execute it. When the Russian fleet first emerged in the Tsushima Strait (which separates Japan from Korea), the Japanese fleet manoeuvred quickly to cross the Russian 'T' – which meant sailing its force across the top of the moving Russian column. With its entire line of ships thus facing the top of the Russian column, the Japanese were able to concentrate their firepower on the leading Russian vessels, while also making it impossible for the Russians to fire on them with all but a handful of their ships.[19]

The result was that the Russians lost all shape, and became sitting ducks for the efficient Japanese. When the battle was over, two-thirds of the Russian fleet had been destroyed, six ships had been seized, six fled to neutral ports and only four reached safety in Vladivostok. It was one of the most one-sided victories in modern naval history.

The success of better-trained and motivated forces over larger armed forces was repeated a number of times in the two world wars. In World War I, the Russian Army was the largest at the start and would remain the largest until 1917. Its size, however, did not correlate to efficient combat performance on the Eastern Front. This was also the case with the second largest military force on the Eastern Front, the army of the Austro-Hungarian Empire.

The Austro-Hungarian armed forces ended up punching below their weight. Part of the problem was the extreme diversity of their soldiers. Austria-Hungary was a polyglot empire with soldiers from more than ten nationalities. It even tried to operate with three official languages – German, Hungarian and Croatian – but soldiers from other areas might learn only a handful of words in the official tongues.[20] However, more than their polyglot nature, it was different operational and human flaws that limited the effectiveness of the Austro-Hungarian armed forces. In particular, the troops suffered from failures in logistics, command and control, and training – which fed into poor morale.[21] They did have relatively good equipment – certainly as good as the Russians for instance – though this did not usually lead to success. When the Austro-Hungarians and Russians met each other in the field, the results were usually messy and indecisive. Indeed, for much of the first few years of the war, the Russians were often able to best the Austro-Hungarians – and occupied a significant slice of Austro-Hungarian territory in 1916.

But if the Russians did well against the large Austro-Hungarian armies, they uniformly struggled against the smaller, but more effective, German armies in the east. Starting with the Battle of Tannenberg in 1914, the Russians normally lost their major engagements with the Germans. The German military's edge over its far larger opponent came from a combination of many operational and human factors. German officers were some of the best trained and drilled officers in the world, and this gave the German Army a flexibility in operations that could hardly be matched.[22] German NCOs were likewise the best or amongst the best in any army. They were trained to the highest standard, given responsibilities that in many other forces would be handled by junior officers, and their morale was supported by excellent career terms and conditions.[23] And the German soldier was arguably the best trained soldier in the war.[24] German training before and during World War I was physically and mentally rigorous. The German soldier was made strong through regular exercise and at the same time was asked to learn a great deal – to understand what would be expected of him once he reached the battlefield. Even British observers, who also came from a well-trained army, were known to remark that a German soldier received 'more training in two years than a British regular in four'.[25]

In World War II, larger militaries could regularly be beaten by smaller ones if they lacked the training and morale to commit to the fight. One of the most remarkable examples of this was the Italian invasion of Greece in October 1940. This was sparked by Mussolini's desire to establish Italy as an independent power not entirely reliant on Nazi Germany for its success. Embarrassed by being seen as a junior partner to Hitler, he determined to invade and seize Greece without German aid – and indeed without even informing the Germans until the last possible moment. He even rather pathetically said, 'Hitler perpetually places me before a *fait accompli*, this time I will pay him back in his own coin.'[26]

The Italian dictator thought it would be an easy campaign – after all, Italy was considered one of the leading powers of Europe while Greece was a small state. Moreover, as Albania was part of the Italian Empire, Mussolini could mass his armies directly on the northern border of Greece. With the moment of invasion approaching, he started dreaming of a quick and decisive war and fantasized about a victory parade in Athens.

Numerically and in terms of modern equipment, the Italians had a clear advantage. Mussolini concentrated more soldiers, aircraft and tanks on the Greek border than the Greeks were able to deploy. However, when the Italians launched their attack it rapidly turned into a military catastrophe. Greek troops, though outnumbered, fought with greater determination and commitment. The Greek Army had actually stressed better training for decades, and was ready to fight.[27] They not only quickly blunted the Italian advance after a few days; they soon began counterattacking.

Soon the smaller, less advanced Greek Army crossed the border into Albania and started to seize large chunks of the Italian colony. Mussolini was left rushing huge numbers of troops from wherever he could find them, including North Africa and the Italian mainland, to try to stop the Greeks.[28] Only when Italian forces vastly outnumbered the better-motivated Greek Army were they able to stem the tide. In the end, the Italians were never able to conquer Greece. It took the intervention of a large, well-trained and motivated German Army in 1941 to do the job the Italians could not.

In World War II, the sophistication of the most advanced weaponry meant its operation required personnel that were able to be trained to a very high standard. Examples previously mentioned include those who served in the CICs of carrier strike forces and those who flew B-29s, but there were many others. Arguably the greatest difference between the British and Americans on the one hand and the Germans on the other was how the former were able to keep giving their pilots detailed and lengthy training periods before sending them into combat – while the latter was rushing them into action with relatively little preparation. In the summer of 1944, for instance, just when German aircraft production was reaching its numerical peak, the number of flying hours that every German trainee pilot was supposed to have before being sent out to fight the British and Americans was cut to only 100. Even then, the Germans struggled to give them that much training. The British and Americans, in comparison, made sure that their pilots received about 300 flying hours in training time.[29] This meant that they had a massive qualitative advantage in pilot skill in the last year of the war.

In some ways this phenomenon became even more pronounced in the post-war period – particularly when it came to the willingness of a military to fight against what seemed to be long odds. The whole series of victories by peoples fighting against colonial authorities was a story that often saw better-armed European and eventually US forces outlasted by less well-armed but more committed local forces, who would be willing to suffer the kinds of losses that no European or American military could have conceived of in the post-war world. That helps explain, for instance, the story of Vietnamese independence. In a period of about thirty years, between the end of World War II and the collapse of the US-backed government in South Vietnam, the Vietnamese fought campaign after campaign, sometimes suffering massive losses and often defeats, only to end up with a complete victory.

First, the North Vietnamese outlasted the French, behaving with such determination that they did something that many thought was impossible by defeating French forces at the Battle of Dien Bien Phu. After the French withdrawal, however, things did not get any easier for the North Vietnamese, as they were soon faced with the might of the US – the 'superpower' of the moment. It is hard to overstate the power differentials between the US and North Vietnam at that time. The US led the world in almost every meaningful economic and military numerical variable. It had air, sea and land power that the North Vietnamese could only dream of – and it used that power to devastating effect.

For almost fifteen years the US military battled with North Vietnamese forces for control of South Vietnam, and inflicted huge casualties on their enemy, far out of proportion to what the US suffered. When the two sides met in combat, US forces could count on excellent artillery support and air power from helicopters and fixed-wing aircraft to support their operations. They even had far superior medical support, allowing for the prompt and often effective treatment of serious wounds. These advantages for the American forces led the Vietnam War to be one of the most lopsided wars in casualty terms in modern history. By the end of their involvement, about 58,000 US soldiers had been killed. In exchange, about 1.1 million North Vietnamese and Viet Cong fighters were dead.[30]

And yet it was the US that eventually decided they'd had enough and withdrew. The commitment of the North Vietnamese military to suffer losses – while losing battle after battle, it should be said – left the

US in a political bind that eventually lessened its society's willingness to continue fighting the war.

Societal Commitment

One key element in sustaining the morale of forces at war is whether they believe their society at large is strongly supportive of their mission. A military reflects many of the strengths and weaknesses of the society from whence it is created – and understanding and taking into consideration the effect of these strengths and weaknesses is one of the most important, and maybe the most difficult factor, to consider in assessing how effective a military will be.

One of the problems is that societal commitment to war is not just active or passive or positive or negative. It can oscillate, often dramatically, between the two. Indeed, it is evaluating the course of this relationship that will tell you a great deal about how a war is going and for how much longer a power is going to fight effectively. One thing that is clear is that dividing societies at war between democracies and autocracies/dictatorships is only partially helpful. It is not the system (though that matters); it is whether a society believes a war is winnable.

A society that believes that it is going to end up on the winning side of a war or that is has no alternative but to fight a war has a significant advantage. On the other hand, a society that loses faith in victory or comes to the conclusion that getting out of the war (even to the point of surrender) is preferable to continuing to fight will almost always seriously weaken its government's ability to continue prosecuting the war.

The specific results of the two world wars and the Vietnam War show how important societal commitment is in shaping the course of a war as well as its eventual outcome. It was a panic in Saint Petersburg about food supplies that started the process that led to the Russian Revolution. In early 1917, the Russian Army was actually in better shape materially than it had been in a while.[31] Internal production of war materiel had gone up significantly, so that Russian forces could count on a regular flow of munitions (when their logistics worked efficiently). However, just when things were looking a little better for the Russian Army, Russian society panicked. Years of inflation had eaten away at people's purchasing power, so that even wartime rises in wages could not keep up with price rises. Then rumours spread like wildfire that the Russian government would not be able to provide enough food for cities like Saint Petersburg. Soon, Saint Petersburg was in crisis, and in March 1917 the Russian Revolution began.

The loss of faith on the home front was very quickly transmitted to Russian military forces in the field. When stories reached the military that much of the population of Saint Petersburg was in revolt against the tsarist government, it was military commanders that persuaded the tsar to abdicate. From that point on, the army divided. Certain elements were loyal to the new provisional government, others remained devoted to the tsar, and some even started sympathizing with elements in society that were calling for even more drastic change. When the Germans launched a powerful attack in the summer of 1917, many Russian soldiers abandoned their posts and ended up supporting the very radical Bolsheviks, led by Lenin, who were advocating the overthrow of the existing order.[32] When the Bolsheviks seized power in November 1917, they were helpfully supported by a number of those who had been soldiers and sailors in the tsarist regime.

Germany experienced something similar in 1918. In this case it would be best to say that the loss of the will to keep fighting at the German home front and amongst the German soldiers at the front was symbiotic. The German people had had an up-and-down experience when it came to the war from the moment the conflict started. Even in August 1914, when it was said there was widespread German war enthusiasm (an idea that was reported more after the fact than during), there were signs that many Germans were more apprehensive than anything else.[33] The German home front also suffered significant food deprivation throughout the conflict. In 1916–17 it endured what was called the Turnip Winter, when food was scarce and people were put on a strictly limited (calories in ration) diet. That being said, the German home front did not lose faith in victory at that time, and the relative success of the German Army in the field provided it with enough hope to keep the country united behind the war.

In 1918, however, there was a catastrophic loss of faith both on the home front and in the army, and this led to a German collapse and surrender. It also happened with extraordinary rapidity. The first half of

1918 actually seemed to be going well for the Germans. Having forced Russia out of the war and seized control of a huge amount of territory to the east, Germany was able to move about 1 million soldiers from the Eastern to the Western Front. These fresh reinforcements combined with battle-hardened German troops already in the west to launch the most tactically successful series of offensives the Western Front had seen since 1914. In a matter of a few months, the Germany Army made a series of large advances against both British and French forces, creeping ever closer to Paris itself. To German soldiers at the front, such as Adolf Hitler, it seemed that Germany was on the cusp of a war-deciding victory. The German home front was equally elated.

And then everything fell apart. To make these advances, the Germans suffered huge losses in a relatively short period of time, estimated at about 800,000 – a rate of loss they could not sustain. Eventually, German advances stopped as the British and French adjusted to the new German form of warfare, and the Americans started to arrive in ever-larger numbers. Almost overnight, Germany went from moving forward to moving backward. The army and home front, faced with this transition, started to crack. With the prospect of victory snatched away and facing a future war against Britain, France and the US, any German hope for eventual victory seemed doomed.

In World War II, on the other hand, German society retained its commitment to the war with greater ferocity until the very end. It was arguably German society's reactions to the last few years of World War I that influenced how it was treated and behaved in World War II. There was the fact that Hitler made sure that the German population was well fed and looked after until relatively late. But there were other considerations as well. Nazi propaganda was extremely skilled in making the German people believe, until very late in the war, that Germany still retained a realistic chance of victory – or at least in striking back against their enemies with devastating blows. This was of course based on mirages – faith in things like the effect of Germany's supposed wonder weapons such as the V-2 rocket or the Me 262 jet – but for all that, it was effective. During the height of the strategic bombing, when the British in particular were nightly attacking and burning large German cities, the German population was recorded asking when the much-awaited 'retaliation miracle' would occur.[34]

Finally, there seems to have been a extreme recognition in German society that the crimes of the regime were so strong that peace, especially a peace under the control of Stalin's Red Army, was bound to be brutal. Even many of those Germans who had no hope for final victory seemed to be motivated by a basic need to keep the Soviets at bay for as long as possible. Knowledge of the concentration camp system was widespread in Germany. Indeed, as the war went on, the concentration camps became so numerous and various that they established economic relationships with the largest cities and smallest villages – ceasing to be an 'abstraction' for most Germans.[35]

These kinds of relationships were an indication of how German society had become integrated into the overall war effort of Hitler and the Nazi Party, through a shared understanding of risk and culpability. And it led to a very different end to World War II than World War I. With many of the German people determined to wage the war until the bitter end, the German armed forces behaved likewise. Unlike in 1918, when Germany surrendered before hardly any of the country was occupied, in 1945 Germans fought street by street in their capital until it was entirely conquered and many more German soldiers and civilians had died.

If societal commitment did not change the war's result, it did affect its course a great deal. When it comes to the US at the height of its power, however, societal commitment has arguably determined the outcome of many of its wars. It has mattered more than US economic/technological strength, military prowess, or the ability and training of American soldiers.

The United States represents something rather extraordinary in history – a global 'superpower', arguably a hegemon for a few decades after 1990, that has lost far more wars than it has won. Indeed, the greatest deployment of US ground forces in the post-1945 world, the Vietnam War, was arguably the greatest military defeat in US history and one of the most extraordinary defeats suffered by a global power at the height of its supremacy. In the case of Vietnam, perhaps the greatest factor that led to the American defeat was that US society eventually decided that the war was unwinnable, even after the expenditure of massive amounts of money and the deaths of many American soldiers.

There has been a great deal of discussion about how society in the

United States reacts to war. For a while during and after the Vietnam War, it was thought that the US population turned against wars when significant casualties were suffered – or, as it can be said, when the body bags started coming home. This seems not to be quite so important in retrospect. Looking at Vietnam and the War on Terror, the real ends of the wars were precipitated when the US population no longer believed that these wars were winnable.

In Vietnam, it was a process that began in 1968. In the first few years of US involvement, support at home for the Vietnam War remained strong, and with this support the administration of President Lyndon B. Johnson was able to steadily increase military involvement. By the end of 1967, there were well over half a million US troops fighting in Vietnam, as well as a massive commitment of air and sea power. This seemed, for a brief moment, to provide Johnson with some validation for his Vietnam policy. In the State of the Union Address which he delivered on 17 January 1968, Johnson was able to portray the war in a positive light and claim that the American people were behind it:[36]

> The enemy has been defeated in battle after battle.
>
> The number of South Vietnamese living in areas under Government protection tonight has grown by more than a million since January of last year.
>
> These are all marks of progress. Yet:
>
> The enemy continues to pour men and materiel across frontiers and into battle, despite his continuous heavy losses.
>
> He continues to hope that America's will to persevere can be broken. Well – he is wrong. America will persevere. Our patience and our perseverance will match our power. Aggression will never prevail.

President Johnson spoke too soon. Just days after this address, the North Vietnamese* launched their largest military operation to date against US forces, the Tet Offensive, in which they attacked all up and down South Vietnam. North Vietnamese forces even got inside the US embassy in Saigon. Johnson had failed to understand that North

---

* It was often said at the time that the US was facing two enemies, the forces of the North Vietnamese government and the Viet Cong – an indigenous military movement of rebels in South Vietnam. It is now clear that the Viet Cong were in no way independent, but were in fact an arm of the North Vietnamese military.

Vietnamese commitment to the war was not one that was going to be broken by some military defeats or the show of American power. There was a shared understanding that they were in the war for the long haul, and they had already seen off the French (and the Japanese, who had occupied Vietnam from 1941 until 1945) and would do the same with the United States.

It was a stunning political rebuke for Johnson – even if it did not change the military status at the time. Within days and at most weeks, US forces had stabilized the situation in South Vietnam, recapturing everything the North Vietnamese forces had seized. However, at home, the attitude of the American people seemed to have taken a decisive turn. In February 1968, for the first time, more Americans thought it was a mistake to send troops to Vietnam than thought it was not.[37] This trend would never be reversed, and US politicians started immediately paying attention.

In the end, the process of the US population turning against the war was actually abetted by the Johnson administration's attempts to keep the public onside. The administration assured the American people that the war was about to be won, but arguably had no strategy to make that happen. When the American people could no longer reconcile the difference between these two positions, they turned against the war. It began the process of politically forcing the US leadership to get out of the conflict. In the 1968 election, both the Republican nominee, Richard Nixon, and the Democratic one, Johnson's VP Hubert Humphrey, ran calling for an end to direct military involvement in Vietnam. The victor, Nixon, would see to it that US forces were out of Vietnam by the end of his first term – and he would gain a significant amount of public support because of it.

Though the US military never lost a battle in the traditional sense of the word in Vietnam, it was defeated by a far less advanced and powerful enemy who was able to take advantage of the fact that US societal commitment to the war was vulnerable. It has been a pattern repeated a few times since Vietnam – one could say that the US population deciding that Iraq was unwinnable forced the Bush administration to opt for the 'surge' and then start a general reduction of US troops in the country.

If larger human questions can lead to the world's greatest 'superpower' losing a war, they can affect any power at war at any time.

The problem remains understanding how and where these human elements will really matter. It is impossible to understand how a war will develop based solely on looking at the military metrics of the armies in the field. It requires the ability to look at how war leadership, the human elements of training and morale, and societal commitment will all interact to change how those armies in the field behave.

9.   Starting vs Sustaining

In 2021, Ukraine could barely build one militarily capable drone – or UAV (unpiloted aerial vehicle) to use its common military abbreviation. And that lack of capacity would have surprised no one. While UAV technology was considered something that would grow in strategic importance, internal Ukrainian production of drones was hardly considered to be a make-or-break capability to help resist a Russian invasion. Ukraine's need for UAVs was thought capable of being met through the purchase of systems from other countries – such as the Bayraktar from Turkey, a UAV that would become famous early in the war. In terms of its own production, Ukraine focused on more famous legacy military systems, such as tanks and artillery based on earlier Soviet designs.

Yet by 2024 the Ukrainian government claimed to be manufacturing 4 million UAVs in a wide range of different configurations.[1] Advanced, long-distance drones that were jet-powered and used to attack high-value military targets deep in Russia itself – from oil refineries to airfields. Large battlefield UAVs that could be used either to drop heavier ordnance on Russian forces or to dive down themselves in a form of suicide attack. And millions of smaller first-person view UAVs, the multipurpose workhorse of the Ukrainian battlefield that could scout, drop grenades, or even attack Russian targets themselves.

In one way, this is an astonishing transformation that very few people would have anticipated. On the other hand, it is also a story that has been seen regularly in modern, industrial and post-industrial war. In other words, it reminds us that even if we don't know what specific technologies or systems will prove ultimately decisive during a war, the ability of a national economy to react to technological developments, adapt, and increase production in those areas as they reveal themselves plays a major role in determining the outcome of a war. And that is because, in all but exceptional cases, wars last longer than expected, become more destructive than expected, and go down different roads than were imagined before the start.

While it has been common in the past to hear of wars presumed to be 'over by Christmas', they rarely are. Wars normally rapidly consume the forces originally brought to the fight and are determined by the militaries assembled in the years after the war starts. These militaries can be – indeed normally are – very different from those in service at the beginning of the war. And this reality highlights that fact that it is not what a state brings to a fight; what really matters is what it can raise and sustain as the fight goes on.

This depends on the ability to do two things. The first is to produce equipment in mass. War consumes massive quantities of material in very short periods of time – often amounts that people cannot imagine before the war starts. The second is to adapt to technological change (which war tends to accelerate), and develop and then produce new systems that also might not have been imagined before the war began.

Mass and the World Wars

Modern war in its most basic form is a struggle between sides to destroy equipment and kill soldiers on the other side. The product which does the destroying or killing in the end is almost always a piece of ammunition, and its overall effect is referred to as 'firepower'. Be it a small cartridge the size of a finger, a mortar shell the size of a fist, or large artillery shells that could reach the weight of a small car, using ammunition to destroy enemy targets is fundamental to warfare. And to get this ammunition to the target, a state needs to manufacture millions of small arms and hundreds of thousands of different larger launching systems, from artillery pieces to multiple-launch rocket systems (MLRS) to missiles and now UAVs.

Looking at how this need to produce and expend mass transformed the British Army is probably the most salutary lesson in how war demands more and more. In 1914, the British Army was what it had been for almost a century: a small if highly proficient European state army. In 1913, for instance, the entire army contained only 247,000 soldiers and officers.[2] The German Army, in comparison, had almost 800,000 active members, and the ability to quickly mobilize more than 1 million experienced reservists.[3] The British were thus only able to dispatch a tiny force to France when the fighting commenced. The original British Expeditionary Force that crossed the Channel when World War I started was made up of about 90,000 men, and would have had a small number of artillery pieces.[4] Much of this force was used up after only a few months of fighting.

Therefore, to cope with the strain of modern war, Britain had to undergo arguably the greatest (and most successful) industrial mobilization of all the powers between 1914 and 1918. British production skyrocketed, to provide its own army – which was growing exponentially – with artillery and shells, while at the same time providing significant military aid to many of Britain's allies as well. By the end of the war, Britain had produced about 25,000 heavy artillery pieces and, astonishingly, more than 170 million artillery shells (to say nothing of 52,000 aircraft, 250,000 machine guns and 4 million rifles).[5]

Britain's ability to mass-produce weapons in all classes helped it stand apart from almost all the other powers, including Germany, during the war. Though people do speak of Germany being a larger power, that was true only in terms of soldiers. When it came to the production of war materiel, the two states were close to equal, with Britain being superior in some important characteristics. Tanks might be the most striking of these. During the war, the Germans were only able to bring one model of tank, the A7V, from design to production and actually put it into battle. It was a large and cumbersome beast, and by the end of the war the Germans had only made about twenty of them.[6] The British, in comparison, had built 2,600 tanks by the end of the war.[7]

The scale of British production was such that Winston Churchill was able to imagine Britain fighting a very different war from any other European power. Churchill, who would become one of the most remembered figures in modern history because of his career in World War II, was also one of the most important – and controversial – British policymakers in World War I. When the war began, he had been in cabinet for years, serving as First Lord of the Admiralty – the civilian head of the Royal Navy. In that role he played a key role in preparing the British fleet for the war against Germany, making sure that they retained a large advantage over the German Navy.

When the war broke out, however, his political star was soon eclipsed. He helped devise the British invasion of the Dardanelles in 1915, also known as the Gallipoli campaign. When this operation turned sour, much of the blame was heaped on Churchill, who was forced to give up his post as First Lord, eventually becoming a powerless backbench MP. Removed from the centre of power, Churchill decided to return to his earlier career. He had entered the cavalry after boarding school, and the first ten years of his career had been spent in or around the British Army. In December 1915, he headed to the Western Front to take over the command of a combat regiment.

What he witnessed changed his ideas of war. Previously, Churchill had possessed a rather boyish view of combat, believing that daring, risk and indeed the shedding of blood was a good thing. A few months on the Western Front blasted that idea out of him. He saw modern industrial weapons, particularly German artillery, cause British losses almost daily – a blockhouse hit here, a trench flattened there, the drip, drip, drip of attritional warfare. For Churchill this was an education in catastrophe. Knowing Britain had a smaller population than most of the other large powers – the US, Germany and Russia for instance – he understood that British forces needed to keep their losses to as small a level as possible. His solution was to greatly accelerate industrial production, in order to build machines to do the bulk of the fighting and keep British casualties down.

He would soon get a chance to try to put his plan into action. In the summer of 1916 Churchill returned to parliament, and in 1917 he was invited back into the cabinet, now led by his great patron, Prime Minister David Lloyd George. He was also given a role that fitted with his vision of modern war – Minister of Munitions – and was thus able to push for the production of modern weaponry on an unprecedented scale.

The main issue facing Churchill was how to restore manoeuvre to the battlefield. He had seen the constant drumbeat of death in the trenches, and feared that any attempt to break through German lines based on infantry was bound to fail. He theorized that the British needed to approach the war in terms of 'moving power' and not just firepower – and judged that the only way to give the British soldier the ability to move forward would be through the application of masses of equipment, not huge numbers of soldiers.[8] He envisaged a war with thousands of aircraft, tanks and artillery pieces all working in combination to break German lines.[9] In the meantime, he wanted to delay all major British offensives until 1919, by which time he believed that British manufacturing strength, combined with growing US military force being deployed to Europe, would provide the Allies with the overwhelming military force needed to put his plan into action. When the British offensives at Passchendaele were finally halted in 1917, after exceptionally high losses, Churchill celebrated and hoped the Germans would next attack. 'Thank God our offensives are at an end. Let them make the pockets. Let them traipse across the crater fields, let them rejoice in the occasional capture of placeless names & sterile ridges.'[10]

In the end, Churchill was unable to see his plan put into action, because the war ended more abruptly than he had anticipated. In 1918, the German Army and people, worn down by their constant losses and having lost the belief that they could win, capitulated more quickly than Churchill had expected. However, having developed the plan, Churchill was able to put it into action in World War II.

Becoming prime minister in 1940, as the German Army was streaking through France, Churchill was soon presented with a situation more perilous than Britain had ever faced in World War I. A few weeks after he became PM, the French asked the Germans for surrender terms and the British had to face a European continent without a reliable, strong ally. In such a situation, Churchill doubled down on production and the preservation of British manpower. Above everything, he stressed the building of aircraft to protect the British Isles, and ships to keep the sea lanes to North America open. He would bide his time until his great, non-European possible ally, the United States, stepped in with an industrial might that could rival all of Europe's put together.

The American production of mass in the war was extreme – not just in terms of the depth but also the breadth of construction. Certain powers were able to concentrate their construction efforts – the USSR on land warfare, the Japanese on naval vessels and aircraft. The US, on the other hand, built up a large air force (then part of the army), navy (with its own air wing) and army. This meant that it needed to produce masses of equipment in a large number of areas, from the most expensive items such as large warships and four-engine bombers, to the smallest such as rounds of ammunition and small arms. Indeed, the story of US ammunition production, particularly artillery ammunition, shows just how pre-war capacity was inadequate for the needs of a modern military and how important it was to be able to scale up production quickly – often for items that were not even being built before the war started.

At the commencement of World War II in Europe, US Army units were commonly provided with some of the oldest artillery pieces to be found in any major army. These included French-designed and -built 75mm and 155mm howitzers, which had come straight out of World War I.[11] Though still serviceable, they would not be up to the task of winning World War II, so the US Army set about having new artillery pieces designed. They settled on three barrel sizes, 75mm, 105mm and 155mm, which they built in large quantities and had mounted on a number of different vehicles – from self-propelled guns to tanks – or had towed. To give one example of this extraordinary expansion, the construction of the new-model 75mm gun barrels went from 50 in the first six months of 1941, to 1,166 in the second six months, to a remarkable 6,431 in the first half of 1942, and 12,454 in the latter half of that year. So, within two years, production had risen by many thousand per cent.

Making ammunition for all these new barrels also required mass production – and quick ramp-ups. In 1941, the US manufactured 777,000 shells for 75mm guns – which might sound like a large number but was only a tiny fraction of what was needed. In 1942, production reached 18,792,000. For the whole war it was over 100 million – of just this one type.

Ammunitions Deliveries to the US Army, 1940–44

Item	1940	1941	1942	1943	1944
75mm, gun & howitzer	310	777	18,792	27,931	20,815
105mm, howitzer	0	353	10,487	14,884	37,790
155mm	0	. . . . . .	4,920	4,914	8,567

Rounds of Ammunition '000

Technological Adaptation and the World Wars

Being able to produce in mass is only part of the creation of a war-winning force. One must also produce the right equipment. And the longer a war goes on, the more military technology progresses, and the more important designing, developing and adaptation becomes in the creation of that equipment. As the story of Ukrainian UAV production shows, systems thought to be more peripheral to military success can become vital as wars develop, and strenuous efforts must be made to design and produce these in larger numbers than ever imagined before the war started. The evolution of aircraft throughout both world wars, for instance, reveals just how rapidly technological developments can accelerate, putting enormous pressure on productive systems to keep pace.

When World War I started, aircraft were flimsy, short-range and low-altitude flying contraptions whose military value was still regularly being questioned. Indeed, there were many who believed that aircraft would be of little use in the upcoming war. These 'pessimists' were quickly proved wrong in one area: it was revealed almost immediately that aircraft had a crucial role to play in military reconnaissance. A pilot could see further behind enemy lines than a land-bound soldier ever could, and soon the powers were all looking for aircraft to scout out enemy positions.

As the war went on, however, it became clear that scouting was only one of the roles for aircraft at war. Aircraft were quickly adapted to attack other aircraft. Seeing that scouting with aircraft was becoming so important, it was thought sensible to try to devise ways to stop the enemy from doing the same thing. This started with the simplest of solutions – arming pilots with small arms – but this was just the beginning. Aircraft were soon armed with machine guns, which themselves required a number of technical solutions.

One of the initial problems with machine guns was that they could damage the propeller of the plane if not placed perfectly. The French came up with the first effective resolution to this problem, when engineer Raymond Saulnier developed a firing synchronizer device that stopped bullets from being fired if they were going to hit the propeller.[12]

Of course, one machine gun was never going to be enough. Efforts were made to develop aircraft with two machine guns, and the British, Germans and French all designed multiple fighters that were so armed – and these would prove some of the most famous and successful aircraft of the war. The Sopwith Camel (British), SPAD S.XIII (French) and Fokker Dr.1 (German – and the preferred aircraft of the

Red Baron, Manfred von Richthofen) were all effective designs with multiple machine guns.

But arming aircraft was only part of the challenge – the war set off a competition to make faster and longer-ranged aircraft, a race that has played a major role in all wars. This required the growth of more powerful aircraft engines, which saw a huge rise in the horsepower being produced. At the start of the war, aircraft engines commonly produced under 100 horsepower, with the absolute best generating just over this.[13] Aircraft powered by these engines were necessarily slow, and most had a top speed well below 100 miles per hour.

The pressures of war, however, led to massive investment in engine production, as suppliers were asked to increase the horsepower generated while not making the more powerful engines that much heavier. This became one of the great goals of US engine producers. By 1917–18, the United States was mass-producing twelve-cylinder Liberty engines, which possessed the ability to create a nominal 421 horsepower and a maximum of 449, while weighing what seemed to be an extreme heavy 844 pounds, but was actually relatively light considering the horsepower produced.[14] The British and French were likewise pushing the frontier of engine development. The result was that aircraft by the end of the war were able to achieve speeds of up to 150 miles per hour.

And as aircraft were getting faster and better armed, their roles were expanding. They were used more and more for ground attacks. This could be done by the machine guns mounted on the airframes, or even, as the war went on, by the dropping of bombs on enemy targets. The history of bombing in World War I is, like that of gun-firing, one of a major technological leap forward. When bombs were first dropped, it was semi-comical and wildly inaccurate. The pilot – or the co-pilot in a double-seated aircraft – would hold a bomb in his hand and drop it from the moving aircraft in an attempt to hit a target on the ground. It was rarely successful.

Soon, however, the advanced powers started developing much larger aircraft with the specific role of bombing enemy targets. The British were one of the most successful bomber aircraft designers. By 1918 they were producing the Handley Page V/1500,[15] which was a massive technological leap forward from earlier in the war. Indeed, in comparing the Handley Page to any widely used aircraft from 1914, it could be argued that several generations of aircraft design had been surpassed in only four years.

One of the first British aircraft to arrive for military duty in France in World War I was known as the B.E.2b.[16] An adaptation of a 1912 design, it was an aircraft that would see action for both reconnaissance and bombing. Its single engine could only produce 90 horsepower, which meant that its top speed was only about 90 miles per hour.[17] Even then, it could not fly particularly far, with a range of fewer than 200 miles and the ability to reach 9,000 feet. It could only carry about 200 pounds of ordnance, above and beyond the weight of the airframe and engines, and a pilot and co-pilot (it was a two-seater aircraft). That being said, it had to do a significant amount of service in 1914 and 1915, and in the end 3,500 were built. Compared to a Handley Page V/1500, however, it was a flying (small) dinosaur.

The V/1500 was a massive aircraft with a wingspan of 126 feet, a length of 64 feet and a height of 23 feet. It was so large that it could accommodate a flying crew of eight or even nine. It had four large Rolls-Royce engines, two mounted on each wing, with every engine capable of generating 375 horsepower. These engines allowed the aircraft to reach an altitude of 11,000 feet and gave it an operational range of 625 miles – meaning it could fly from south-east England to Berlin and back. It also had up to eight different machine guns for protection and could carry approximately 7,500 pounds of bombs. It was the kind of aircraft that was a precursor to the heavy bombers of World War II. And it was the kind of technological change that only a handful of the most advanced economic and technological powers were capable of producing.

In World War II, if anything, the technological leaps that were achieved and put into production were even more extreme. While it would be impossible to discuss all aircraft design during the war, it is worth highlighting three areas where aircraft saw extreme changes between 1939 and 1945: jet engines, Long Range Bombers and unpiloted flight. These elements, which remain key parts of aircraft and air power today, all moved from the abstract to the actual in combat aircraft during World War II. It was a sign of just how important the air war was in the economic/technological competition between the World War II powers. Though the war is often seen as being determined by the outcome of land battles, this is a popular myth writ large. In fact all the powers (with the possible exception of the more technologically backward USSR) spent far more effort and expense building aircraft than any other weapon of war, usually by a factor of many times. Germany, for instance, usually devoted more than 50 per cent of its war output to the building of aircraft and the weapons needed to arm them. In comparison, the Germans spent less than 10 per cent of their output building and arming tanks and other AFVs.[18]

This choice was deliberate and considered, as it became apparent in the war that control of the air led to victory in other domains. However, with that stress on aircraft development, it was crucial to get things right, and that was not easy. The development and use of jet-powered aircraft revealed just how important getting the design process right could be – and what could happen, even with massive investment, when it went wrong.

The jet engine was actually a British design, though it would be the Germans who first developed it for a mass-produced aircraft capable of combat. This was, most famously, the Messerschmitt Me 262, which entered service in 1944 and quickly revealed itself to be a formidable weapon of war. It was faster than any non-jet fighter of the day, even the legendary P-51 Mustang, which played a major role helping the western Allies win the air war over Germany. The Mustang could reach a speed of just over 430 miles per hour, which was impressive until the Me 262 appeared with a top speed of 540 miles per hour.[19]

However, the great failure for the Germans was that they were only able to make the Me 262 operational quite late into the war – by which point they could do nothing to change the course of events. One of the reasons it arrived so late was because of Adolf Hitler's interference in the design process. Always stressing the offensive aspect of aircraft, when Germany started getting close to making an operational jet-powered military plane, he at first insisted that it be developed as a dive bomber. He wanted a weapon to try to strike back at Britain in 1943, as at that point the British and Americans were hammering German domestic targets with their large four-engine bombers almost every day.

It was a stupid idea. Dive-bombing had shown itself to be effective very early in the war, as it could place a small amount of ordnance quite accurately on a small target. However, it also left the aircraft extremely vulnerable, as they had to hold course and get close to the ground. Designing a jet dive bomber was also superfluous to Germany's immediate need, which was defence against British and American bombers. But Hitler delayed the appearance of the Me 262 as a fighter for a considerable period. Even though what would become the Me 262 did its first test flight in the spring of 1941, it did not appear as a fighter over Germany until the summer of 1944 – by which time the strategic air war was all but lost. It was a salutary lesson in investing wisely in your strategic needs. Germany had the opportunity to develop the best air-interception fighter of the war, but threw it away. Something similar happened with the development of VLR bombers for the Germans, but didn't for the US, which shows how being able to develop new systems in war is important.

The German story is short and expensive. For years, the Germans tried to develop a VLR bomber, at one point even imagining an aircraft that was nicknamed the *Amerikabomber*. It never came close to fruition, however, as Germany even struggled to build a four-engine bomber to compete with the US B-17 or British Lancaster. The US, however, set up a multi-layered and extremely well-funded operation to come up with a VLR bomber and eventually succeeded in producing arguably the most advanced operational aircraft of the war, the B-29.

The American VLR bomber programme – sometimes also called the Very Heavy Bomber (VHB) – produced a workable aircraft far more quickly than most. Though the specifications desired by the US air force were only passed to US aircraft manufacturers in early 1940, the first B-29 was delivered by Boeing in September 1943.[20] It was a technological leap in many ways, and required resources on a grand scale – both money and the willingness to use some of the scarcest of raw materials. The B-29 was so large that its production required the equivalent materials of eleven P-51 Mustangs. In 1944, when production ramped up, it still cost more than $600,000 to build one B-29 – compared to about $51,000 for a Mustang.[21] Overall, the cost of developing and building the B-29 was by far the most expensive weapons programme of the war – costing more than the atomic bomb project, for instance.

Average Unit Cost of Combat and Transport Aircraft Models,
US Army Air Forces, 1939–45

Model	1939–41	1942	1943	1944	1945
B-29	......	893,730	......	605,360	509,465
B-24	379,162	304,391	......	215,516	......
B-17	301,221	258,949	......	204,370	187,742
P-51	......	58,698	58,824	51,572	50,985
P-47	113,246	105,594	104,258	85,578	83,001
C-47	128,761	109,696	92,417	88,574	85,035

Prices in US Dollars

The B-29 was able to play a key role in cutting Japan off from the outside world in 1944 and 1945. Though it is controversially known for its role in the firebombing of Japanese cities (which was both ethically and strategically questionable), it also helped cut off all sea communications into and out of Japan, through the mining of Japanese harbours and the bombing of Japanese railways. In addition, it was the only aircraft capable of dropping the atom bomb. It did all of this from the Marianas Islands, about 1,500 miles from Tokyo (a city which was heavily bombed a number of times).

If the Germans struggled on this front during the war, they were able to develop one very important weapons system – not for winning World War II but for showing the future of war. This was the unpiloted aircraft or missile. They created two such systems, which they put into operation in 1944. These were the so-called V-weapons ('vengeance weapons', or *Vergeltungswaffen* in German): the V-2 rocket and the V-1 flying bomb. The latter was arguably the first operational cruise missile.

They were an interesting contrast. The V-2, which was formally entitled the A4 rocket before propaganda needs took over its name, required massive investment. It was a completely new attempt to build the world's first offensive ballistic rocket and took years of effort and cost – it was probably the most expensive German weapons system of the war. Under the design control of Wernher von Braun, who after the war would be spirited off to the US where he would play a key role in the US space programme, the Germans eventually developed and even started mass-producing a missile that could be fired from western Europe and hit Britain.

As a technological achievement, it is worthy of note. The V-2 could launch a payload weighing 1,600 pounds for 220 miles, and quite amazingly for the time could reach a ceiling of about 60 miles and travel faster than the speed of sound, reaching more than 3,000 miles per hour.[22] It was so fast and travelled so high that it was impossible to intercept, and the people unlucky enough to be killed by the V-2 would have had no idea that it was even descending on them before they were obliterated.

That being said, the key thing about the V-2 as a weapons system was that it did not justify its enormous cost. It has been estimated that the V-2 programme was, in relative terms, as expensive for Germany as the Manhattan Project designing the atomic bomb was for the US. However, like the Me 262, it appeared too late in the war and in too few numbers to make a difference. First launched against Britain in September 1944, just over 1,000 hit the UK (many others were launched against Antwerp once it was liberated by Allied forces).[23] And those that hit did no damage to British production, while thankfully killing only a relatively small number of British civilians – approximately 2,500.[24] Tragically, far more people were killed building the V-2 in the slave labour factories set up for their construction.

Overall, if the V-2 was a technological marvel but a strategic failure due to its exorbitant cost and small effect, the V-1 was a far greater success as a technological innovation – partly because it cost so much less and achieved, if anything, a greater strategic effect.

Developed quite late in the day, the V-1 (sometimes called the buzz bomb) was a far cheaper Luftwaffe response to the German Army's plan to build the V-2. (Even though it was a rocket, the A4 rocket programme was from the start funded as an army effort.) The V-1 was both advanced and simple. It was an unpiloted, winged missile powered by a small pulse-jet engine that could propel the missile at over 350 miles per hour. The V-1's flight was controlled by a compass and gyroscope, and it was a 'fire and forget' system – pointed at a target up to 150 miles away and launched off a ramp, and from there any human control was dispensed with.[25] A gyroscope would correct any flight changes and the compass would keep it on target, and the V-1 would fly on its way until it ran out of fuel and crashed to the ground with its 1,870-pound payload (larger than the far more expensive V-2).

The V-1's simplicity allowed for it to be developed and produced in a very short period. It was launched at Britain months before the V-2, in early July 1944, having been ordered into development by the Luftwaffe two years earlier.[26] And it caused an enormous reaction, even before the first one was ever launched. Arguably the largest Allied bomber effort in 1944 and 1945 was directed at trying to stop these V-weapons. More than 5 per cent of all the bombs dropped by large British and American bombers in this last part of the war were targeted on V-weapon sites, from production to launch – under what was known as Operation Crossbow.[27]

The lesson of all these different developments is clear: a power needs to have the ability to develop new technologies and the ability to spend enough money on them to make them come into reality – and to do so quickly. Along with that, a power needs to have the combination of sagacity and understanding to invest in technologies that will have a strategic effect on the enemy. Successfully passing these tests requires the sensible applications of all elements of a power at war: its economic/technological strength, its leadership choices, even its societal engagement. When it works out, it can provide a crucial advantage in capability and mass. When it doesn't, it can hobble a war effort through huge and inefficient expenditure.

Mass and Adaptation since 1945

What makes the world wars so extraordinary is that they witnessed the powerful economic/technological powers in the world mobilizing to an extreme degree, to build (almost) as much as they possibly could while prosecuting each war for many years. They thus saw massive rises in production so that most war equipment was, a few years after each world war started, being churned out in quantities exponentially larger than before the fighting started. Crucially, the equipment was also, until very late in the wars, being produced in such quantities that it was capable of not only making up but normally exceeding the losses of equipment suffered in direct engagement.

These rises in production allowed the different powers to augment significantly their military strengths, particularly during the first few years of each war. Armies, navies and air forces were all able to become larger and equipped with better weapons between, say, 1914 and 1916 and 1939 to 1943. As such, the world wars were not at first cases of one side making the other absolutely weaker; they were cases of one side growing its military capabilities relatively more quickly than the other – which is eventually what determined the outcome of the war. In other words, German strength in World War I did not become absolutely weaker until sometime in the summer of 1918, while Japan could be argued to have become materially stronger in amounts of fighting equipment until the summer of 1944.

After 1945, however, such large growth in strength in the course of a war was not the norm (though it might very well become the norm again if the US and China end up in full-scale conflict). Many wars, particularly state-to-state combined arms conflicts, consumed equipment at a rate far above the replacement capabilities of the states to manufacture them and even mostly to acquire them from outside. And this fundamental weakness played a huge role in influencing how they progressed.

This can be best seen in a series of wars in the Middle East: the 1967 and 1973 wars between Israel and a coalition of Arab states, and the Iran-Iraq War of the 1980s. The wars between Israel and Arab states seem on the surface to show the reality of short wars. However, that is deceptive for two reasons. The first is that they ended not long after they started not because there had been a decisive result, but because the losses made continuing the conflict all but impossible as neither side had the ability to generate replacement forces in the quantity needed. What could be said to have happened is, because of this, the Arab-Israeli wars have actually been one very long, decades-in-duration war punctuated by regular moments of intense combat and then long periods of more limited (but always ongoing) fighting. As this book is being written, military action is taking place in Israel, Gaza, the West Bank, Lebanon and Syria. Sometimes short wars are really not short.

When it comes to equipment losses, it is easy to see why the moments of intense combat only lasted for short periods. After a few days of fighting, both sides had normally lost so much equipment that continuing on the same track became practically impossible. This was the case in the 1967 Six-Day War and in particular the Yom Kippur War in 1973. The loss of expensive-to-replace equipment in a short period of time was decisive.

In 1967, the Six-Day War saw Israel launch a pre-emptive strike against Egyptian, Syrian and Jordanian-Palestinian forces in short order. The opening stages of the war were almost entirely militarily tactically successful for Israel (whether they were strategically success-ful is far more debatable). By the time a ceasefire was declared, under firm pressure from both the USSR and US, the Israeli military had seized the Sinai Peninsula from Egypt, the Golan Heights from Syria and the West Bank from Jordanian forces.[28]

Israeli military success was reflected in the very lopsided casualty differences. Where Israel lost 700–800 dead, the combined total for the Egyptians, Syrians and Jordanians was closer to 20,000.[29] That being said, the course of the war was determined as much by the equipment losses, which exceeded replacement levels by a very large margin – on all sides. Egypt, Syria and Jordan all used tanks and aircraft provided from outside, and even though combined they had the ability to generate far more soldiers than Israel they lost so much equipment in such a short period that they were compelled to stop fighting. A US intelligence estimate written a few months after that war ended claimed that, in a few days, 'Syria lost most of its 85 fighter aircraft and about 100 of its 425 tanks. The small Jordanian air force was com-pletely destroyed; two-thirds of Jordan's 200 tanks were destroyed or captured. The UAR [Egypt], with the largest Arab armed force, lost about two-thirds of its 365 fighter aircraft, 55 of its 69 bombers, and about half of its 1,000 tanks.'[30] Overall, it has been estimated that Egypt lost all but 15 per cent of its military hardware.[31] Such losses required many months of resupply from primarily Soviet sources, and with no such ability to make up the losses quickly, the Arab states were forced to accept Israeli control over the newly occupied territories. Israel, on the other hand, though its losses were smaller, hardly got off lightly. In only six days of war, it lost approximately 20 per cent of its air power.[32] This would of course have been unsustainable in any kind of longer war.

This destruction of equipment on both sides was even more deter-minative in the Yom Kippur War of 1973. This time, the Arab states, particularly Egypt and Syria, attempted to strike back after their failures in 1967. They launched an offensive against Israeli forces on the most important Jewish holiday, catching their enemy by surprise. The war itself was longer than in 1967, but still extremely short, lasting less than three weeks, from 6 October to approximately 25 October. Though the Arab forces did well at first, after a few days the Israelis were able to stabilize the situation and in some ways recovered quite quickly.[33] The Israelis were eventually able to blunt the different attacks against them. They then launched multiple counterattacks on all fronts, and arguably on the map seemed poised for a comprehensive victory. They pushed the Egyptians out of the Sinai Desert and were on the road to taking the Syrian capital of Damascus.

What stands out, however, was that all sides were losing equipment at unsustainable rates. The Israeli military lost approximately 1,000 tanks (destroyed or damaged) and more than 100 aircraft, while Arab forces lost 2,400 armoured vehicles and over 400 aircraft.[34] Once again, the domestic production base of Israel, Egypt and Syria could make nothing like this amount of equipment, and there was no option but for the war to be brought to a temporary conclusion. To win a more decisive victory, one needs the ability to produce enough in mass to secure more grand strategic objectives than the Israeli military, for all its efficiency, has ever been able to do.

And the Israeli military has partly understood that. Their losses were so high in 1973, and the expense so dramatic as much of the equipment had to be sourced from outside, that they had to change their way of doing business. Israel spent approximately $7 billion to fight the 1973 war for only a few days – an entirely unsustainable clip, as the entire Israeli economy was worth less than $12 billion.[35] Understanding the huge cost of not being able to produce its own equipment, Israel moved to create a much larger domestic military-industrial base, including the ability to design and manufacture its own tanks. They were not alone. Egypt pivoted from working with the Soviet Union to working with the US, and was able to get its hands on more effective weapons going forward. As part of the deal with the US, Egypt is actually the location for a production facility for US-designed Abrams tanks.

Of course, not having the ability to make up losses doesn't just lead to regular, arguably indecisive, short wars. It shaped the course of the Iran-Iraq War (1980–88), which was one of the most horrible conflicts

of the twentieth century and saw Iran and Iraq fight for control over
the oil reserves of much of the Persian Gulf. The opening phase of the
war was one of mass destruction, as much of the equipment both sides
went to war with was chewed up in the opening months.

The war started with an Iraqi invasion of Iran, with expectations,
as always, of a swift victory. The Iraqi leadership believed that the
Iranians, weakened by the chaos of their 1979 revolution and with a
military dependent on US weapons (which they now couldn't replace
because of the breakdown in US-Iranian relations brought on by
the overthrow of the US-backed Shah of Iran), would be a foe that
they could overwhelm.[36] And again, as always, the short war idea was
shown to be nonsense.

Though Iraq destroyed a large number of Iran's western tanks, its
own losses were so high that after making only small advances into
Iran, the war entered a stalemate. Neither side could operate its air
power systems effectively, and with their armour too vulnerable, the
fighting evolved into a form of trench warfare not entirely dissimilar
from World War I. Eventually, the Iranians counterattacked.[37] Believing that they would have an advantage with the supposed fervour
of their population, the Iranians massed a large amount of infantry
and began a series of offensives. These often involved human-wave
assaults, which resulted in very high casualties.[38] The Iraqis in return
used poison gas and mustard gas increasingly as the war went on.[39]
Ultimately, however, defensive lines proved to be too strong to overwhelm, and so advances were kept to a relative minimum – especially
when the defender had time to prepare.[40]

In this case, the two sides stayed fighting so long that their outside supporters could provide significant support to allow them to
regenerate their armed forces. Both relied on oil exports to provide
the capital needed to buy arms, as both lacked a highly developed
military-industrial base to make a great deal of their own weapons.[41]
This ability to get arms from outside was particularly vital for Iraq.
After the original advance petered out and the war entered the trench
warfare stage, the Iranians slowly pushed the Iraqis back. Had outside
support not come to Saddam Hussein's aid, the Iraqis might have lost.

As it was, by the late 1980s the Iraqis had been helped so much that they
had assembled one of the larger military forces in the world. Between
1981 and 1988, the USSR provided Iraq with military support worth

more than $20 billion.[42] This included thousands of tanks, hundreds of military aircraft, and masses of artillery systems and ammunition. Such vast amounts of military support eventually allowed the Iraqis to stabilize the situation, and by 1988 both sides were so exhausted and had lost so many soldiers and pieces of equipment that the war was for all intents and purposes over. And arguably there was no winner in what could be said to be the largest war in the world between World War II and the Russo-Ukraine War.[43]

In the end, the Russo-Ukraine War is just the latest example of how important the ability to regenerate military force is in determining the course of a war. What happened between 2022 and 2024 is that both sides relatively quickly worked through most of the force with which they started the war, and then strenuously tried to source war materiel from wherever they could. That involved increasing their domestic production but also gaining support from allies. Neither Russia nor Ukraine, as it turned out, had the capacity to support their own war efforts without the provision of masses of materiel from outside.

Ukraine's partners, mostly NATO countries in Europe as well as the US, provided a range of artillery, tanks, anti-air systems and millions of pieces of ammunition. Much of this aid was defensive and short-range in nature, and there were strict limits placed on its usage, but it was vital in allowing Ukraine to keep fighting. What was perhaps even more surprising was how Russia, reportedly a great power before 2022, equally needed masses of military aid from its allies to keep fighting. For instance, it needed thousands of Shahed drones to be supplied from Iran (as well as the construction of whole new factories to produce them in Russia itself). In what might be an even more astonishing move, North Korea had reportedly supplied Russia with 8 million artillery shells by October 2024 – far more than the number of shells provided by Ukraine's partners.[44]

Wars consume materiel at unimaginable rates, and metastasize to become horrific competitions in weapons that were not considered vital at the start. To try to understand how a state will perform in a war, therefore, don't look at what they bring to the fight, look at what they can raise and equip of their own accord during the conflict. And pay attention to what their allies can raise and equip as well – for as the next chapter shows, allies can and often do make the difference between winning and losing a war.

10. States vs Alliances

One of the greatest problems with the great power version of international relations is that it places too much emphasis on a few strong states – which supposedly determine the course of world events, including wars. It creates a subject—object relationship where the great powers can bestride the world like colossi, with the small powers peeping out from under their legs just trying to survive.

In reality, however, this vision is time and time again shown to be flawed.

Far from being decided by individual powers, most wars are won and lost by coalitions. Though this book looks primarily at the twentieth and twenty-first centuries, the earliest recorded wars for which we know details – such as the Peloponnesian War – were almost all won or lost by coalitions in which the role of a number of allies mattered a great deal. Sparta's cooperation with the Persian Empire, for instance, was crucial to its triumph over Athens. And the importance of allies in determining the outcome of wars has probably only grown over the last few centuries, as technology has allowed militaries to be globalized. The ability to move large amounts of military force rapidly around the globe has meant that groups of states that can do this more efficiently have a major advantage.

The reason allies matter so much is that they can participate in a war in many different ways. There are active allies who participate directly in the fighting, committing both their armed forces and mobilizing their economies in the struggle. Both world wars, for example, were won by large international coalitions who pooled their efforts successfully, and lost by other alliances who operated far less effectively.

However, these are the most extreme examples, as allies can also be vital without directly joining in a war. In many cases, allies can make a major difference in shaping the outcome of war not by fighting but through the provision of aid, military equipment, money or diplomatic support. That was often the norm in the Cold War, when the USSR and the US did not want to fight each other directly, but were more than happy to support third parties who were willing to do so instead. Soviet aid for North Vietnam and US aid for the mujahideen rebels in Afghanistan played a major role in shaping the course of both those wars. In fact, it is worth comparing these two cases to provide an illustration of what worked for both large powers in the Cold War – and what decidedly did not work.

It must also be kept in mind that while good allies are invaluable, weaker allies can not only not help – they can be a significant impediment to success in war. Allies who lack the will to fight, or have incompetent or unreliable leadership, or overrated militaries, can lead to wasteful and destruction diversions of force and also suck away strength from other powers in the coalition. In extreme cases of this type, weaker allies can even lead to military losses where victory was a possibility. The role of Mussolini's Italy in World War II leads one to ask if it was at all useful as an ally to Hitler's Germany.

Overall, it is the huge variety of ways in which alliances can matter that makes them worthy of deep consideration when trying to judge how a war will develop and eventually conclude.

Winning the World Wars

In the first part of the book, it was shown how the creation of the British, French and Russian alliance (the Allies) before 1914 allowed them to enter the war in a superior position to wage war over Germans and Austro-Hungarians. The Allies had the largest combined economic output, armies and navies. This strength allowed them to persevere even when the war militarily did not develop necessarily in their favour in the first few years.

From 1914 to 1917, Germany held its own, with far less in-depth aid from its allies – Austria-Hungary and the Ottoman Empire (the Central Powers). Certain strengths in the German Army, particularly in terms of its training, morale and ability to operate its systems, allowed the Germans to hold off the British and the French on the Western Front, while pressing the Russians in the east. And yet the strength of the Allies in controlling world trade meant that no matter what happened on the battlefields, their basic strength remained untouchable for the Germans. They were able to continually outproduce the

Germans in most of the major categories of war production (as discussed in chapter 9).

The strength of the Allies also meant that they were able to secure the support of the US, even when Russia was being pushed to the state of failure. Because the Allies controlled the seas through the Royal Navy, the only way that the US could ever join the war was in combination with them. All US trade with Germany was stopped very early on in the war, whereas trade with the Allies boomed. Soon the trade accompanied loans, and the US built up a massive economic stake in an Allied victory. However, that was just one reason the US was drawn into the Allied camp. The World War I alliance structures meant that the only way Germany could strike back was with unrestricted submarine warfare, which further inflamed American opinion and in particular that of President Woodrow Wilson – who had already shown himself to be instinctively sympathetic to the Allies (particularly Britain and France) when the war started. It was the total package of interactions that the different alliance structures unleashed that left Germany in the position of triggering US involvement in the war, by believing it had to restart unrestricted submarine warfare in 1917 to have any chance to win – the decision that sealed its fate.

And even though the Germans could win some battles after that moment, at the time causing real headaches in the war at sea and then in 1918 having some successes with their Spring Offensives, there was no way that they could ever hope to win the war. These fleeting successes only temporarily masked the fact that they were soon to be overwhelmed by the creation of a massive military force. Indeed, by the time the Germans surrendered, they really had no option – the balance of forces was moving decisively against them.

Even though Germany had, through great effort, almost 4 million men under arms in the second half of 1918, each of the major Allies (Britain, France, the US and Italy) had more than 2 million each, with a combined strength that was nearing 10 million.[1] The US figure was even set to grow. The alliance against Germany was simply too strong for it to resist.

World War II repeated World War I on a grander scale. It also had fascinating contrasts showing how to run, and not run, alliances to achieve maximum strategic effect. The Axis might be an example of one of the most powerful and yet dysfunctional alliances in history. It started in Europe with the alliance between Nazi Germany and Fascist Italy. Before the war started it had functioned quite well, as the two cooperated (mostly to Hitler's benefit, it must be said) in allowing Nazi Germany to expand at the expense of Austria-Hungary and Czechoslovakia. However, from the eve of the German invasion of Poland, it showed how poorly constructed it really was – and from that point on it could be argued that Hitler put on a masterclass with all his allies on how not to run a strategic partnership.

One of Hitler's regular mistakes was not to coordinate actions with his allies. He did not, for instance, let Mussolini know of his plan to attack Poland until a few days before the invasion was scheduled to begin. When Mussolini, much to Hitler's enormous shock, refused to join the war at this time, it caused such turmoil in the German dictator's mind that he almost did not go to war. Then, in May 1940, when Mussolini saw Hitler was winning and decided that now indeed Italy could join the war, Hitler reacted with something close to derision. The German dictator told a group of his officers that Mussolini's move was 'the worst declaration of war in this world . . . I would not have thought the Duce so primitive'.[2]

It was a textbook example of how the two dictators, ostensibly close comrades, actually worked together extremely poorly at the key moments of the war. Mussolini, for instance, as much for ego as anything else, decided a few months later to surprise Hitler by not informing him of his plan to invade Greece. As it was, when the invasion deteriorated, it was the Germans who had to bail out Mussolini, with war-affecting results. In early 1941, partly because of Mussolini's ill-fated decision, the Balkans became worryingly unstable for the Germans. There were British troops showing up in large numbers in Greece, and then Yugoslavia exploded when a pro-German government was overthrown. These developments forced Hitler to delay his impending invasion of the USSR, Operation Barbarossa, which had originally been scheduled for April 1941. He had to take a large strike force away from the Soviet border and use it to invade Yugoslavia and Greece. Though this force was militarily successful, the result was that Barbarossa was delayed by two months, and did not commence until 22 June.

There is some debate about how important this delay was in keeping the Germans from reaching Moscow that year (they got to the gates of the Soviet capital but could not take it). If the Germans had attacked in April they might have been slowed by the spring muds. However, the reality is that they did not have enough time to seize Moscow in 1941, and the two extra months would not have hurt. That they lost that time is to a large degree down to poor alliance communication and coordinating.

Things just went downhill from there. Instead of using the debacle to try to work together as allies, the European Axis for the rest of the war devolved into a dominant Germany and a supplicant Italy. Showing just how low Italy was in his mind, Hitler didn't bother to inform Mussolini about Barbarossa until German troops had practically crossed the border. From then on, Germany looked at Italy merely as a source of supplies and at times manpower for the German war effort. It was not an alliance but an imperial relationship – and when the US and Britain invaded Sicily in 1943, there was a coup against Mussolini. The erstwhile dictator was arrested and the new Italian government tried to change sides. In the end, Hitler rescued Mussolini from captivity and installed him as a puppet, but any idea of there being an alliance was over.

Hitler's relationship with the Japanese leadership was a little better in that it was not imperial – but that was as much because they were many of thousands of miles apart and were basically fighting two different wars. Even their enemies were different. Hitler was at war with the USSR from 1941 onwards, while the Japanese were actually close partners of the USSR until just before World War II ended (when Stalin went to war against the Japanese to try to get as much territory as possible).

This kind of disequilibrium meant that the German-Japanese alliance was haphazard and distant. The Germans did not consult the Japanese before major operations, though sometimes would inform them, and vice versa. The Japanese only let Hitler know that they were contemplating a major attack in early November 1941, a few weeks before it occurred. However they gave no details and at that point there was little Hitler could do to affect the operation anyway – even if he had been so inclined.[3] Moreover, at the time, the Japanese, showing how little they understood their new ally, urged Hitler to cut a deal with Stalin, so the Axis could concentrate on a war against the British and Americans. This proposal was so outside Hitler's ability to comprehend that he didn't bother to reply to it for a long period of time.[4]

Once the Japanese entered the war, there was little coordination or even exchange between the two sides. Small technological developments were shared, though the distance involved made even this tricky. Getting goods back and forth between them could require a submarine voyage, which rather limited intercourse.

And this difficulty in communication meant that neither ally understood just how dire the position of the other was. The Germans heard Japanese claims of (non-existent) military successes from the summer of 1942 onwards and thought that the war in the Pacific was more finely balanced than it ever was. Indeed, Hitler himself seemed completely unsure how to understand his Japanese allies. On the one hand, he had an extremely strong prejudice against non-white Europeans, and on racial and cultural grounds believed that the Germans had no 'affinities' for the Japanese.[5] On the other hand, he seemed to have extremely unbalanced views of what the Japanese could achieve militarily. He had been pushing them to attack the British and Americans for months before Pearl Harbor. When the attacks were announced, Hitler then rejoiced that, by having Japan at his side: 'We can't lose the war at all. We now have an ally which has never been conquered in 3,000 years.'[6]

The situation with the Grand Alliance against Hitler and the Japanese, particularly involving the leadership of Winston Churchill, Joseph Stalin and Franklin Roosevelt, was entirely different. In many ways these three were more suspicious about the motives of each other than the Germans and Japanese were about each other. However, that in the end didn't mean that they could not cooperate and even coordinate military actions to great effect.

The relationship between Churchill and Roosevelt is sometimes assumed to have been personally much closer than it actually was. While the two did grow fond of each other (up to a point), they also approached the world very differently. Churchill, the British prime minister, was determined to defend the longer-term viability of the British Empire and very much tried to shape the grand strategy of the Grand Alliance with that in mind. He wanted a great deal of aid from the US, to fight in the Pacific as little as was practicably possible, and to use air and sea power mostly in the war against Germany. He saw no need to fight large land battles against the German Army, as he wanted to keep British casualties as low as he could, seeing as Britain had the smallest population of the leading powers (not including Italy as a leading power in the war). To achieve all these strategic goals, Churchill wanted to limit British land-fighting in Europe to Italy or the Balkans, to let Stalin's Red Army handle the bulk of the land war, and to have the western allies strangle Germany through strategic bombing and blockades.

Churchill's favoured war strategy was materially different from that being pushed by Franklin Roosevelt. While Roosevelt also wanted to start with a naval blockade and the strategic bombing of Germany, the American president believed that when the time was right (and it would be right in 1944), the western allies would need to invade north-western Europe in a D-Day operation, thus sandwiching Germany between the Red Army in the east and a mass Anglo-American army in the west. In the interval before D-Day could be launched, Roosevelt saw little need to make the Mediterranean a large area of US commitment, always seeing it as secondary to US interests, as opposed to British – and a theatre from which Germany could not be fully defeated.*

Roosevelt's suspicions about the Mediterranean were also down to the fact that he did not believe that the US was fighting the war to protect the British Empire. Far from it – he was becoming an even more convinced anti-imperialist as he aged. Once the US entered the war, it could be argued that Roosevelt saw his role as America's war leader to help ease the ending process of the British Empire. Certainly exposure to the British Empire did not endear him to the idea of its long-term existence. As part of his long and arduous journey to the Casablanca Conference in January 1943, Roosevelt passed through the British colony of the Gambia, on Africa's west coast. The deprivation he saw there led him to make a sputtering, anti-imperial tirade. Speaking of the African workers he saw, Roosevelt said, 'They're given half

---

* Churchill and Roosevelt also disagreed significantly over strategy in the Pacific. Roosevelt was a big believer that China would be a future power in the world, and wanted to get force into China as soon as possible. Churchill was much more sceptical about the value of China, and wanted to focus British resources overwhelmingly on the war against Nazi Germany.

a cup of rice . . . Dirt. Disease. Very high mortality rate. I asked. Life expectancy – you'd never guess what it is. Twenty-six years. Those people are treated worse than the livestock. Their cattle live longer!'[7]

At times in the war, their fundamental differences could lead Roosevelt and Churchill to great fights and even depression, and 1943 was arguably the crisis year between the two. At the start of that year, Churchill seemed very much to be in the ascendant. During the Casablanca Conference he had convinced Roosevelt to make the Mediterranean a major theatre of operations in the coming months (Roosevelt did not believe that the US would be ready to launch a D-Day operation until the following year). However, after this one success, the rest of the year saw Roosevelt putting Churchill under enormous pressure to prepare to invade the continent in 1944.

In the end, Roosevelt teamed up with Stalin to force Churchill to agree to D-Day. At the Tehran Conference in November–December 1943, the American and Soviet leaders made it perfectly clear that they both expected there to be an invasion of France in the coming months. Churchill was dead-set against the invasion, but also believed it was better to keep the alliance together, and went along with a decision that he very much worried about.

Stalin also learned to work within the alliance structure, despite a deep distrust of his Anglo-American partners. He had chosen to be a proto-ally of Hitler's from 1939 to 1941. During that time, the USSR had provided Germany with massive amounts of vital raw materials, even when the Germans did not reciprocate and provide the USSR with the finished goods they were supposed to send in return.[8] It was another failing of Hitler's as an alliance manager that he did not understand what benefits he could accrue by keeping Stalin onside until the war with Britain was over. Regardless, once Hitler invaded the USSR, Stalin pivoted with extraordinary speed and energy. He worked assiduously to cultivate both US and British connections, and in particular to win over Roosevelt and Churchill.

It was a pivot that paid enormous strategic dividends. Stalin was able to extract a massive amount of aid from the US and Britain between 1941 and 1945. In raw material terms, the US handed over to the Soviet Union as much aluminium as was allocated to the US Navy for new production. This was the only reason the Soviets were able to build aircraft in such numbers in the war. However, it was in providing the USSR with trucks that Stalin might have achieved his most impressive results. Through Lend-Lease, Stalin basically made the Red Army one of the most mobile military forces in the world.[9] In 1942, the US provided the Soviets with 120,000 trucks, and in 1943 this number jumped to 132,000. By 1944 the US was handing over almost 160,000 trucks, in a range of sizes from the standard 2.5-ton workhorse Studebakers to massive vehicles capable of carrying 5 tons. In the end the US provided the USSR with more trucks than the Germans were able to build themselves. All of this aid meant that much of the Red Army's mobility came directly from the United States.

Stalin, however, did not always succeed in getting what he wanted from Roosevelt and Churchill. The Soviet dictator was desperate for the western allies to start a land campaign against the Germans as early as possible, and lobbied for an invasion of north-west Europe in 1942 and 1943. But until Roosevelt was ready, he had to wait.

Roosevelt never trusted Stalin – though he was determined to try to find a way to work with the Soviet dictator. The president had determined that while Stalin was not to be trusted, the Soviet Union was not as much of a threat to the global system that he wanted to create as was Nazi Germany. Thus Roosevelt would aid Stalin, as in his mind he was convinced that this was what was best for the US and best for the world. He did start to waver on this very much near the end of this life. Once victory in Europe was all but assured, with Hitler trapped in his bunker awaiting perdition, Roosevelt and Stalin reached a crisis in their alliance. At this point, Stalin made the baseless accusation that Roosevelt might be willing to collaborate with Germany against him, and Roosevelt in return started doubting whether Stalin really was a partner.

Overall, however, what stands out is that from 1941 to 1945, except for periodic moments of tension and some fundamental disagreements in outlook, the three leaders did act together in a remarkably successful way. They agreed on different grand strategic options, planned the start of operations, and trusted each other with certain military secrets far more than the Axis powers. Stalin was kept apprised of the starting time for D-Day, so that he could plan for the launching of a Soviet offensive in the east at about the same time, catching the Germans in a bind. This coordination worked exceedingly well. In the summer of 1944, through this coordination, the Allies made the Germans try to defend in both France and on the Eastern Front; the result was a two-front catastrophe as the Germans found themselves caught between the British and Americans, who had landed in Normandy, and the large Red Army offensive codenamed Operation Bagration. It resulted in the greatest battlefield catastrophe that the Germans would suffer during the war.

Alliances and the Cold War

The Cold War period (approximately 1947–89) witnessed an extraordinary phase in warfare. The two alliance leaders, the US and USSR, usually ended up losing the wars that they took the lead in fighting. The US was the lead combatant in both the Korean and Vietnam wars. While the first ended up with a satisfactory strategic draw (though one that still has certain negative repercussions to this day), the latter was one of the greatest strategic calamities in US history. For the Soviet Union, on the other hand, the invasion of Afghanistan ended up being an expensive failure that helped drain Soviet resources in the 1990s and hastened the collapse of the whole Soviet construct.

If taking the lead in such wars was usually a problem, supporting an ally who wanted to do the fighting ended up being by far the smarter strategy. The Soviet Union, for instance, received far more strategic benefit from aiding the North Koreans and the North Vietnamese than they did by directly invading Afghanistan – and the US situation was that, for relatively inexpensive aid to anti-Soviet Afghan sources, they helped enmesh the USSR in an expensive long-term conflict that it could not win.

This also shows the pitfalls powerful states face when they don't understand the limitations of their own power and the benefits of certain kinds of allies. Those who are willing to fight are to be particularly valued, while those whose forces lack this basic willingness usually cause far greater problems and expenses that provide no strategic benefit. Indeed, one of the most difficult and often futile things a power can do is try to make an unwilling ally fight for it. What that usually results in is the larger power taking over more and more of the fighting, which usually/often leads to strategic and eventual defeat.

The US intervention in Vietnam ended up being one of the most

expensive and disastrous wars in US history, and remains the greatest
strategic defeat that the United States would ever suffer. It started, as
many wars do, with very different expectations from what it would
become years later.

After the French had been militarily defeated by the Vietnamese
Communists, whose strength was primarily in the north of the country, Vietnam was divided into a Communist North with its capital in
Hanoi (known as the People's Republic of Vietnam) and a pro-western
government in control of the South, known as the Republic of Vietnam, which had its capital in Saigon. When the United States first made
the decision to get militarily involved with the South Vietnamese, it
was supposed to be to help them build up their own military in the
face of a growing insurgency being controlled by the North.[10] However, once the process started of getting the US involved, which began
under the presidency of John F. Kennedy, the United States started
to creep up the military involvement ladder. Instead of just training
and equipping South Vietnamese forces, US military personnel started
going on operations to observe their ally in action. When South Vietnamese forces still struggled to impose themselves, US personnel were
given the green light to engage Communist forces directly.[11]

In 1964, the hotly debated Gulf of Tonkin incident was used by
the administration of the now president Lyndon Johnson to get congressional approval for whatever he wanted to win the war.[12] At
that point, with the US becoming a combatant, the gradual growth
of American forces became a rush – moving from 23,000 in 1964 to
more than half a million in 1968. Hand in hand with this growth of
force numbers in Vietnam went an increase in expense. US defence
spending rocketed from just over $50 billion in 1964 to more than $80
billion in 1968.

And yet, no matter how much the US spent and how many US
forces were sent to Vietnam, the South Vietnamese forces struggled to
evolve into a credible military force that could fight the North on its
own. Arguably the opposite occurred, and South Vietnamese forces
seemed to become infantilized and more dependent on the US the
longer the Americans were involved. By 1968, the situation seemed so
intractable that the American people lost faith that the war could be
won, and this had profound political repercussions. The victor in the
1968 presidential election, Richard Nixon, announced that he would

try to turn the war over to South Vietnam in a policy that was called Vietnamization.

Nixon went to extreme lengths to try to make this policy work. He flooded South Vietnam with weapons and strongly increased the use of US air power to try to bomb the North into acquiescence. It all failed.[13] When US troops pulled out, the ability of the South Vietnamese military to defend the South Vietnamese government withered in relatively short order. On 29 March 1973, the last US combat troops left Vietnam. Just over two years later, in April 1975, Saigon fell to attacking North Vietnamese forces and the Republic of Vietnam ceased to be.

It was a humiliation for the US that in some eyes represented a moment of real relative decline. Unfortunately for the Soviets, the USSR might have believed this the most. It had sat back during the Vietnam War and watched its ally, North Vietnam, take on the combat duties while the Soviets sent a great deal of equipment. Indeed, it was while the US was floundering that the USSR upped its aid. From the mid-1960s onwards, the USSR sent North Vietnam on average about $450 million in military aid annually.[14] They also trained large numbers of North Vietnamese soldiers and sent military observers to watch their ally in action.

It was a mutually beneficial relationship precisely because the USSR did not take over a combat role. It provided a great deal of effective aid, risked few Soviet lives, and in return saw its great opponent humbled while learning some lessons about warfare. That being said, the USSR did not learn the most important lesson, which was not to do what the US had done. Only four years after the fall of Saigon, the USSR launched its own version of the Vietnam War when it invaded Afghanistan.

This 1979 invasion had many similar justifications to the US involvement in Vietnam. Like the US, the Soviets said that they were sending in military force to help a friendly (in this case pro-Communist) government. Like in Vietnam, the Soviets also said that they were getting involved to help their ally government be better able to exercise control, and that Soviet forces would be withdrawn when they had secured the situation.

It was a pipe dream. The Afghan government the Soviets were propping up was fighting a group of insurgents called the mujahideen, who were motivated by both religious and ethnic differences with the Kabul Communist regime. They were determined to resist the Soviet invasion, even when things started poorly. At first, using brutally effective tactics and lots of air power – particularly helicopters – to hammer the mujahideen, the Soviet Army was able to exert control over a large part of the country. The US, however, decided to respond to the invasion by tremendously increasing its support for the mujahideen.

The US, under the administration of Jimmy Carter, had begun planning to aid Afghanistan rebels before the Soviet invasion.[15] At that point the USSR was trying to protect a pro-Soviet government that was coming under pressure. It was only when those efforts seemed to be failing that the USSR opted for a full-scale invasion in December 1979.

What happened shows once again the difficulty of fighting for a weak government and a people who really do not want you there. At first, much like the US in Vietnam, the Soviets used modern firepower and advanced technology to begin imposing themselves where they wanted. Arguably they fought intelligently, if brutally. They improved in areas such as convoy protection, but probably their most successful innovation was the growing use of helicopters to both move quickly around the country and apply firepower on mujahideen positions.[16]

At the same time, the US had started providing the mujahideen with significant aid, at first mostly economic but later also involving weapons. The story of this aid is often distorted by a debate over the 1986 arrival of American Stinger anti-air missiles.[17] These missiles were very effective in shooting down Soviet helicopters. However, their exact value in ending the war is believed by some to be overrated as they arrived quite late, by which point the USSR was already enmeshed in a war it could not win and wanted to get out of.

And it is the overall story that undoubtedly makes the difference. From 1981 until the eventual Soviet withdrawal from Afghanistan in 1989, the US provided the mujahideen with more than $20 billion of military assistance, and billions more in economic aid.[18] The overall impact of the aid was part of the process of allowing the mujahideen to fight the war as they wanted, and the war they wanted was one the Soviets were always going to struggle to win. For instance, some US aid went to providing for Afghan refugees in Pakistan.[19] Their care freed up other Afghanis to fight.

Like the US in Vietnam, the USSR spent a massive amount of money to keep the fight going in the hope that it would get better. In the ten years of war, the Soviets lost 15,000 soldiers, and many more were wounded.[20] Overall financial cost is hard to calculate, but up until 1986, it was estimated conservatively, the Soviets had spent 15 billion roubles in Afghanistan.[21]* This figure is hard to confirm as Soviet military spending was so opaque, however it is worth comparing it to the annual Soviet defence budget at the time, which was claimed to be 21 billion roubles in 1988.[22]

The key thing is that it was not a sustainable conflict, considering the economic situation of the USSR.[23] And it ended with pretty much the same result that the US had in Vietnam. The Soviets withdrew their military from Afghanistan in February 1989, and from that point relied on aid to try to keep their imposed government, led by Najibullah, in power. In some ways they did slightly better than the Americans in Vietnam, as the Najibullah government clung on until 1992, but the end result was the same. The power that had tried to create an ally ended up doing the fighting – and when they left, the government they had backed fell. Meanwhile the power that stayed out of the fighting, but helped an ally that was willing to do the fighting, had one of the greatest strategic successes of the Cold War.

Both the Vietnam and Afghanistan wars show how smaller allies can make a major difference if they work well with their partners – in many ways far more than more statistically larger and more technologically advanced ones. Both Vietnam and Afghanistan were amongst the poorest and least developed parts of the world when the US and Soviet militaries started their interventions. Indeed, the disparity between the US and Vietnam and between the USSR and Afghanistan could hardly have been more stark. Both intervening powers were nuclear behemoths, with the ability to destroy the globe many times over. Both had also spent more on their militaries for decades than any other powers (other than each other). The Americans and Soviets had

---

* Giving this value a dollar equivalence is not easy. The USSR liked to keep the official conversion rate for 1 rouble at more than 1 US dollar. However the actual purchasing power of the rouble on a free market would have been much less.

stores of modern weapons that far exceeded anything their opponents in Vietnam or Afghanistan could have dreamed about, including thousands of the best aircraft and tanks in the world.

And yet in both cases the supposedly dominant power lost, at least partly because the far weaker power received enough military aid to draw out the war and fight effectively. Certainly at the end of the Cold War, when the balance was taken of the four-decades-long struggle, more Americans had died fighting the Vietnamese than had died fighting the USSR; and likewise more Soviet soldiers had died fighting the mujahideen than died fighting the Americans. The value of both of these smaller powers as allies to the larger was far more than, say, the value of Mussolini's Italy to Hitler's Germany.

The Failure to Learn the Lessons

You might think that after two such powerful and clear examples as Vietnam and Afghanistan, powers would learn the lessons about how difficult it is to create an ally out of a people or nation that does not want to fight; and, on the other hand, recognize the great value of allies who do want to do their own fighting. In the case of the US, however, any learning was less than skin deep. Indeed, it would be hard to construct a poorer example of how to work with allies than the US in the post-Cold War period, or more specifically from 2001 onwards.

In the 1990s, the US worked quite well with its allies. The two largest US military interventions of the decade were done with, and arguably for, the strategic needs of US allies as much as for those of the US itself. This was the First Gulf War of 1991–2, discussed earlier, and the intervention over Kosovo in 1999. The First Gulf War saw the US assemble the most impressive international coalition of the post-World War II world, with thirty-four states sending military forces to liberate Kuwait.[24] It is important to note that the US did not strictly need so many allies, as it had the military force itself to evict Saddam Hussein from Kuwait – but it chose to do so for reasons of international politics and gathered major advantages from that.

When it came to the military operation against Serbia over Kosovo, once again the US worked with and, arguably, in the interest of its allies. The fate of the Balkans was hardly an issue of high American concern in 1999. However, it was for America's European allies, who were struggling to deal with the ongoing bitter ethnic divisions in the area that had been set off by the dissolution of Yugoslavia.

Kosovo was a province of Serbia that was populated mostly by Albanians. The Serbs and Albanians had a difficult history, to say the least, and by the late 1990s the situation in the province was tense. When Serbia sent a large military force into Kosovo (legally recognized as part of Serbia, it must be remembered), this was seen as a possible trigger to a wider conflict in the region, and the decision was made to try to protect the Albanian population using outside power.

In this case the US was as much pushed into the war by its European allies as it was doing the pushing. In the end, however, the administration of Bill Clinton, heavily influenced by Secretary of State Madeleine Albright, decided it was better to use US military force in concert with its European partners to get the Serbian military out. The result was a true coalition-wide bombing campaign against the Serbs that lasted for two and a half months, from 24 March 1999 to 10 June. The operation even had the support of a number of Middle Eastern states, as the Kosovan Albanians were Muslims and the operation's purpose was to protect them.

It was a good thing that the operation did have coalition support, because it was actually more protracted than expected. The first part of the campaign involved attacking Serbian targets in Kosovo, and as it turned out it had very limited success. When it became clear that this was not going to work, the decision was made to escalate and attack targets in Serbia itself, including bridges and civilian communications. Such an escalation was only possible because of widespread European support.

In the end the escalation worked (even with one problematic moment when the coalition bombed the Chinese embassy in Belgrade, the Serbian capital), as the Serbian government folded under the pressure of the attacks. Still, it was a close-run thing, and had they resisted, the plan was to send in ground forces, which could have led down many unknown paths. The work of so many allies means that there has been decades-long support since to protect the Kosovan population.

If the 1990s showed that the US could work productively for and with its allies (and gain significant advantages from that), the period after 2001 showed how little the country had actually internalized about this. The War on Terror, unleashed by the terrorist attacks on the World Trade Center and Pentagon on 11 September 2001, revealed just how little the US thought about alliances when the chips were down. The decision to invade Iraq, one of the most controversial in US foreign policy history, was made over the objections of many of America's most loyal post-war allies. While the US administration of George W. Bush came to the conclusion that overthrowing the regime of Saddam Hussein (still in power) would serve American interests by allowing the US to construct a pro-American regime in one of the most powerful Arab countries, many of their allies baulked – considering the whole plan impracticable and dangerous. This lack of international support meant that when the war went badly, the US was very much on its own, with unfortunate results.

Still the US persisted. What happened afterwards was a debacle. The invasion of Iraq, which started in 2003, ended up as a strategic catastrophe for the US. Not listening to its allies, the US pressed ahead and went for regime change. It ended up with an extremely expensive, multi-year occupation that saw Iraq descend into chaos. Even after the US upped its military presence significantly to stabilize the situation, it was left having created a situation that gave it no benefit and cost massive amounts. The Muslim opposition to the US in the region became even more extreme than that manifested by the 9/11 attackers, and the new Iraqi government became closer to America's greatest strategic opponent in the area, Iran. It is hard to think of a single positive that emerged from the entire US intervention. It would have been better if the US had heeded the warnings of its allies and partners.

The experience of the war in the Middle East also revealed that the US had forgotten its failure in South Vietnam and the extreme difficulty of trying to create an ally who will fight for you. The United States' intervention in Afghanistan started in 2001, just days after 9/11. Over the next two decades, the US is estimated to have spent an eye-watering $2.3 trillion on the intervention.[25] This is larger than the GDP of all but a handful of nations. At the same time, the human cost was large. The US lost 2,324 military personnel and 3,917 contractors, and 1,144 allied troops died as well. Afghani deaths were exponentially higher; considering those who died on all sides and civilians killed, the number would probably reach into the hundreds of thousands.[26] All this expense was in vain. Different US governments from both parties, including the Bush, Obama, Trump and Biden administrations, tried many different strategies to try to establish a workable Afghanistan government that could outlast the US occupation. In other words, the United States tried to create an ally where none existed. The results made the American intervention in Vietnam and the earlier Soviet intervention in Afghanistan look like relative successes. The US-installed regime, with its large army well equipped with US weapons, outlasted the occupation by a few hours. Without US military force, America's putative Afghan ally was doomed. It was one of the most disastrous attempts to create an ally in human history.

And it had a further disaster in that it led to the US failing to understand that Ukraine offered the exact other case – a possible ally who wanted US friendship and support and would be willing to do the fighting. In Ukraine, the US was presented with a chance to help a people who wanted to build a democratic system and were more than willing to risk their own lives and futures to do so. At the same time, the Ukrainians were fighting the greatest threat to US security in Europe – Vladimir Putin's Russia. However, the US seemed to have totally lost any ability to properly judge its own interest and the strength of its possible allies, and instead prepared to sacrifice Ukraine to Russia before the Russian Army had even crossed the border.

The assumption that the Biden administration had made (and those around Donald Trump had as well) was that Ukraine would be quickly conquered. Indeed, the administration thought so little of the Ukrainians' willingness to fight for themselves that they engaged in a bout of self-pity. On the eve of the Russian invasion, the president bemoaned his own fate, saying: 'Jesus Christ! Now I've got to deal with Russia swallowing Ukraine?'[27]

Sadly for the US and the democratic world, the Biden administration was never able to adjust its understanding of the value of Ukraine as an ally. It continued to view Russia as some great power that should not be defeated and Ukraine as a small power that needed modest support, but who could never be a true ally. Biden kept Ukraine from being given a clear path to NATO membership and also strictly limited the military aid given to the Ukrainian military. Crucially, Ukraine was given US aid to fight only a limited-range war, and was forbidden to attack Russian military targets in Russia (even those which were being used almost daily to attack civilian targets in Ukraine). The result was that the Biden administration transformed what could have been a Ukrainian victory into a long-term, bloody and grotesque attritional struggle that resembled World War I (with drones) more than anything else.

It was a catastrophic view that stretched the gamut of failure from all aspects of war and power. Biden had, like US presidents before him such as Trump and Obama, failed to understand that Ukraine was not some insignificant state whose people would give up in the face of Russian power. The Ukrainians had a strong sense of identity and the economic/technological ability to create their own effective military force. Moreover, their growing, open system allowed for a more flexible military culture that had enabled them to plan effectively for the Russian invasion. In other words, Ukraine had a number of areas of strength, and many of the qualities needed to be an effective ally.

In the end, though, this underrating of allies has been one of the great failures of the post-World War II world. While it was widely understood that both world wars were won by alliance groupings, after 1945 too much attention was paid to the supposed 'great' or even 'super' or 'hegemonic' powers. It has been a tragic mistake that has led continually to wars that should never have been fought. As a rule of thumb, it is normally the case that you cannot make an ally fight for you if they do not wish to, but an ally that does want to fight is worth its weight in gold.

Conclusion: War and Power in the Indo-Pacific

This book has presented what might be called a 'methodology' for understanding national power, and then what matters when that power is employed in the conduct of war. It argues that reliance on pre-conflict military metrics is not helpful in understanding either war or power – and that it is far more important to look holistically at a number of fundamental variables that create military power in times of peace and then regenerate and support that military power in times of war. This methodology calls for the dropping of the phrase 'great power' to describe states, because it fails on a number of grounds. The term assumes 'great' powers are, in fact, more powerful than they are; it assumes 'great' powers are driven by identical concerns; and it almost always fails, as it did before the Russian invasion of Ukraine, because of the assumption that a 'great' power is to be judged primarily on the outward manifestation of its military strength. 'Great' powers are rarely great – they almost always have major flaws and regularly lose wars – but in labelling them as 'great', we place them on a pedestal and create a natural instinct to defer to them – often with disastrous results.

A far better term for judging power is not 'great' but 'full-spectrum'. This automatically puts the emphasis on the components that create power as opposed to its outward manifestations. It also allows for the possibility of understanding the limits and problems for even the largest states, highlighting the fact that they can be well-endowed in some of the important elements of power, but far less stout in others.

The starting element to understand a full-spectrum power, as discussed in chapter 1, is its economic/technological strength – in both peace and war. To be a powerful nation, to influence others kinetically and non-kinetically, a state needs to be an economic and technological leader. It needs to have the ability to develop and make the most advanced 'stuff' in very large numbers. It needs to have the ability to raise capital quickly and efficiently. In other words, it needs to be able to make the best military equipment in mass, and then develop more and better systems when the time comes to use that equipment.

If a state cannot do that, it will fail to qualify as a full-spectrum power at the first hurdle.

However, just being an economic/technological leader does not in and of itself mean that a state will be a full-spectrum power. There are a number of factors that strongly influence how that economic/technological strength is employed, ranging from political leadership and system to social cohesion. These factors can make an economic/technological leader punch above its weight, or even far below.

Leadership is one of the most complex yet important variables to add to the equation. The problem with a great deal of theoretical constructs around power is that they fail to account for the human elements. Certain leaders can be prudent, sensible, and marshal resources effectively. Others can be dangerous, wasteful, and construct showy but foundationally weak manifestations of power. And some leaders can excel in certain areas but be weak in others.

Of course, leaders don't operate in a vacuum. They operate within political systems and are in a constant relationship with the societies that they are trying to rule. Certain political systems exercise restraint on their leader; others bestow almost unlimited power. Also, societies themselves can be very different. Some are aggressive and desirous of power; others are far less concerned. Some societies are welcoming to new technologies, while others are cautious or even opposed to change. As part of that, some societies are open to debate and discussion, while others can be more apathetic or even downright disobedient.

One of the best ways to see how these different factors interact and how they are all important is to look at the kind of military a power creates. Militaries are products, though often they are studied as standalone institutions. A military can only be as strong and resilient as the economic/technological resources that underpin it; it will reflect the leadership choices made by those who were in power when it was built; and the society that serves in it (and that it is supposedly there to protect) can influence it in numerous ways.

Finally, a full-spectrum power is never a power existing on its own. All powers operate in a world where friendly and allied states can be an enormous support to their goals. This is true in times of peace as well as war. In peacetime, alliances are enormously important in providing deterrence against outside threats and support for changes that can be enacted without resorting to military force. At the same time, being in league with weak or reluctant allies can create far more headaches and commitments than the benefits they bring.

In the end, a full-spectrum power is one that has advantages in every one of these categories. That being said, all the categories do not matter equally. The foundation of national power is economic/technological prowess. A state that cannot produce a large amount of the best material will *always* struggle to impose itself on the international stage. From Mussolini's Italy to Putin's Russia, powers that try to punch above their economic/technological weight usually run into trouble.

A full-spectrum power is one that can harness that economic/technological power through a combination of effective leadership, a supportive society and a flexible political system. It can then add to its own power through cooperating with allies of substance, particularly those who want to be allies and are willing to fight if needs be.

And this brings up how to assess the military potential of a full-spectrum power and what might happen when it goes to war. Making definite judgements about a war is a fool's errand, but there are ways to analyse what might happen when a power or group of powers goes to war. The first thing to remember is not to look at war as a battle-decided encounter – a war game, as it were – that will be determined by the first events when militaries meet. Battles, especially at the start of a war, almost always decide very little and are often fought over land of minimal or no strategic value. Instead, to try to understand how a war might develop, look at the powers involved as possessing different military systems, and examine the factors that will govern not only how those systems will operate at first, but how they can be regenerated, adapted and improved as a war goes on.

One of the most important tests of such a vision is whether a military can undertake complex operations effectively. Complex operations are actions that require the close coordination of many different steps, pieces of equipment, personnel, etc., so that they have their greatest impact. The ability to successfully undertake complex operations usually separates advanced militaries from those who have advanced equipment but can't utilize it to its full potential.

Of course, one of the key aspects of the execution of complex operations is the people involved. The human element of war is multi-faceted, and is often overlooked in the focus on machinery. But humans influence war profoundly – through both emotional and professional elements of human interaction. The former is about people's commitment to the struggle, as well as morale and identity. A willingness to fight, to take risks to the point of death – and keep taking risks even in the face of what seems like large odds – has been a hugely important factor in many victories.

At the same time, the specific role of training and preparation – the professional element of human interaction – can separate two militaries that on paper look quite similar. Training influences all aspects of military operations – from the ability to operate systems, to the ability to react to stressful situations, and even to the maintenance of morale. It is easy to overlook training as a factor, or assume that a force is well-trained when it is not.

Training and preparation are about the operation of military forces – but that, of course, only reveals what is happening at a moment in time. Keeping a military force constantly supplied and equipped with more and better equipment in the future is just as important as a military's current strength. This ability to sustain military operations is dependent on having the capacity to manufacture equipment in mass and continuing to develop improved systems, by either adapting existing ones or creating entirely new ones, in a continual cycle. Wars are rarely won with the equipment that is on hand when they start. Indeed, that equipment is normally used up or destroyed at a rate that would have been impossible before the war started. Stocks that were assumed to be enough for years can be eaten up in months, or even weeks.

Finally, rarely does one power win a war – they are almost always won by coalitions, often large and wieldy ones, where a range of allies bring different strengths to the table. Indeed, the ability of a large power to work with allies is one of the greatest tests it can face in war. If it tries to either dominate them or work entirely separately from them, as Nazi Germany did with Fascist Italy and Imperial Japan, usually the best that happens is that the alliance brings little benefit – if any benefit at all. On the other hand, if a larger power can work well with smaller ones, this often provides enormous benefits – particularly if the smaller powers can help tie down opposing states.

Having a proper understanding of war and power is vital in order to try to lessen the chance of another disaster like the Russo-Ukrainian War. One of the great problems for this war – which seemed to be the case across the board, from the leadership councils of Vladimir Putin to the White House of Joseph Biden, and the numerous think-tanks whose job it was to supposedly study these things – was how the concepts of war and power became something so definite. Russia was thus seen as a great power with an awesome military; Ukraine was not. A full-scale war between them was confidently said to be one that Russia would win in a few weeks, maybe even days or in extreme cases hours/minutes. Indeed, the war was predicted to be so clinical and short that people were already wondering what the impact would be from Russia's swift victory. This included the President of the United States, Joseph Biden, who lamented the fact that he would have to deal with the Russians swallowing Ukraine.

If there is one general truth in war, it is that how a war ends bears very little resemblance to how people imagine it will end when it starts. Very rarely have the opening battles of a war decided its outcome. A battle is more a snapshot in time – a moment when two armed forces reveal their current strengths and weaknesses. What to take from a battle is not so much its result (which is often ambiguous and hardly ever decisive), but what it reveals about the direction of travel of the armed forces involved. It is the adaptations that occur during a war – in terms of leadership, societal commitment, technological developments, mass production and international alignments – that play a greater role in determining the outcome of a war. What we need to do is step back from the battlefield – and the heroism and horror that are such compelling human stories, but tell us little about victory and defeat – and try to understand how a war is evolving.

War is the ultimate reflection of power, and power is so much more than just military power – because military power is itself a product of the complex variables laid out above. Therefore, to try to have some idea of how 'powerful' a state is, it is important to study those variables as much as the weapons and manpower that they end up producing. Moreover, it is important to move away from studying individual 'great' powers as the determinants of international relations and look as much at alliances and coalitions. These can either amplify power or – if poorly constructed, with reluctant allies – make it less than the sum of its parts.

When states do meet in war, what is important is not to look at the engagement as some war game to be decided through the interaction of the armies that are in existence when the conflict starts. More often than not, wars expand greatly and become something far more horrible – consuming and changing in many ways that would have seemed outlandish at their start. As such, it is the ability to continue fighting that matters most. And once again, the role of allies in helping support this force generation (or limit it) usually plays a great role in a war's outcome. The longer a war goes on, the more likely it is to draw in other countries.

One of the purposes of this book is to try to understand war and power from these larger perspectives. And one of the best ways to do so is to apply them to the US and China in the Indo-Pacific today.

Power in the Indo-Pacific Today

The United States and China are the two most powerful states in the world, and a war between them (with their allies) would be a cataclysm not seen since World War II – and maybe even larger. That is because both of these states have many of the strengths that make for an effective full-spectrum power in a way not seen since World War II – more so, I would argue, than we saw in the Cold War – and they are definitely flirting with direct confrontation. It has been a long time since the globe has witnessed anything similar.

By any metric, these are the two largest economic/technological powers in the world today. During the Cold War, the USSR never rivalled the US as an economic/technological power. Napoleonic France and early nineteenth-century Britain were the two largest economic powers in Europe, but China at that time had arguably the largest economy in the world. Indeed, the last time there were two economic/technological powers in anything like a similar situation, it was the US and Great Britain in the late nineteenth and early twentieth centuries. However, in that case, the two powers – particularly Britain – went out of their way not to have dangerous confrontations (which rather undermines the idea that all states will try to maximize their power in the international system).

Not only do China and the US possess the two largest GDPs, both in absolute and PPP terms; they also lead the world in technological developments. They have, for instance, most of the world's leading high-tech companies, from Apple in the US to Huawei in China.

Moreover, they produce most of the world's highest-rated scientific and technological papers. The US and China are basically racing each other for control of the technologies that will lead to more powerful military systems in the future. Artificial intelligence (AI) might be the most pointed. If either side could develop a workable AI system that could actually make different military (and civilian) systems autonomous, it would transform warfare. Machines from aircraft to land and sea vehicles that could be sent out without human crews, and even operate without human control at a distance, would arguably end warfare as we have known it for millennia – leaving the outcome of the struggle over force destruction and regeneration in the hands of those who could best the other in the race for autonomous forces.

The issue that both sides face is that making such autonomous weapons poses massive challenges in terms of power supply, the creation of neural networks, and the building of chips small but powerful enough to run autonomous programming. All the signs are that this race will be intense. The US seemed to have a major advantage in this area with the work being done by its large high-tech companies. However, in early 2025, a small Chinese start-up, DeepSeek, released an AI program that was much simpler than any US version available at the time – an announcement that Chinese companies were making some of the most important advances, and ones that could have a major military impact, in this vital area.

The economic/technological strength of the US and China is far from identical, and these differences could make a significant, even determinative difference, in a war. The US has come to dominate world services, while China is a manufacturing powerhouse. The US would have an advantage in raising and spending money in any conflict, but China can make almost anything in a far greater mass than the US.

If these are the two largest economic/technological powers of the time, and it is assumed they will remain so for a number of decades at least, their leaderships are very different and these contrasts will play a role in their actions as global powers. The US, with its democratic system that changes leaders every four or at most eight years, has thrown up an uneven list of leaders in the last twenty-four years (and over the country's history as a whole). Indeed, it could be argued that over the past quarter-century, American foreign policy has been a catalogue of bipartisan failure – whereas before that, the US had far more success (and in a bipartisan way). The foreign policies from George W. Bush through Obama, Trump, Biden and now back to Trump, have been uneven – prone to dramatic changes, often reflecting the personal prejudices of the sitting president – and mostly a failure. Getting far too enmeshed in areas that are not actually of great security interest, such as Afghanistan and Iraq, while failing to understand where the US could have supported allies that are willing to fight, such as in Ukraine, has revealed the capriciousness of American policies. The US policy towards Syria is a textbook case of this, with swings and inconsistency leading to instability. During the War on Terror, under George W. Bush, the US helped exacerbate the chaos in Syria. A growing civil war between the government of Bashir al-Assad and a range of different actors – including ISIS, Sunni groups, and Kurds – gripped much of the country. When Barack Obama became president, he then declared that the US had a clear red line in policy: that if Assad (and his Russian allies) used chemical weapons to assert their control, then the US would militarily intervene. When Assad and the Russians did just that, the Obama administration showed that its red-line claim was meaningless and did nothing. The US then watched on as Assad seemingly entrenched his power and, under Trump, actually ended up bombing other parties in the Syrian Civil War – such as ISIS. The US actually ended up improving the position of a regime that used chemical weapons. And then, when that regime fell in 2024, it was almost entirely a bystander.

Overall, leadership changes of opinion have also meant that the American preparations for any large war have been spasmodic. There has been talk about a realignment in the Indo-Pacific, but at the same time US leadership has allowed certain vital strategic capabilities – such as shipbuilding and other military manufacturing – to weaken dangerously.

The Chinese situation is not much better. There can be a tendency to overrate the 'strength' and purpose of dictatorial rulers, but the truth of the matter is that dictators are the sharpest of double-edged swords when it comes to exercising national power – and they become even more so the longer they are in office. Certainly, dictators like Chinese president Xi Jinping often get more intransigent and less willing to listen to counterarguments the longer they stay in power (and Xi has been in power for more than a decade).* Vladimir Putin is a salutary lesson. The disastrous invasion of Ukraine was based, it seems, mostly on his personal vision than any rational understanding of the risks he was taking. And this is the issue with the leaderships in both countries. The US has clearly shown how unstable leadership can lead to unstable policies, while China, with its predilection towards dictatorial rule, might ultimately opt for something far more dangerous.

The way the two states act towards Taiwan is a textbook example of this. The Chinese state under Xi has increasingly ramped up its pressure on Taiwan for many years now. It has steadily and threateningly increased its military preparations and military exercises – showing a growing ability to interdict trade on all sides of the island and even to attempt an invasion. The US, on the other hand, has been inconsistent, particularly recently under Donald Trump. The traditional US policy of strategic ambiguity towards Taiwan (not making it clear whether the US would fight for Taiwan or not) has been replaced by statements that Taiwan is a threat to the US economy. So the Taiwanese are faced with a China leadership that has presented a consistent and growing threat, and a US leadership that has alternately been friendly or dismissive. It makes defensive planning a nightmare.

If leadership adds an air of unpredictability to both China and the US, the role of their different societies and political structures if anything amplifies instability. American society is probably the greatest advantage the country would have in any conflict with China: it has shown dynamism, is technologically conversant, and can innovate more than almost any other on earth at this time. You would have said around 2014 that it represented one of the most reliable pillars of US strength. At the same time, in the past ten years it has also divided against itself and has been unexpectedly influenced by outside forces that have been effective in feeding it different narratives – from anti-vaccine to anti-Ukraine/pro-Russian – and it has shown itself to be easily taken in by the arguments of its greatest enemies.

In comparison, the strength of Chinese society in supporting China

---

* The exact date that Xi Jinping became dictatorial is up for debate. He became general secretary of the Communist Party in 2012, president of the PRC in 2013, and in 2018 scrapped all term limits on the office of president, allowing himself to keep power for as long as he can hold it.

as a power remains more under the surface. One-party or dictatorial societies are normally told to not express themselves, to let the state structure do their thinking for them, and to immerse themselves in either the material or distracting parts of the human experience. China is no exception. The Chinese people are encouraged to better themselves materially or distract themselves as much as possible, while leaving politics and international relations to the Communist Party. As part of this, the party has brought into being arguably the most comprehensive surveillance-state structure in human history, with almost all movements, physical or online, being watched.

What we don't know, and can never know until a real crisis occurs – such as a war with the US in the Indo-Pacific – is to what degree Chinese society supports its rulers in their foreign affairs. This is a huge question. Probably, as in the case of Russia, Chinese society has been so shaped and cowed that it will do what its rulers say. That being said, there is a chance that – as with a number of dictatorial societies over the years, from Mussolini's Italy to Bashir al-Assad's Syria – when given the opportunity, many Chinese who seemed loyal to the state actually harboured serious doubts about the policies of their own rulers. The fact that the Chinese state has such strict surveillance is a sign that they know such hidden opposition is a possibility.

The two nations' strengths, weaknesses and instabilities when it comes to leadership, society and structure have all interacted with their economic/technological strengths to create the two largest militaries in the world today. Looking at them, it is remarkable how much larger and more comprehensive they are than any other military on the planet.* The US and China are the only states who maintain large forces in all four domains (land, air, sea and space). They have millions of military personnel under arms and, we assume, the ability to operate their equipment in complex operations.

It is here where some of the difficulties in assessment occur, particularly in relation to the human aspects of war and power. The US military has been at war for most of the last eighty-five years, and

---

* Going forward, the interesting question will be how/whether the Indian military attempts to strengthen itself to reach the level of the US and Chinese militaries. Going by present trends, India should possess the economic/technological means to try this in the coming decades.

this has given it tremendous experience in the complex operation of its systems in times of war. It has, in that time, waged campaigns of all sorts, including the most difficult amphibious landings and complex air campaigns involving extensive SEAD (suppression of enemy air defences). It has also deployed large forces in numerous places around the world at relatively short notice, and it has practice in using its high-tech goods in combat conditions. The different branches of the US military all have their own traditions and experiential hinterlands, which generally prove an asset when they are utilized. All of this experience should continue to provide a significant leg-up to the US as its military undertakes its assigned tasks at the start of any war.

That being said, the US military is experiencing some worrying trends when it comes to the more human aspects. It is becoming increasingly reliant on, and in many cases reflective of, one particular part of American society. It now comes more and more from the parts of the country that support the Republican Party, and the US military as a whole seems far more religiously minded than the rest of the country – which is actually seeing a significant drop in religious practice. While this is extremely difficult to quantify, a military that is not representative of the society it serves as a whole can end up being distrusted by that society – with potentially corrosive results.[1]

The Chinese military, on the other hand, is about as inexperienced as that of a full-spectrum power has ever been, and has no meaningful experience operating its systems under wartime conditions. The last significant war it fought was against Vietnam in 1979, and during this conflict it performed very poorly. Of course, the Chinese military has also been remade into an entirely different beast since then – which in and of itself presents challenges. It has gone from a mass conscript force that relied overwhelmingly on land power of the more basic type, to a smaller (by Chinese standards), more professional military force with some of the most advanced equipment in the world. In this transition what has been entirely lacking is any real-world experience of waging a war.

What we also don't know is just how much corruption has impacted the readiness of China's military. While it is probably not as bad as for the Russian military, which was and is deeply affected by corruption, the Chinese government is acting as if it has been a problem. In 2024, the government instituted a very active crackdown on corruption and a number of very high-ranking officers, including the commander of China's strategic rocket forces (amongst the most technologically advanced parts of the Chinese military), were arrested. Of course, this opens up another question – of leadership and political system. What we don't know is to what degree this crackdown was inspired by a genuine desire to stop corruption, or whether it was staged to strengthen the Communist Party's or even President Xi's hold on power.

So, the US and Chinese militaries, emerging from the different factors that create national power, have their distinct strengths and weaknesses. Of course, neither of these powers interacts in the world alone. They both lead different groups of alliances or looser power groupings which, surprisingly, bear resemblance to the situation in Europe before World War I. The alliances then were not in many cases hard and fast commitments that obligated one power to fight for another – but rather larger diplomatic groupings that indicated likely fighting partners if a war did break out. The British, for instance, were in no way obligated to fight for France and Russia in 1914. They chose to in the end, but even then there were voices very much opposed to such action.

On the surface, the US alliance structure in the Indo-Pacific is considerably stronger than China's. The US has defence pacts with Japan, South Korea and Australia, and has defence ties (but no obligation to defend) Taiwan. The US also has strong established relations with Thailand, the Philippines, Vietnam and Singapore, all of whom are uncomfortable with China trying to dominate the South China Sea. Even in terms of 'neutrals' the situation is not unfavourable to the US. India, a coming international power, shares a border with China that is the site of regular military clashes. If the US had the ability to coordinate relations with its different allies, find ways to have them work together, and reassure them of its strategic commitment to the region, this could help expand its influence in the area.

Alas for America, in this case, issues of leadership, society and structure seem to be working overtime to keep this from happening. The swings in US politics, the rise of populists such as Donald Trump, and the general unreliability that the US is projecting as an international partner undermine this American advantage. What the US is doing, particularly under Trump, is defining its relationship with its allies from a zero-sum perspective. What does the US pay versus the ally in terms of defence, and what is the trade balance between the US and the ally? In this version, even historic partners can be shamed as 'public parasites' who are shirking their responsibilities and taking advantage of American beneficence.

In the Indo-Pacific, this could be particularly destructive. What the US has in the Indo-Pacific is a group of bilateral relationships with its allies, and it is not clear which, if any, trust the US enough to fight for any other US friend in the region. Japan, for instance, is not pledged to fight for Taiwan, nor is Australia committed to defend South Korea. And the more the US turns under its populist politics to view its relationship with these countries from a financial cost—benefit basis, the less these countries will trust the US to lead them as a group. Even South Korea, which is the site of the second-largest deployment of US forces outside of the United States (to Japan), has serious concerns about US commitment. The South Koreans, because of their worries, are wondering if they should start constructing their own nuclear deterrent. Needless to say, Taiwan, which is operating with no firm US defence commitments, is even more concerned. This is being made worse by Donald Trump, who is turning the US relationship with Taiwan from one of friends and allies into one between economic competitors.

If the US has a potentially powerful group of allies staring it in the face, the situation is not so comforting for the Chinese – though they at least seem to be able to get more concrete support from theirs. Chinese policy in its region, which has been heavy-handed and aggressive in the assertion of Chinese rights, has left the PRC with only a small number of possible defence partners in its area – primarily Russia and North Korea. Russia, it is now clear, has been terribly overrated as a power, and has suffered grievously during its bloodthirsty invasion of Ukraine. North Korea is likewise an economic basket case. Even adding in more distant states, such as Iran, provides China with allies whose standing lately has been damaged or weakened.

And yet, what China does have through this group are a number of states that are reliant on China for their existence and provide at least more stability than the far wealthier and more powerful group that the US could – but has failed to – organize. Russia is absolutely reliant on China for its continuing ability to function economically, and has basically stripped the long Russo-Chinese border of all defensive forces. It has and will continue to support all Chinese claims in the area. North Korea likewise is to a great extent reliant on China for its continuing existence. So China has fewer and poorer partners than the US, but structurally can ask a great deal from them.

War in the Indo-Pacific Tomorrow

Overall, the power balance between the US and China is finely weighted, so much so that any war between them would almost certainly metastasize into an event with dramatic global repercussions. They are both full-spectrum powers, with the ability to act around the world and possessing military forces capable of doing a great deal of damage. That being said, it is the differences in the elements of their full-spectrum power structures that could prove decisive in any war.

In the opening stages of a conflict in the Indo-Pacific involving the US and China, the US should have some noticeable advantages. Its real-world experience of war-fighting and its probable technological advantage should allow it to exert its influence over the Chinese in certain areas. This could be amplified by ongoing developments or Chinese action. If the US, for instance, could leap ahead in the race for autonomous systems (as it is attempting with the Replicator Initiative*), there is the possibility of a step-change advantage in targeting speed and accuracy.[2]

If the Chinese were rash enough to attempt an amphibious assault on Taiwan, the US would also have the ability to work with the well-armed Taiwanese, who have access to stocks of anti-ship and anti-air missiles, and so could make such an operation as difficult and destructive as possible for the inexperienced Chinese military. A decisive mass Chinese amphibious assault on Taiwan is one of the most common war scenarios proposed by western war-gamers (as it fits with the battle-centric view of conflict that they prefer). One of the most reputable US think tanks has run a series of war games of this initial action,

---

* The Replicator Initiative is one of the most ambitious US weapons systems initiatives that has been publicly acknowledged. It is an effort to equip US forces with all-domain, autonomous (AI) weapons to help counter the Chinese advantage in mass.

and in most the Chinese lose to a combined US-Taiwanese force.[3] The difficulty of launching an invasion into the teeth of US-Taiwanese defensive firepower, including anti-ship and anti-air missiles and UAVs, means that Chinese vessels and aircraft, which would have to work with an extremely high level of complex operational success for an invasion to succeed, would be lost in very high numbers.

It is probably safe to assume (for now – but not in the medium term) that the US would maintain a technological advantage at the start of any war. The Chinese are in many ways building up a replica force (with aircraft carriers and fighter aircraft such as the Chinese J-35) that seem to be 'bootleg' versions of US equipment – though with what are assumed to be inferior capabilities.* The US also maintains a suite of more advanced technological systems that it won't share even with its closest allies. If properly organized and coordinated with its allies, the US military with its advanced equipment should have the ability to deal heavy blows to China's front-line military forces at the start of any war – to such a degree that the Americans should probably hope for an aggressive Chinese opening to any conflict, as that would play into its operational advantages.

That being said, the Chinese might choose not to be so rash early in the conflict, and instead play to their strengths in a long-war scenario. China's ability to regenerate military force, in mass, is much superior to that of the US. It is in this area that the economic differences between the two very much favour the Chinese. Though the US economy might still be larger and arguably more technologically advanced, it is much smaller than the Chinese economy when it comes to the ability to manufacture goods. The US is primarily a service-based economy, and it has seen a collapse in many crucial, strategic areas over the last few years – such as ammunition production. The Chinese, on the other hand, even as they are experiencing economic difficulties today with a bankrupt real-estate sector and a declining working-age population, can manufacture goods in a manner that is entirely superior to what is possible in the US. For instance, while the US basically has no domestic production of civilian shipbuilding left,

---

* The J-35 seems almost like a carbon copy of the F-35 – almost identical in shape and design, with what is assumed to be Chinese attempts to replicate the American systems.

the Chinese are the world leaders by a long way – making almost half the world's new shipping.[4]

If any war in the Indo-Pacific therefore became a long struggle, the early advantages that the US would possess could easily be erased not only by Chinese manufacturing strengths but also certain leadership and societal factors. As this book has hopefully shown, in most major wars it is not what you start with that decides the contest; it is what you make during the war that determines the military outcome. The Chinese can make more of everything – and even if their equipment might not be as good on an individual basis as that of the US, the mass that they can deploy is sobering. Russia and Ukraine are at present trying to source UAVs of all kinds, from the simplest to the most advanced, from anywhere in the world – and China is supplying both sides. One study has estimated that the Chinese control about 80 per cent of world UAV production.[5] If that percentage were maintained in a war, it would not bode well for the US. If it turns out that the Chinese can make equipment as effective as the US', then the mass they can produce would probably be overwhelming.

Winning a battle rarely wins a war – and any US-Chinese struggle needs to be placed in this broader context. If the story of war and power over the last century and a half (and longer) tells us anything, it's that gaining advantage in a long war matters much more than winning opening battles. Unfortunately the US seems more geared to the latter than the former. It would be under great pressure to try to end any war as quickly as possible, and that would come from a combination of economic, leadership and societal factors. Its military would struggle to regenerate itself with mass; its leadership is inconsistently interested in the region; and the likelihood of the US population believing that a longer-term war against China could be won is questionable. China would not have such pressure, or at least not to the same degree.

The US might be able to redress some of its deficiencies in long-term output and mass if it could harness the productive abilities of its much stronger allies. Japan and South Korea, for instance, are the second- and third-largest shipbuilding powers in the world, and could help match China in this regard. US allies also deploy large and powerful military forces in their own right. Certainly a fighting alliance involving the US, Japan, South Korea, Taiwan, Australia and the Philippines would be one of the most powerful in human history, with the ability to deploy and regenerate force on a massive scale. A fighting alliance involving China, Russia and North Korea would be much weaker in comparison.

However, the US, as previously mentioned, has so far failed to create a fighting alliance with its friends. Australia seems more than likely to step aside from any fighting in the Indo-Pacific and has gone out of its way to say that it is not committed to fighting for Taiwan, even if the US decides to do so.[6] There are strong signs that both Japan and South Korea are deeply reluctant to commit themselves to fighting over Taiwan as well.[7] It is hard to blame them. The US has shown itself to be unreliable as an alliance leader and they can in no way count on the US to commit itself to actually fight for their freedom. On the other hand, Russia and North Korea, if their present regime types remain in power, seem to believe that China will help them fight for their dictatorships. Certainly, they can count on China being with them for the long haul in the region over an increasingly isolationist and capricious United States.

One final question to examine is the likelihood of any longer war between the US and China seeing the use of nuclear weapons. Both the US and China would have strong disincentives against the use of nuclear weapons in any such war. China would be aiming to assert its control over extended areas of the Indo-Pacific, so would not want to make them into radioactive wastelands. The US, on the other hand, is already acting like there is every chance it would abandon its friends in the region to China if needs be – and if so, the idea that it would resort to nuclear weapons to try to wage such a war seems far-fetched. It is hard to see what either side would gain from the use of nuclear weapons in any scenario.

This is another reason to be sceptical of a war-game, battle-view of conflict. Before the Russian invasion of Ukraine, the US and its partners ran many war games that saw such a scenario or similar conflict relatively quickly escalate to the use of nuclear weapons.[8] This idea echoes earlier war-gaming experiences from the 1960s onwards, many of which saw the world obliterated by gamers acting as war leaders. Certainly the Biden administration seemed to think that there was every chance Putin would use nuclear weapons when his initial assault on Ukraine proved far less effective than many expected. It has been claimed that the administration thought there was a 50 per cent chance that Putin would use nuclear weapons in the second half of 2022.[9]

Yet at no time has Russia actually taken any steps to use such weapons. Even though Russia constantly threatened, blustered and acted like it might do so if the US or any other of Ukraine's supporters did something they didn't want them to do, once these 'red lines' were crossed, the Russians did precious little to escalate. One of the reasons is that China itself has been resolutely opposed to the use of nuclear weapons by Russia. The Chinese seem to see little benefit and huge risks in the use of such weapons, and when it comes to a war with the US in the Indo-Pacific, it's difficult to see them changing their position.

Overall, during the last few decades – and particularly recently – the US has taken what should very well be a winning hand in any war with China and thrown away many of its advantages. Though economically strong overall, it has allowed certain strategic areas of strength to wither. It possesses a technologically sophisticated and in some ways dynamic society, but it is also one riven by divisions and surprisingly unable to resist outside influences – as has been seen with Russian influence operations and their impact on US politics. Its leadership, which demonstrated real strength and bipartisan consensus in the Cold War and the immediate period after, has shown itself more recently to be unstable and unable to act in the best interests of the nation. Finally, though it has a very powerful group of possible allies with whom to work, the US seems determined not to make as much of this advantage as it could.

And these failures all give the Chinese a significant opportunity in any war, if they can find a way to compensate for probable US technological and experiential advantages at present – and possibly in terms of adaptation as any war went on. Time could favour China in terms of economics (mass production), leadership (commitment to the war) and society (willingness to support or at least not oppose its leadership in the war). If China could help keep the US from forming a strong alliance structure to fight a long war, it would probably achieve many of its strategic goals in the end.

The United States is presently set up to win the opening battles in any conflict with China, but China might very well triumph in any longer war.

Afterword

This book was written almost entirely over the course of 2024 and the final draft was submitted to the publisher in November of that year. As such, it was composed almost entirely before the election of Donald Trump – though as readers will be able to tell, very much written with that possibility in mind. It is now early April 2025, fewer than three months after the second Donald Trump Administration started. This, I believe, needs some comment and acknowledgement. What we have seen so far in this extraordinary if short period has confirmed, indeed arguably strengthened, the central ideas of the book.

Most obviously, what Trump has done in reorienting many of the fundamentals of US foreign policy, reveals the important role that specific leaders play in determining policy and events and how this needs to be more widely acknowledged and integrated into our concepts of national power. That was the central argument of chapter two. Though much of traditional great power and other international relations thinking stresses similarities in state behaviour and de-emphasizes the role of individuals, what we have seen in just a few months underscores the gaps in such analysis. Under the personal rule of Trump, and a Cabinet that is very much operating under his thumb, the United States has started to reconfigure its entire vision of foreign policy-making, including fundamental questions of what makes for a friendly state and what makes for a possible enemy. He has pushed the United States to have a series of bilateral confrontations with states that used to be friendly and at the same time made the United States far more supportive of the Russian dictatorship of Vladimir Putin, which until his presidency was almost always seen as one of the most likely enemies of the USA.

Trump's behaviour has been exacerbated by certain societal and systemic factors in the United States such as those discussed in chapter three. He has benefited greatly from (indeed he has cleverly exacerbated) the political fragmentation of the American population, which has left him with a committed base that has allowed him today to dominate the Republican Party almost completely. His strength in the party means that even though he won what is in historical terms a small election victory, and even though the Republicans have a very small majority in the House of Representatives (three seats as this is being written), there is little willingness in Congress to try to interfere with Trump's dramatic changes in policy. Even when many Republicans in the past have identified themselves as strong backers of the US alliance system – most famously the transatlantic NATO alliance, as Trump moves to weaken (perhaps entirely defang) those alliances, they have shown little or no willingness to try and stop him. It is worth noting that in the very short time between Trump becoming president and writing this a large percentage of self-identified Republicans have changed their outlook according to opinion polls, and now see dictatorial Russia as a potentially strong US ally.

If it is too early to discuss any fundamental changes to the structure of US military forces, such as are discussed in chapter four, in just two months we have seen glimpses of important changes that will affect military power. The Defense Department is de-emphasizing the thinking and inclusive parts of the military and stressing what it calls a 'warrior culture'. In its fanaticism to eradicate anything that smacks of DEI initiatives and its eagerness to cut research and educational bodies, it has started the process of making the US military less reflective and analytical. If it follows through with such changes, the US military might become a more obedient and bloody-minded organization, but at the same time less flexible and adaptive. In fighting modern wars, that would be a distinctly negative trade-off.

If its unclear if there will be any fundamental changes in military force creation, there have already been fundamental changes in the US alliance structure, which was the focus of chapter five. Since World War II the US has underpinned its global predominance through close work and mutual defence relationships with a group of mostly democratic states in Europe, North America and East Asia. Already these relationships are being severely damaged, perhaps fatally. Trump has, as this is being written, unleashed a potentially devastating trade war which has placed most US allies under punitive tariffs if they want to trade with the USA. More specifically, Trump has incessantly talked about ending Canada's independence by using US economic strength to coerce Canadians into becoming the '51st State'. At the same time he has talked if anything more aggressively about conquering Greenland and making it a US protectorate. As this is being written the United States is preparing to send a high-level delegation to Greenland, including the Vice President, J. D. Vance, to make its intentions towards the island clear. This threatening of Greenland, still legally part of Denmark, and the public demands on Canada represent a Trump-led 180 degree turn in US policy, which has already destabilized the US relationship with two of the USA's best allies since World War II (both of whom saw their soldiers die fighting alongside US forces in Afghanistan).

All of these different changes and developments could very well spill over into US position in the Indo-Pacific. In one way, Trump has made war (discussed in chapters six to ten) involving the USA less likely. This is for the simple fact that Trump is pushing US policy in a more pro-China and anti-Taiwan direction. Trump has been noticeably critical of Taiwan, as he has been of many of the US's democratic allies, reframing the US relationship with the Taiwanese into an economic zero-sum game which has, supposedly, seen the Taiwanese take advantage of the USA by stealing the US microchip production industry. At the same time, Trump is regularly reaching out to China, to try and improve relations. Overall it seems that the US is now de-emphasizing working with its allies, and is under Trump consciously destroying decades of strategic relationships.

If, as seems likely, the Chinese understand that Trump would not fight for Taiwan, it means the fate of the island is very much in question – though without the US playing a direct combat role. That alone could have a major impact on the entire US position in the western Pacific. If the Chinese seize Taiwan they could then project power outwards far more effectively, threatening the US ability to deploy force anywhere from the Marianas Islands, to Japan, to the South China Sea. That alone would be transformative.

If the US did decide to try and defend Taiwan, Trump's moves to weaken US alliances alone could be determinative. Whether Japan, South Korea or Australia would actually fight for Taiwan before a Trump presidency was very much up in the air. They are now even less likely to do so – and moreover Europe is certainly less likely to help the US as well. Weakening the US alliance structure means that the US alone might end up fighting for Taiwan, and in any kind of longer war, against China, the world's largest manufacturing power by a long way, that alone could be telling.

Of course it is still very early days for the new Trump administration. Yet, in such a short period he, and those who work for him, have already had an impact on many of the different variables that make up national power and which then determine the outcome of wars.

April 2025

Acknowledgements

The writing of this book coincided with the most intense chapter of my academic life. While working on *War and Power*, I was simultaneously serving as Head of School for the School of International Relations at the University of St Andrews, coordinating the Russia-Ukraine Military Assessment Project with Professor Eliot Cohen (one of the most important research endeavours of my career), and even launching a new Substack. I made it through this period intact, owing entirely to the constant support and joy provided by my wife Mathilde and son Payson. They kept me going through moments of exhaustion and anxiety, when I doubted that I could get everything done. Knowing they were in my corner made what so often seemed impossible, *possible*.

I also need to thank my family and those close friends I leaned on during this process – and who added to the cheer when it was most needed. Family back in America were always there and, though brief, my visits to Boston buoyed my spirits each time. Thanks and love to Mom, Aunt Anne, Liz, Sarah, Bill, Jamie, Sam F., Andrew, Sam W., Ben and Marilyn.

Roddy and Anne, the Highland trips were much needed (even when the power went out). Matt, as ever, it was wonderful to see you in Glasgow. Will and Kate, I didn't make it to Dublin as promised but will soon. Ina and Guy, my gratitude, as always, for hosting me in London – now come north sometime. Gary and Joan, thanks for introducing me to College Station, which was great fun when I really needed it. Eliot and Judith, you put me up in Washington DC for longer than Ben Franklin advised, but always with good grace. Simon, thank you for the vegetarian meal; next time do bring Helen.

Also, many thanks to the group in the Back Room. You know who you are, but no one else does . . .

In St Andrews I relied on a lovely and steadfast group of friends. Stephen and Anya, I never saw either of you in a bad mood, which was remarkable and regularly comforting. Thanks also go to many members of the School of International Relations and the University of St Andrews for their friendship, support, and help in freeing up enough time to let this book be written. I am grateful, in particular, to Gurch, Fiona, Tony, Kristen, Marc, Lynne, Sally, Brad, Ineke and Hew.

I would also like to thank my agent, Ellen Levine, for her unerringly sage counsel. And, of course, the book would never have seen the light of day without the backing of Daniel Crewe and Penguin UK. The whole team at Penguin has been brilliant.

Lastly, I would like to thank a group of individuals that I have not spoken to for decades but who could be said to have instilled the earliest ideas for this book. As a young boy at Dexter School in Brookline, Massachusetts, I was lucky enough to have my historical imagination fired by a set of kind-hearted and passionate teachers, including Misters Rossiter, Lee, Reed and Putnam. When they first introduced me to the story of Alcibiades and the siege of Syracuse they not only unleashed a passion for Sicily, they taught me very adult lessons on the stupidity of war and the perils of power. Though I do not imagine they are still around to read this book, they bear much of the inspiration.

February 2025

Notes

Introduction: The Failure

1 'Zelensky refuses US offer to evacuate, saying "I need ammunition, not a ride"', CNN, 26 February 2022, https://edition.cnn.com/2022/02/26/europe/ukraine-zelensky-evacuation-intl/index.html.

2 'Near-Peer Threats at Highest Point Since Cold War, DOD Official Says', US Department of Defense, 10 March 2020, https://www.defense.gov/News/News-Stories/Article/Article/2107397/near-peer-threats-at-highest-point-since-cold-war-dod-official-says/; 'Near-Peer Adversaries Work to Surpass U.S. In Technology, Official Says', US Department of Defense, 4 May 2018, https://www.defense.gov/News/News-Stories/Article/Article/1512901/near-peer-adversaries-work-to-surpass-us-in-technology-official-says/.

3 According to the *Washington Post*, in early February, US intelligence estimates were that, if Russia launched a full-scale invasion, Kyiv would fall in 'days': 'Russia could seize Kyiv in days and cause 50,000 civilian casualties in Ukraine, U.S. assessments find', https://www.washingtonpost.com/world/2022/02/05/ukraine-russia-nato-putin-germany/.

4 'Gen. Milley says Kyiv could fall within 72 hours if Russia decides to invade Ukraine: sources', Fox News, 5 February 2022, https://www.foxnews.com/us/gen-milley-says-kyiv-could-fall-within-72-hours-if-russia-decides-to-invade-ukraine-sources; 'Ukraine Crisis: Deterring Putin is expensive but much cheaper than war', Atlantic Council, https://www.atlanticcouncil.org/blogs/ukrainealert/ukraine-crisis-deterring-putin-is-expensive-but-much-cheaper-than-war/.

5 'Secretary of Defense Austin and Chairman of the Joint Chiefs of Staff Gen. Milley Press Briefing', Department of Defense, Department of Defense, 28 January 2022, https://www.defense.gov/News/Transcripts/Transcript/Article/2916567/secretary-of-defense-austin-and-chairman-of-the-joint-chiefs-of-staff-gen-milley/; https://www.bbc.co.uk/news/world-60177929.

6 'Gen. Milley says Kyiv could fall within 72 hours', Fox News, 5 February 2022.

7 'U.S. Military Aid to Ukraine: A Silver Bullet?', Rand Corporation, 21 January 2022, https://www.rand.org/blog/2022/01/us-military-aid-to-ukraine-a-silver-bullet.html.

8 *The Russo-Ukraine War: A Study in Analytic Failure*, September 2024, CSIS report, https://csis-website-prod.s3.amazonaws.com/s3fs-public/2024-09/240924_Cohen_Russia_Ukraine.pdf.

9 Charap regularly presented Russia as a Great Power, and liked to envisage Russian international politics within a great power paradigm. Samuel Charap, John Drennan and Pierre Noël, 'Russia and China: A New Model of Great-Power Relations', *Survival*, 59/1 (2017), 25–42, https://doi.org/10.1080/00396338.2017.1282670.

10 *The Russo-Ukraine War: A Study in Analytic Failure.*

11 Leopold von Ranke, 'The Great Powers (1833)', in *The Theory and Practice of History*, ed. Georg G. Iggers, 1st ed. (Routledge, 2010).

12 Daniel Costa, 'Great Power', *Encyclopaedia Britannica*, 2 October 2023, https://www.britannica.com/topic/great-power.

13 Charles Brandon Boynton, *The Four Great Powers: England, France, Russia, and America* (Hardpress Publishing, 2020).

14 Paul Kennedy (ed.), *The War Plans of the Great Powers* (Routledge, 2014), https://www.routledge.com/The-War-Plans-of-the-Great-Powers-RLE-The-First-World-War-1880-1914/Kennedy/p/book/9781138812772.

15 Edward H. Carr, *The Twenty Years' Crisis 1919–1939* (Macmillan, 1940), 109.

16 Phillips O'Brien, *How the War Was Won: Air–Sea Power and Allied Victory in World War II* (Cambridge University Press, 2015), 484–5

17 Ibid., 90, 359.

18 Michael C. Williams, 'Why Ideas Matter in International Relations: Hans Morgenthau, Classical Realism, and the Moral Construction of Power Politics', *International Organization* 58/4 (2004), 633–65, http://www.jstor.org/stable/3877799.

19 'An Introduction to Realism in International Relations', ND International Security Center, 21 July 2022, https://ndisc.nd.edu/news-media/news/an-introduction-to-realism-in-international-relations/.

20 Hans J. Morgenthau and Kenneth W. Thompson, *Politics among Nations: The Struggle for Power and Peace* (McGraw Hill, 1993), 127–158 contains a description of all these points.

21 The founder of structural realism, Kenneth Waltz, in his major work *Theory of International Politics*, uses the phrase 'great power', but never provides a clear definition except to imply that it has to do with national 'capabilities'. Kenneth Neal Waltz, *Theory of International Politics* (McGraw-Hill, 1979), 72–3.

22 John J. Mearsheimer, *The Tragedy of Great Power Politics* (Norton, 2001), 5.

23 Stephen M. Walt, 'Liberal Illusions Caused the Ukraine Crisis', *Foreign Policy*, 19 January 2022, https://foreignpolicy.com/2022/01/19/ukraine-russia-nato-crisis-liberal-illusions/.

24 'Transcript: John Mearsheimer on Handling Russia and China', *The Weekly Dish* (Substack), 3 March 2022, https://andrewsullivan.substack.com/p/transcript-john-mearsheimer-on-handling.

25 https://www.youtube.com/watch?v=o9A-u8EoWcI.

26 Michael Kofman and Andrea Kendall-Taylor, 'The Myth of Russian Decline', *Foreign Affairs*, 19 October 2021, https://www.foreignaffairs.com/articles/ukraine/2021-10-19/myth-russian-decline; Michael Kofman, 'Raiding and International Brigandry: Russia's Strategy for Great Power Competition', War on the Rocks, 14 June 2018, https://warontherocks.com/2018/06/raiding-and-international-brigandry-russias-strategy-for-great-power-competition/; Maxim Trudolyubov, 'Guns, Butter, and Russia's Enduring Military Power', *Moscow Times*, 26 September 2019, https://www.themoscowtimes.com/2019/09/26/guns-butter-and-russias-enduring-power-a67461.

27 'Air Strikes or Invasion: What are Putin's Military Options for Ukraine', *Financial Times*, 30 December 2021.

28 'Ukraine Commanders Say a Russian Invasion Would Overwhelm Them', *New York Times*, 9 December 2021, https://www.nytimes.com/2021/12/09/world/europe/ukraine-military-russia-invasion.html.

29 Lancelot Farrar, *The Short War Illusion: German Policy, Strategy & Domestic Affairs August–December 1914*, (ABC-Clio, 1973).

30 Holger H. Herwig, 'Germany and the "short-war" illusion: Toward a new interpretation?' *Journal of Military History*, 66/3 (2022), 681–93.

31 Raphael S. Cohen and Gian Gentile, 'America's Dangerous Short War Fixation', Rand Corporation, 31 March 2008, https://www.rand.org/pubs/commentary/2023/03/americas-dangerous-short-war-fixation.html.

32 'The Bomber Will Always Get Through' speech, https://www.airandspaceforces.com/article/0708keeperfile/; 'Walt Disney's *Victory Through Air Power*: A Behind-the-Scenes Look at the Making and Impact

of the Film', Walt Disney Museum, 20 July 2020, https://www.
waltdisney.org/blog/walt-disneys-victory-through-air-power-behind-
scenes-look-making-and-impact-film; School of Advanced Airpower
Studies, *The Paths of Heaven: The Evolution of Airpower Theory*, ed. Phillip
Meilinger (Air University Press, 1997), 256–8, https://www.airuniversity.
af.edu/Portals/10/AUPress/Books/B_0029_MEILINGER_PATHS_
OF_HEAVEN.pdf.

33 O'Brien, *How the War Was Won*, 1944 chapter.

34 Phillips O'Brien, 'The New Appeasement', *The Critic*, 14 January 2022,
https://thecritic.co.uk/the-new-appeasement/.

1. Economic/Technological Strength

1 https://worldpopulationreview.com/.

2 Carolin Pflueger and Pierre Yared, 'Global Hegemony and Exorbitant Privilege', 11 September 2024, https://bfi.uchicago.edu/insights/
global-hegemony-and-exorbitant-privilege/.

3 'How Did the United States Become a Global Power?', Council on
Foreign Relations, 14 February 2023, https://education.cfr.org/learn/
reading/how-did-united-states-become-global-power.

4 Wilson Center, 'A short history of America's economy since World
War II', 23 January 2014, https://medium.com/the-worlds-economy-
and-the-economys-world/a-short-history-of-americas-economy-since-
world-war-ii-37293cdb640.

5 Lieutenant Colonel James G. Lacey, 'Trafalgar: A Predestined Victory',
U.S. Naval Institute Proceedings (October 2005), https://www.usni.org/
magazines/proceedings/2005/october/trafalgar-predestined-victory.

6 'The Nelson Bullet', Royal Collection Trust, https://www.rct.uk/col-
lection/61158/the-nelson-bullet.

7 Roger Parkinson, *Dreadnought: The Ship that Changed the World* (IB Tauris,
2015), 89–92

8 Arthur J. Marder, 'Fisher and the Genesis of the Dreadnought', *U.S.
Naval Institute Proceedings* (December 1956), https://www.usni.org/maga-
zines/proceedings/1956/december/fisher-and-genesis-dreadnought.

9 Phillips O'Brien, *British and American Naval Power: Politics and Policies
1900–1936*, (Praeger, 1998), 62–7.

10 Matthew S. Seligmann, 'The Anglo-German Naval Race, 1898–1914', (Oxford University Press, 2016), 22. https://doi-org.ezproxy.st-andrews. ac.uk/10.1093/acprof:oso/9780198735267.003.0002, pp. 21–40

11 Parkinson, *Dreadnought*, 118.

12 Nicholas A. Lambert, *Sir John Fisher's Naval Revolution* (University of South Carolina Press, 1999), 279–80.

13 *Jane's Fighting Ships of World War I* (Studio Editions, 1990), 35–6.

14 'Bayern Class vs. Queen Elizabeth Class Dreadnoughts', Navy General Board, 29 July 2018, https://www.navygeneralboard.com/bayern-class-vs-queen-elezabeth-class/.

15 Andrew K. Blackley, 'The Barr and Stroud Rangefinder', *U.S. Naval Institute Naval History* (February 2024), https://www.usni.org/magazines/naval-history-magazine/2024/february/barr-and-stroud-rangefinder.

16 '*Titanic* facts and figures', BBC Bitesize, https://www.bbc.co.uk/bitesize/articles/zng8jty.

17 *Jane's Fighting Ships of World War I*, 35–6.

18 'The Woolworth Building (est. 1913)', https://www.woolworthsmuseum.co.uk/1910s-wwbuilding.htm.

19 This 35 is made up of all battleships (25) and battlecruisers (10) launched from January 1915 backward – so starting with *Queen Elizabeth* and counting back to *Dreadnought*. This includes two battleships, *Agincourt* and *Erin*, that were originally being built for other countries.

20 *The Paths of Heaven*, 9–10.

21 'The Bomber Will Always Get Through' speech.

22 Manfred Griehl and Joachim Dressel, *Heinkel: HE 177, 277, 274* (Air Life Publishing, 1998).

23 'Stuka Attack! The Dive-Bombing Assault on England during the Battle of Britain', Air University Press, 5 November 2020, https://www.airuniversity.af.edu/AUPress/Book-Reviews/Display/Article/2406538/stuka-attack-the-dive-bombing-assault-on-england-during-the-battle-of-britain/.

24 USSBS, Milch Interview, 23 May 1945, 8.

25 Heiber and Glantz (eds), *Hitler and His Generals: Military Conferences 1942–1945* (Enigma Books, 2003), 414.

26 O'Brien, *How the War Was Won*, 28–30.

27 Charles Webster and Noble Frankland, *Strategic Offensive Against Germany* (Naval and Military Press), vol. 3, 307.

28 W. F. Craven and J. L. Cate (eds), *The Army Air Forces in World War II* (University of Chicago Press, 1955), vol. VI, 203–4.

29 Ibid., 206.

30 Richard Hollingham, 'V2: The Nazi rocket that launched the space age', BBC, 7 September 2014, https://www.bbc.com/future/article/20140905-the-nazis-space-age-rocket.

31 Craven and Cate, vol. VI, 209.

32 Curtis Lemay, *Superfortress: The Boeing B-29 and American Airpower in World War II* (Westholme Press, 2007), 34.

33 Major Gerald S. Gorman, *End Game in the Pacific: Complexity, Strategy and the B-29*, monograph, https://apps.dtic.mil/sti/tr/pdf/ADA370327.pdf

34 Graham Simons, *The Boeing B-29 Superfortress* (Pen and Sword, 2012), 23–4.

35 Gorman, *End Game in the Pacific*.

36 Kenneth Werrell, *Blankets of Fire: US Bombers over Japan in World War II* (Smithsonian Institute Press, 1966), 82.

37 Scott Mall, 'B-29 Superfortress Pulled the Trigger on World War II in the Pacific', *Flying Magazine*, 5 September 2022, https://www.flyingmag.com/b-29-superfortress-pulled-the-trigger-on-world-war-ii-in-the-pacific/.

38 O'Brien, *How the War Was Won*, 304–5.

39 'This Russian Aircraft Carrier Was Built to Kill Navy Submarines and Carriers', *The National Interest*, 1 August 2018, https://nationalinterest.org/blog/buzz/russian-aircraft-carrier-was-built-kill-navy-submarines-and-carriers-27442.

40 https://www.history.navy.mil/content/dam/nhhc/research/histories/naval-aviation/dictionary-of-american-naval-aviation-squadrons-volume-1/pdfs/Appendx3.pdf.

41 'Chinese Aircraft Carrier *Fujian* Commences Catapult Testing', *Naval News*, 26 November 2023, https://www.navalnews.com/naval-news/2023/11/chinese-aircraft-carrier-fujian-commences-catapult-testing/.

42 'Aircraft Carriers: The New Battleship (As in Old and Obsolete)?', *The National Interest*, 13 December 2023, https://nationalinterest.org/blog/buzz/aircraft-carriers-new-battleship-old-and-obsolete-207914.

2. Leadership

1 'Summary of Hitler's Meeting with the Heads of the Armed Services on November 5, 1937 (Hossbach Protocol of November 10, 1937)',

https://germanhistorydocs.org/en/nazi-germany-1933-1945/summary-of-hitlers-meeting-with-the-heads-of-the-armed-services-on-november-5-1937-hossbach-protocol-of-november-10-1937.

2 'Judgement: The Aggression Against Poland', The Avalon Project, Lillian Goldman Law Library, https://avalon.law.yale.edu/imt/judpolan.asp.

3 Ibid.

4 'Letter from Mussolini to Hitler, August 25, 1939', The Avalon Project, Lillian Goldman Law Library, https://avalon.law.yale.edu/20th_century/ns058.asp.

5 Ian Kershaw, *Hitler 1936–1945: Nemesis* (Allen Lane, 2000), 214–15.

6 Julian Amery, *The Life of Joseph Chamberlain*, vol. 4, (Macmillan, 1951), 137.

7 https://core.ac.uk/download/pdf/41994008.pdf, 208.

8 Thomas Kohut, *Wilhelm II and the Germans: A Study in Leadership* (OUP, 1991), 97.

9 Jonathan Steinberg, *Bismarck: A Life* (OUP, 2011), 328–9.

10 Giles MacDonogh, *The Last Kaiser: William the Impetuous* (Weidenfeld & Nicolson, 2000), 168–9.

11 Christopher Clark, *The Sleepwalkers: How Europe Went to War in 1914* (Penguin, 2012), 147.

12 Ibid., 148.

13 Patrick J. Kelly, *Tirpitz and the Imperial German Navy* (Indiana University Press, 2011), pp. 128–33.

14 Clark, *Sleepwalkers*, 160–61.

15 Keith M. Wilson, *Policy of the Entente* (Cambridge University Press, 1985), 75.

16 Ibid., 35.

17 Keith Robbins, *Sir Edward Grey: A Biography of Grey of Fallodon* (Cassell London, 1971), 132–4.

18 Thomas G. Otte, *Statesman of Europe: A Life of Sir Edward Grey* (Penguin, London, 2023), 357.

19 Joseph Heller, *British Policy Towards the Ottoman Empire: 1908–1914* (Frank Cass, 1983), 79–81.

20 Aleksandar Rastović, 'Edward Grey and the First Balkan War', *SDU Faculty of Arts and Sciences Journal of Social Sciences*, https://dergipark.org.tr/tr/download/article-file/117969.

21 S. J. Valone, '"There Must Be Some Misunderstanding": Sir Edward Grey's Diplomacy of August 1, 1914', *Journal of British Studies*, 27/4 (1988), 405–24, https://www.jstor.org/stable/175713?seq=6.

22 James Cronan, 'The lamps are going out all over Europe', National Archives, 4 August 2014, https://blog.nationalarchives.gov.uk/lamps-going-europe/.

23 'Stock Market Crash of 1929', https://www.federalreservehistory.org/essays/stock-market-crash-of-1929.

24 Kershaw, *Hitler*, 420–25.

25 A. J. P. Taylor, *The Origins of the Second World War* (Penguin, 1964), 12–13.

26 Quote comes from the end of Chapter 4/Book 1 of *Mein Kampf*. Here is an online version: https://gutenberg.net.au/ebooks02/0200601h.html#ch1-04.

27 O'Brien, *British and American Naval Power*, 230–32.

28 'Appeasement and "Peace for Our Time"', National WWII Museum, 15 October 2024, https://www.nationalww2museum.org/war/articles/appeasement-and-peace-our-time.

29 'The Formation of the United Nations, 1945', US Department of State Archives, https://2001-2009.state.gov/r/pa/ho/time/wwii/17604.htm.

30 https://www.macrotrends.net/global-metrics/countries/CHN/china/gdp-per-capita.

31 https://data.worldbank.org/indicator/NY.GDP.PCAP.CD?locations=NG; https://data.worldbank.org/indicator/NY.GDP.PCAP.CD?locations=KE.

32 https://data.worldbank.org/indicator/NY.GDP.PCAP.CD?locations=US.

33 https://www.imf.org/external/datamapper/NGDPDPC@WEO/CHN/HKG/JPN/KOR/SGP/TWN.

34 Jude Blanchette, *China's New Red Guard: The Return of Radicalism and the Rebirth of Mao Zedong* (OUP, 2019), 96.

35 Maurice Meisner, *Mao Zedong, A Political and Intellectual Portrait* (Polity, 2007), 140–41.

36 Edward E. Rice, *Mao's Way* (University of California Press, 1974), 159.

37 Frank Dikotter, *Mao's Great Famine: The History of China's Most Devastating Catastrophe: 1958–62* (Bloomsbury, 2010), 325.

38 Alexander Pantsov, *Mao: The Real Story* (Simon & Schuster, 2012), 507–8.

39 Song Yongyi, 'Chronology of Mass Killings during the Chinese Cultural Revolution (1966-1976)', SciencesPo, 25 August 2011, https://www.sciencespo.fr/mass-violence-war-massacre-resistance/en/document/chronology-mass-killings-during-chinese-cultural-revolution-1966-1976.html.

40 From Daniel Yergin and Joseph Stanislaw, *Commanding Heights*, https://www.pbs.org/wgbh/commandingheights/shared/minitext/prof_dengxiaoping.html.

41 Michael Dillon, *Deng Xiaoping: The Man who Made Modern China* (Tauris, 2015), 175–85.

42 Alexander Pantsov, *Deng Xiaoping: A Revolutionary Life* (OUP, 2015), 374–5.

43 'Tiananmen Square: What happened in the protests of 1989?', BBC, 23 December 2021, https://www.bbc.co.uk/news/world-asia-48445934.

44 Ezra F. Vogel, *Deng Xiaoping and the Transformation of China* (Belknap, 2011), 630–32.

45 'Tiananmen Square protest death toll 'was 10,000', BBC, 23 December 2017, https://www.bbc.co.uk/news/world-asia-china-42465516.

3. Society and Structure

1 'Taiwan's dominance of the chip industry makes it more important', *The Economist*, 6 March 2023, https://www.economist.com/special-report/2023/03/06/taiwans-dominance-of-the-chip-industry-makes-it-more-important.

2 https://www.yahoo.com/news/chinas-military-corruption-crackdown-explained-034656021.html.

3 Chris Laudati, 'The Precarious State of U.S. Defense Stockpiles (UPDATED)', *National Defense*, 18 November 2022, https://www.nationaldefensemagazine.org/articles/2022/11/18/the-precarious-state-of-us-defense-stockpiles.

4 Selwyn Parker, 'The US wakes up to China's latest threat – big ships', *The Interpreter*, 11 October 2024, https://www.lowyinstitute.org/the-interpreter/us-wakes-china-s-latest-threat-big-ships.

5 Susan G. Sample, 'Power, Wealth, and Satisfaction: When Do Power Transitions Lead to Conflict?' *The Journal of Conflict Resolution* 62/9 (2018), 1905–31, https://www.jstor.org/stable/48596880.

6 Bernard Elbaum and William Lazonick, 'The Decline of the British Economy: An Institutional Perspective', *The Journal of Economic History* 44/2 (1984), 567–83, http://www.jstor.org/stable/2120731 (569).

7 https://www.statista.com/chart/20342/peak-land-area-of-the-largest-empires/.

8 Lara Kriegel, *The Crimean War and Its Afterlife* (Cambridge University Press, 2022), 7.

9 Howard Jones, *Blue and Gray Diplomacy: A History of Union and Confederate International Relations* (UNC Press, 2010), 38.

10 For much of the discussion of Britain recognizing Southern independence, see ibid., 29, 34, 125–6.

11 Philip E. Myers, *Caution and Cooperation: The American Civil War in British American Relations* (Kent State University Press, 2008), 56, 60.

12 Ibid., 205.

13 https://encyclopediaofalabama.org/article/css-alabama/.

14 Adrian Cook, *The Alabama Claims: American Politics and Anglo-American Relations, 1865–1872*, 27–8.

15 Ibid., 239.

16 'Venezuela Boundary Dispute, 1895–1899', Office of the Historian, https://history.state.gov/milestones/1866-1898/venezuela.

17 Kori Schake, *Safe Passage: The Transition from British to American Hegemony* (Harvard University Press, 2017), 144–5.

18 Donald J. Lisio, *British Naval Supremacy and Anglo-American Antagonisms 1914–1930* (Cambridge University Press, 2014), 16–36.

19 Duncan Andrew Campbell, *Unlikely Allies: Britain, America and the Victorian Origins of the Special Relationship* (Hambledon, 2007), 204.

20 Arthur Link (ed.), *The Papers of Woodrow Wilson*, vol. 30, (Princeton University Press, 1979), 472.

21 https://www.statista.com/statistics/1334676/wwii-annual-war-gdp-largest-economies/.

22 Simons, *The Boeing B-29 Superfortress*, 23–4.

23 Table 2, page 2, https://worldsteel.org/wp-content/uploads/Steel-Statistical-Yearbook-1980.pdf.

24 Odd Arne Westad, *The Cold War: A World History* (Allen Lane, 2017), 507.

25 Ibid., 509.

26 John C. Dewdney, Richard E. Pipes, Martin McCauley and Robert Conquest, 'Soviet Union', *Encyclopedia Britannica*, 11 February 2025, https://www.britannica.com/place/Soviet-Union.

27 David Reynolds, *One World Divisible: A Global History Since 1945* (Allen Lane, 2000), 569.

28 William Inboden, *The Peacemaker: Ronald Reagan, the Cold War and the World on the Brink* (Dutton, 2022), 457–9.

29 John Lewis Gaddis, *We Now Know: Rethinking Cold War History* (Clarendon, 1997), 293.

30 Mike Sewell, *The Cold War* (Cambridge University Press, 2002), 118–19.

31 Paul Kennedy, *The Rise and Fall of the Great Powers: Economic Change and Military Conflict from 1500 to 2000* (Random House, 1987), 459.

32 'US high-tech firms redeem the past', *Christian Science Monitor*, 3 August 1994, https://www.csmonitor.com/1994/0803/03081.html.

33 https://www.statista.com/statistics/1350976/leading-tech-companies-worldwide-by-market-cap/.

34 'Economics: why Europe is falling behind the USA', *Polytechnique Insights*, 11 June 2024, https://www.polytechnique-insights.com/en/columns/economy/economy-why-europe-is-falling-behind-the-usa/.

35 *The Future of European Competitiveness*, Part A (September 2024), https://commission.europa.eu/document/download/97e481fd-2dc3-412d-be4c-f152a8232961_en?.

36 Stefan Lehne, 'Has the "Hour of Europe" come at last? The EU's strategy for the Balkans', https://www.jstor.org/stable/pdf/resrep07054.11.pdf.

37 'Transforming European Defense', Center for Strategic and International Studies brief, 18 August 2022, https://www.csis.org/analysis/transforming-european-defense.

38 https://core.ac.uk/download/pdf/225129904.pdf.

39 'More than 1 in 10 people in Japan are aged 80 or over. Here's how its ageing population is reshaping the country', Wrold Economic Forum, 28 September 2023, https://www.weforum.org/stories/2023/09/elderly-oldest-population-world-japan/.

40 Myles Carroll, *The Making of Modern Japan: Power, Crisis and the Promise of Transformation* (Haymarket Books, 2021), 167–8.

4. Constructing a Military

1 Michael Kofman and Jeffrey Edmonds, 'Russia's Shock and Awe: Moscow's Use of Overwhelming Force Against Ukraine', *Foreign Affairs*, 22 February 2022, https://www.foreignaffairs.com/articles/ukraine/2022-02-21/russias-shock-and-awe.

2 'Russian Military Forces Dazzle after a Decade of Reform', *The Economist*, 2 November 2020, https:// www.economist.com/europe/2020/11/02/russian-military-forces-dazzle-after-a-decade-of-reform.

3 'Russia says a fifth of defense budget stolen', Reuters, 24 May 2011, https://www.reuters.com/article/world/russia-says-a-fifth-of-defense-budget-stolen-idUSTRE74N1YX/.

4 Howard T. Anderson, 'Corruption and War: Russian's Invasion of Ukraine', International Anti-Corruption Resource Center, https://iacrc.org/in-the-news/corruption-and-war-russians-invasion-of-ukraine/.

5 Philip Wasielewski, 'The Roots of Russian Military Dysfunction', Foreign Policy Research Institute, https://www.fpri.org/article/2023/03/the-roots-of-russian-military-dysfunction/.

6 'Mobilized Strength and Casualty Losses', https://www.loc.gov/collections/world-war-i-rotogravures/articles-and-essays/events-and-statistics/mobilized-strength-and-casualty-losses/.

7 Graydon A. Tunstall Jr, 'Austria-Hungary', in Richard Hamilton and Holger Herwig, *The Origins of World War I*, (Cambridge University Press, 2003), 126.

8 Martin Samuels, *Doctrine and Dogma, German and British Infantry Tactics in the First World War* (Greenwood Press, 1992).

9 David Stone, *The Kaiser's Army in World War One* (Bloomsbury, 2015), 46–8.

10 Holger Herwig, 'The Dynamics of Effectiveness', in Allan Millett and Williamson Murray (eds), *Military Effectiveness, Vol. I, The First World War* (Allen Unwin, 1988), 84.

11 David R. Jones, 'Imperial Russia's Forces at War', in ibid., 275.

12 Holger Afflerbach, *On a Knife Edge: How Germany Lost the First World War* (Cambridge University Press, 2022), 57.

13 Robert B. Asprey, *The German High Command at War: Hindenburg and Ludendorff and the First World War* (Little, Brown, 1993), 80.

14 https://battleofbritain1940.com/messerschmitt-bf-109/.

15 Templewood Mss (Cambridge University Library), Beaverbrook to Hoare, 30 August 1940.

16 Volker Ullrich, *Hitler: Ascent 1889–1939* (Bodley Head, 2016), 503–5.

17 Jak P. Mallmann Showell (ed.), *Fuehrer Conferences on Naval Affairs: 1939–1945* (Greenhill Books, 1990), 33.

18 Franklin D. Roosevelt, 'State of the Union Address', 6 January 1942, https://www.presidency.ucsb.edu/documents/state-the-union-address-1.

19 'Research Starters: US Military by the Numbers', The National WWII Museum, https://www.nationalww2museum.org/students-teachers/student-resources/research-starters/research-starters-us-military-numbers.

20 Research Starters: US Military by the Numbers, https://www.nationalww2museum.org/students-teachers/student-resources/research-starters/research-starters-us-military-numbers.

21 'WW2 Germany Population, Statistics, And Numbers', Feldgrau, https://www.feldgrau.com/ww2-germany-statistics-and-numbers/.

22 'Research Starters: Worldwide Deaths in World War II', The National WWII Museum, https://www.nationalww2museum.org/students-teachers/student-resources/research-starters/research-starters-worldwide-deaths-world-war.

23 Ray Stokes, *Ruins to Riches: The Economic Resurgence of Germany and Japan after 1945* (Cambridge University Press, 2024), 11–56.

24 Ibid., 57–136.

25 https://www.visualcapitalist.com/cp/the-worlds-largest-economies-1970-2020/.

26 https://data.worldbank.org/indicator/MS.MIL.XPND.GD.ZS?locations=DE.

27 https://data.worldbank.org/indicator/MS.MIL.XPND.GD.ZS?locations=DE-JP.

28 'Defence Expenditure of NATO Countries (2014–2024)', NATO press release, June 2024 https://www.nato.int/nato_static_fl2014/assets/pdf/2024/6/pdf/240617-def-exp-2024-en.pdf.

29 'Japan's Defense Budget Rising Toward NATO Target of 2% of GDP', Nippon.com, 26 September 2024, https://www.nippon.com/en/japan-data/h02121/japan%E2%80%99s-defense-budget-rising-toward-nato-target-of-2-of-gdp.html.

30 'Nord Stream 2 – Symbol of failed German bet on Russian gas', Clean Energy Wire, 8 March 2023, https://www.cleanenergywire.org/factsheets/gas-pipeline-nord-stream-2-links-germany-russia-splits-europe.

31 'Russia's Nord Stream 2 Natural Gas Pipeline to Germany Halted', Congressional Research Service, 10 March 2022, https://crsreports.congress.gov/product/pdf/IF/IF11138.

32 'Geopolitical implications of Nord Stream 2', UK Parliament research briefing, 2 March 2022, https://commonslibrary.parliament.uk/research-briefings/cbp-9462/.

33 'Remarks by President Biden on the United Efforts of the Free World to Support the People of Ukraine', 26 March 2022, https://sg.usembassy.gov/remarks-by-president-biden-on-the-united-efforts-of-the-free-world-to-support-the-people-of-ukraine/.

5. Allies

1 Foreign, Commonwealth & Development Office, 'UK and Portugal celebrate the world's longest diplomatic alliance', UK Government press release, 15 June 2023, https://www.gov.uk/government/news/uk-and-portugal-celebrate-the-worlds-longest-diplomatic-alliance.

2 David Crane, 'The Franco-Prussian war changed the map of Europe – so why are we so ignorant about it?', *Spectator*, 17 June 2023, https://www.spectator.co.uk/article/the-franco-prussian-war-changed-the-map-of-europe-so-why-are-we-so-ignorant-about-it/

3 P. J. V. Rolo, *Entente Cordiale: The Origins and Negotiations of the Anglo-French Agreements of 8 April 1904* (Macmillan, 1969), 271.

4 Alan Sharp and Glyn Stone, *Anglo-French Relations in the Twentieth Century: Rivalry and Cooperation* (Routledge, 2000), 16.

5 D. N. Collins, 'The Franco-Russian Alliance and Russian Railways, 1891–1914', *Historical Journal*, 16/4 (1973), 777–88, http://www.jstor.org/stable/2638282.

6 John H. Morrow, *The Great War: An Imperial History* (Routledge, 2004), 13.

7 Collins, 'The Franco-Russian Alliance and Russian Railways'.

8 Gary E. Weir, 'Tirpitz and Technology', *Naval History* 4/1 (January 1990), https://www.usni.org/magazines/naval-history-magazine/1990/january/tirpitz-and-technology.

9 Robbins, *Sir Edward Grey*, 161–4.

10 'The Anglo-Russian Entente – 1907', The Avalon Project, Lillian Goldman Law Library, https://avalon.law.yale.edu/20th_century/angrusen.asp.

11 Wilson, *Policy of the Entente*, 75.

12 T. G. Otte (ed.), *British World Policy and the Projection of Global Power, c. 1830–1960* (Cambridge University Press, 2019), 129–46.

13 William Mulligan, 'Restraints on Preventative War before 1914', in Jack Levy and John Vasquez (eds), *The Outbreak of the First World War* (Cambridge University Press, 2014), 132–31.

14 John C. G. Rohl, *Wilhelm II: Into the Abyss of War and Exile, 1900–1941* (Cambridge University Press, 2014), 329–31.

15 Ibid., 798–9.

16 Alma Hannig, 'Austro-Hungarian Foreign Policy and the Balkans Wars', in Dominik Geppert, William Mulligan and Andreas Rose (eds), *The Wars Before the Great War* (Cambridge University Press, 2015), 235.

17 O'Brien, *British and American Naval* Power, Naval Crisis chapter.

18 Matthew Seligmann, Frank Nagler and Mikhael Epkenhans, *The Naval Route to the Abyss: The Anglo-German Naval Race 1895–1914* (Boydell, 2015), 349–50.

19 'Adolf Hitler: Address on the anniversary of 'Day of Coburg', 15 October 1937.

20 George Peden, *Churchill, Chamberlain and Appeasement* (Cambridge University Press, 2022), 182.

21 Andrew David Stedman, *Alternatives to Appeasement: Neville Chamberlain and Nazi Germany* (IB Tauris, 2019), 232.

22 Franco Amatori and Andrea Colli (eds), *The Global Economy: A Concise History* (Routledge, 2020) 211–19.

23 Richard N. Cooper, 'Economic Aspects of the Cold War', in Mervyn Leffler and Odd Arne Westad, *Cambridge History of the Cold War*, vol. 2, (Cambridge University Press, 2010), 50.

24 Giovanni Arrighi, 'The World Economy and the Cold War, 1970–1991', in ibid., 39.

25 Michael Schaller, 'Japan and the Cold War', in ibid., 179.

26 Jian Chen, *Mao's China and the Cold War* (UNC Press, 2001), 64–8.

27 S. Mahmud Ali, *US-China Cold War Collaboration, 1971–1989* (Routledge, 2005), 198.

28 Odd Arne Westad, *The Global Cold War: Third World Interventions and the Making of Our Times* (Cambridge University Press, 2005), 158.

6. Battles vs Wars

1 Courtney Kube, 'U.S. Intel: Nine Probable Russian Routes into Ukraine in Full-Scale Invasion', NBC News, 10 February 2022, https://www.nbcnews.com/news/world/u-s-intel-nine-probable-russian-routes-ukraine-full-scale-n1288922.

2 Heinrich and Sabes, 'Gen. Milley says Kyiv could fall within 72 hours'.

3 'Revisiting RAND's Russia Wargames After the Invasion of Ukraine', Rand Corporation, 21 November 2023, https://www.rand.org/pubs/research_reports/RRA2031-1.html.

4 Stephen Blank, 'The Illusion of a Short-War', *SAIS Review (1989–2003)*, 20/1, 2000, 133–51, http://www.jstor.org/stable/45345874.

5 Eliot Cohen and Phillips O'Brien, *The Russia-Ukraine War: A Study in Analytic Failure* (CSIS, 2024), 23, 27–8.

6 Ibid.

7 Jack Watling and Nick Reynolds, 'The Plot to Destroy Ukraine', RUSI,
   15 February 2022, https://www.rusi.org/explore-our-research/publica-
   tions/special-resources/plot-destroy-ukraine, 17. For more discussion of
   Ukraine's need to stave off corruption in its institutions, see Watling and
   Reynolds, 'Putin Has Put Ukraine on the Horns of a Dilemma', RUSI,
   4 February 2022, https://rusi.org/explore-our-research/publications/
   commentary/ putin-has-put-ukraine-horns-dilemma.

8 For a good overview of all the different pre-war plans, see Richard Hamilton and Holger Herwig (eds), *War Planning 1914* (Cambridge University
   Press, 2010).

9 Annika Mombauer, 'German War Plans', in ibid., 52–3.

10 Ibid., 73.

11 Zara Steiner and Keith Neilson, *Britain and the Origins of the First World
   War* (Palgrave, 2003), 223.

12 'The Commonwealth and the First World War', National Army Museum,
   https://www.nam.ac.uk/explore/commonwealth-and-first-world-war.

13 'Mobilized Strength and Casualty Losses', https://www.loc.gov/
   collections/world-war-i-rotogravures/articles-and-essays/events-and-
   statistics/mobilized-strength-and-casualty-losses/.

14 Ibid.

15 'Surviving the Deluge: British Servicemen in World War', *Economics &
   Human Biology* 49 (April 2023), https://www.sciencedirect.com/science/
   article/pii/S1570677X22001125.

16 Afflerbach, *On a Knife Edge*, 149.

17 https://history.stackexchange.com/questions/37864/was-falkenhayn-
   the-first-commander-to-recommend-defeating-an-enemy-by-bleeding-t.

18 Shawn T. Grimes, *Strategy and War Planning in the British Navy, 1887–1918*
   (Boydell Press, 2012), 181–9.

19 Matthew Seligmann, *The Royal Navy and the German Threat: 1901–1914*
   (Oxford University Press, 2014), 163.

20 Edwyn A. Gray, *The U-Boat War* (Leo Cooper, 1994), 269.

21 O'Brien, *The Strategists*, 129.

22 Malcolm Brown, *The Imperial War Museum Book of 1918: Year of Victory*
   (Sidgwick and Jackson, 1998), 167.

23 J. H. Johnson, *1918: The Unexpected Victory* (Arms and Armour, 1997), 195.

24 Horst Boog, Werner Rahn, Reinhard Stumpf and Bernd Wegner (eds), *Germany and the Second World War*, vol. VI, (Oxford University Press, 2001), 1060–65.

25 Christer Bergstrom, *Stalingrad: The Air Battle: 1942 Through January 1943* (Midland Press, 2007), 122.

26 https://www.statista.com/statistics/1336929/wwii-combat-aircraft-production-annual/.

27 'How the Luftwaffe Lost the Battle of Britain', *Air & Space Forces*, 1 August 2008, https://www.airandspaceforces.com/article/0808battle/.

28 Karl-Heinz Frieser (ed.), *Germany and the Second World War*, vol. VIII (Oxford University Press, 2017), 121–8.

29 'As Allies Recall D-Day, Russians Say It Was Just a Sideshow to Their War', *New York Times*, 2 June 1984, https://www.nytimes.com/1984/06/02/world/as-allies-recall-d-day-russians-say-it-was-just-a-sideshow-to-their-war.html.

30 *Germany and the Second World War*, vol. VIII, 132.

31 O'Brien, *How the War Was Won*, 310–11.

7. *Weapons vs Complex Operations*

1 Cole Livieratos, 'From Complicated to Complex: The Changing Context of War', Modern War Institute, 14 June 2022, https://mwi.westpoint.edu/from-complicated-to-complex-the-changing-context-of-war/.

2 Thomas Hone, Norman Friedman and Mark Mandeles, *Innovation in Carrier Aviation* (Naval War College Press, 2011), 26–9.

3 Worrall R. Carter, *Beans, Bullets and Black Oil: The Story of Fleet Logistics Afloat in the Pacific During World War II* (Naval War College Press, 1998), 355.

4 'The U.S. Navy Fleet Train in WW2', Royal Canadian Logistics Service Association, https://rclsa-asrlc.org/stories/the-u-s-navy-fleet-train-in-ww2/.

5 Carter, *Beans, Bullets and Black Oil*, 343.

6 'CIC Operation in an AGC', https://www.history.navy.mil/research/library/online-reading-room/title-list-alphabetically/c/cic-combat-information-center-operation-agc.html.

7 S. W. Roskill, *The War at Sea*, 3/2, 374.

8 Ibid., 340.

9 James Brungess, *Setting the Context* (Air University Press, 1994), https://www.airuniversity.af.edu/Portals/10/AUPress/Books/B_0054_BRUNGESS_SETTING_CONTEXT.PDF.

10 'How Radar Changed the Second World War', Imperial War Museum, https://www.iwm.org.uk/history/how-radar-changed-the-second-world-war.

11 'What Was the Dowding System', Imperial War Museum, https://www.iwm.org.uk/history/what-was-the-dowding-system.

12 'Stuka Attack!'

13 'Schweinfurt–Regensburg Raid: August 17, 1943', The National WWII Museum, 17 August 2023, https://www.nationalww2museum.org/war/articles/schweinfurt-regensburg-raid-august-17-1943.

14 'Black Thursday: Schweinfurt, October 14, 1943', National Museum of the U.S. Air Force, https://www.nationalmuseum.af.mil/Visit/Museum-Exhibits/Fact-Sheets/Display/Article/1519661/black-thursday-schweinfurt-october-14-1943.

15 Michael Paul, *Location, Suppression, and Destruction of Enemy Air Defenses: Linking Missions to Realize Advanced Capabilities*, Master's thesis, https://apps.dtic.mil/sti/tr/pdf/ADA490673.pdf.

16 Nathan J. Barlow. *Multi-Domain Suppression of Enemy Air Defense* (School of Advanced Military Studies, 2021), https://apps.dtic.mil/sti/pdfs/AD1160617.pdf.

17 Brungess, *Setting the Context*, 40–44.

18 Martin Van Creveld, 'World War I and the Revolution of Logistics', in Roger Chickering and Stig Forster (eds), *Great War, Total War: Combat and Mobilization on the Western Front 1914–1918* (Cambridge University Press, 2000), 67.

19 Herwig, 'The Dynamics of Effectiveness', 85, 94.

20 David Stone, *The Kaiser's Army in World War One* (Bloomsbury, 2015), 341–4.

21 https://www.tankograd.com/cms/website.php?id=/en/British-Military-Trucks-of-World-War-One.htm.

22 Jonathan Boff, *Winning and Losing on the Western Front: The British Third Army and the Defeat of Germany in 1918* (Cambridge University Press, 2012), 86.

23 Ian Malcolm Brown, *British Logistics on the Western Front 1914–1919* (Praeger, 1998), 109–11.

24 Ibid., 140.

25 Ibid., 174.

26 O'Brien, *The Strategists*, 227.

27 Boff, *Winning and Losing on the Western Front*, 91.

28 Martin Windrow, *The Last Valley: Dien Bien Phu and the French Defeat in Vietnam* (Weidenfeld & Nicolson, 2004), 616–18.

29 Craven and Cate, vol. V, 78.

30 Phillips O'Brien, 'Logistics by Land and Air', in Ferris and Mawdsley, *The Cambridge History of The Second World War*, vol. 1 (Cambridge University Press, 2015), 632.

31 'Airlift During the Vietnam War', Air Mobility Command Museum, https://amcmuseum.org/history/airlift-during-the-vietnam-war/.

32 Anton Troianovski, Michael Schwirtz and Andrew E. Kramer, 'Russia's Military, Once Creaky, Is Modern and Lethal', *New York Times*, 27 January 2022, https://www.nytimes.com/2022/01/27/world/europe/russia-military-putin-ukraine.html.

8. Human vs Metrics

1 Bernhard R. Kroener, Rolf-Dieter Muller and Hans Umbreit (eds), *Germany and the Second World War*, vol. V/II (Oxford University Press, 2003), 515.

2 Ibid., 528.

3 Ibid., 529.

4 Jorg Echternkamp (ed.), *Germany and the Second World* War, vol. IX/II (OUP, 2014), 368.

5 Justin Q. Olmstead, *The United States' Entry into the First World War* (Boydell, 2018), 80.

6 MacDonogh, *The Last Kaiser*, 387.

7 Afflerbach, *On a Knife Edge*, 235–6.

8 'Unrestricted U-boat Warfare', National WWI Museum and Memorial, https://www.theworldwar.org/learn/about-wwi/unrestricted-u-boat-warfare.

9 Afflerbach, *On a Knife Edge*, 240–42

10 Christian Goeschel, *Mussolini and Hitler: The Forging of the Fascist Alliance* (Yale University Press, 2018), 159.

11 Ibid., 182–3.

12 John Gooch, *Mussolini and His Generals: The Armed Forces And Fascist Foreign Policy 1922–1940* (Cambridge University Press, 2007), 512–13.

13 Jonathan Parshall, 'Ignoring the Lessons of Defeat', *Naval History* 21/3 (June 2007), https://www.usni.org/magazines/naval-history-magazine/2007/june/ignoring-lessons-defeat.

14 'Address to a Joint Session of Congress and the American People', September 2001, https://georgewbush-whitehouse.archives.gov/news/releases/2001/09/20010920-8.html.

15 Christopher Martin, *The Russo-Japanese War* (Abelard Schuman, 1967), 34.

16 Quintin Barry, *Command of the Sea: William Pakenham and the Russo-Japanese Naval War* (Helion, 2019), 111.

17 Richard Hough, *The Fleet that Had to Die* (Hamish Hamilton, 1958), 30.

18 Nicholas Papastratigakis, *Russian Imperialism and Naval Power* (IB Tauris, 2011), 256–7.

19 Lieutenant George Hageman, 'Battle of Tsushima: The First Naval Battle of the 21st Century', 2020 https://www.history.navy.mil/get-involved/essay-contest/2020-winners/hageman-cno-essay.html.

20 Alexander Watson, *Ring of Steel: Germany and Austria-Hungary at War, 1914–1918* (Allen Lane, 2014), 115.

21 Ibid., 117.

22 Ibid., 109.

23 Ibid., 110.

24 Samuels, *Doctrine and Dogma*, 98–9.

25 Ibid., 99.

26 R. J. B. Bosworth, *Mussolini* (Hodder Arnold, 2002), 376.

27 Thanos Veremis, 'Some Observations on the Greek Military in the Inter-War Period, 1918–1935', *Armed Forces & Society*, 4/3 (Spring 1978), 527–41.

28 Max Gallo, *Mussolini's Italy: Twenty Years of the Fascist Era* (Abelard-Schuman, 1973), 322.

29 O'Brien, *How the War Was Won*, 336.

30 'Vietnam War Background, Casualties & Statistics', https://study.com/academy/lesson/casualties-of-the-vietnam-war-causes-statistics.html.

31 David R. Stone, *The Russian Army in the Great War, The Eastern Front 1914–1917* (University Press of Kansas, 2015), 231.

32 'Russian Civil War', Army Heritage Center Foundation, https://www.armyheritage.org/soldier-stories-information/russian-civil-war/.

33 Jeffrey Verhey, *The Spirit of 1914: Militarism, Myth, and Mobilization in Germany* (Cambridge University Press, 2000), 58–71.

34 *Germany and the Second World War*, vol. IX/1, 451.

35 Ibid., 283–4.

36 'January 17, 1968: State of the Union Address', https://millercenter.org/the-presidency/presidential-speeches/january-17-1968-state-union-address.

37 'Polling Wars: Hawks vs. Doves', Pew Research Center, 23 November 2023, https://www.pewresearch.org/2009/11/23/polling-wars-hawks-vs-doves/.

9. Starting vs Sustaining

1 Olenea Harmash, 'Ukraine ramps up arms production, can produce 4 million drones a year, Zelenskiy says', Reuters, 2 October 2024, https://www.reuters.com/world/europe/ukraine-ramps-up-arms-production-can-produce-4-million-drones-year-zelenskiy-2024-10-02/.

2 Ministry of Defence, 'Size of army, navy, and air force from 1700 to 2016', 28 April 2017, https://assets.publishing.service.gov.uk/media/5a81d66740f0b623026996e1/2017-04440.pdf.

3 'The Year 1913 in Foreign Armies, Germany', *Royal United Services Institution Journal*, 58/435 (1914), 619–30. https://doi.org/10.1080/03071841409420112.

4 '1914: Mons to Christmas', National Army Museum, https://www.nam.ac.uk/explore/1914-mons-christmas.

5 'The Factories That Fed the Front in the First World War', Imperial War Museum, https://www.iwm.org.uk/history/the-factories-that-fed-the-front-in-the-first-world-war.

6 'Tanks and Tank Warfare', https://encyclopedia.1914-1918-online.net/article/tanks-and-tank-warfare/#toc_german_tanks.

7 'How Britain Invented the Tank in the First World War', Imperial War Museum, https://www.iwm.org.uk/history/how-britain-invented-the-tank-in-the-first-world-war.

8 Winston Churchill, *The World Crisis: Vol. 3 1916–1918* (Thornston Butterworth, 1927), chapter XII.

9 O'Brien, *The Strategists*, chapter 6.

10 *WSC*, vol. 4, companion 1, Churchill to Sinclair, 29 December 1917, 222.

11 'U.S. and German Field Artillery in World War I: A Comparison', The Army Historical Foundation, https://armyhistory.org/u-s-and-german-field-artillery-in-world-war-ii-a-comparison/.

12 John F. Guilmartin and John W. R. Taylor, 'Military aircraft', *Encyclopedia Britannica*, 24 June 2024, https://www.britannica.com/technology/military-aircraft.

13 B. Sanbongi, 'The Aircraft Engine: An Historical Perspective of Engine Development through World War I', *Journal of Aviation/Aerospace Education & Research*, 8/3 (1999), https://doi.org/10.58940/2329-258X.1224.

14 Ibid.

15 'The most successful British Bomber Aircraft of The First World War', Western Front Association, https://www.westernfrontassociation.com/world-war-i-articles/the-most-successful-british-bomber-aircraft-of-the-first-world-war/.

16 'B.E.2c', *The Aerodrome*, https://www.theaerodrome.com/aircraft/gbritain/raf_be2c.php.

17 'Royal Aircraft Factory B.E.2', Fluzeug, https://www.flugzeuginfo.net/acdata_php/acdata_raf_be2_en.php.

18 For a full description of the production balances of all the major powers, and to see just how much more was spent on aircraft than other systems, see: O'Brien, *How the War Was Won*, chapter 1.

19 'Messerschmitt Me 262A Schwalbe', https://www.nationalmuseum.af.mil/Visit/Museum-Exhibits/Fact-Sheets/Display/Article/196266/messerschmitt-me-262a-schwalbe/.

20 Craven and Cate, vol. VI, 208–9.

21 Ibid., 360.

22 'V-2 Rocket', National Museum of the U.S. Air Force, https://www.nationalmuseum.af.mil/Visit/Museum-Exhibits/Fact-Sheets/Display/Article/195894/v-2-rocket/; The Editors of Encyclopaedia Britannica, 'V-2 rocket', *Encyclopedia Britannica*, 16 January 2025, https://www.britannica.com/technology/V-2-rocket.

23 'British Response to V1 and V2', National Archives, https://www.nationalarchives.gov.uk/education/resources/british-response-v1-and-v2/.

24 'Fact File: V-weapons Attack Britain', BBC, https://www.bbc.co.uk/history/ww2peopleswar/timeline/factfiles/nonflash/a1143532.shtml.

25 'V-1 Cruise Missile', National Air and Space Museum, https://airandspace.si.edu/collection-objects/v-1-cruise-missile/nasm_A19600341000.

26 'Missile, Cruise, V-1 (Fi 103, FZG 76)', Smithsonian Institute, https://www.si.edu/object/missile-cruise-v-1-fi-103-fzg-76%3Anasm_A19600341000.

27 O'Brien, *How the War Was Won*, 347–8.

28 Guy Laron, *The Six-Day War: The Breaking of the Middle East* (Yale University Press, 2017), 303–4.

29 Michael B. Oren, *Six Days of War: June 1967 and the Making of the Modern Middle East* (Oxford University Press, 2002), 305.

30 '414. Special National Intelligence Estimate', 10 August 1967, https://history.state.gov/historicaldocuments/frus1964-68v19/d414.

31 Oren, *Six Days of War*, 305.

32 Ibid., 306.

33 David Rodman, *Israel in the 1973 Yom Kippur War* (Liverpool University Press, 2016), 126.

34 Sebastien Roblin, 'In 1973, the Yom Kippur War Gave the World a Horrifying Glimpse of What a Modern Mechanized Warfare Would Look Like', *The National Interest*, 14 October 2018, https://nationalinterest.org/blog/buzz/1973-yom-kippur-war-gave-world-horrifying-glimpse-what-modern-mechanized-warfare-would?.

35 Uri Kaufman, *Eighteen Days in October: The Yom Kippur War and How it Created the Modern Middle East* (St Martins Press, 2023), 309.

36 Williamson Murray and Kevin Woods, *The Iran-Iraq War* (Cambridge University Press, 2014), 90–91.

37 Rob Johnson, *The Iran-Iraq War* (Bloomsbury, 2010), 71–2.

38 Ibid., 73–4.

39 Michael Brill, 'Part II: "We attacked them with chemical weapons and they attacked us with chemical weapons": Iraqi Records and the History of Iran's Chemical Weapons Program', Wilson Center, 31 March 2022, https://www.wilsoncenter.org/blog-post/part-ii-we-attacked-them-chemical-weapons-and-they-attacked-us-chemical-weapons-iraqi.

40 Murray and Woods, *The Iran-Iraq War*, 212.

41 Nigel Ashton and Bryan Gibson (eds), *The Iran-Iraq War: New International Perspectives* (Routledge, 2013), 94–5.

42 Rachel Schmidt, *Global Arms Exports To Iraq, 1960–1990*, A Rand Note, https://www.rand.org/content/dam/rand/pubs/notes/2009/N3248.pdf, 13.

43 Murray and Woods, *The Iran-Iraq War*, 336–9.

44 Donato Paolo Mancini and Andrea Palasciano, 'North Korea to Send More Troops to Russia, South Korea Spies Say', Bloomberg, 25 October 2024, https://www.bloomberg.com/news/articles/2024-10-25/north-korea-to-send-more-troops-to-russia-soon-intelligence-documents-reveal.

10. *States vs Alliances*

1 'Strength of Armies at the Armistice, 1918', https://www.ctevans.net/WorldWar1/Data/Visuals/Armistice.html.

2 Goeschel, *Mussolini and Hitler*, 184.

3 *Germany and the Second World War*, vol. VI, 173.

4 Ibid.

5 7 January 1942, *Hitler's Table Talks (1941–1944)*, 1953.

6 Peter Grier, 'Pearl Harbor Day: How did Adolf Hitler react to the attack?', *Christian Science Monitor* (December 2011), https://www.csmonitor.com/USA/2011/1207/Pearl-Harbor-Day-How-did-Adolf-Hitler-react-to-the-attack

7 Elliott Roosevelt, *As He Saw It* (Duell, Sloan and Pierce, 1946), 75.

8 *Germany and the Second World War*,. IV, (OUP, 1998), 126-8.

9 US Department of State, *Soviet Supply Protocols*, 20, 57, 97–9.

10 Mark Atwood Lawrence, *The Vietnam War: A Concise International History* (Oxford University Press, 2008), 71.

11 Bruce O. Solheim, *The Vietnam War Era: A Personal Journey* (Praeger, 2006), 49–51.

12 Brian VanDeMark, *Road to Disaster: A New History of America's Descent into Vietnam* (Custom House, 2018), 248–9.

13 Gregory A. Daddis, *Withdrawal: Reassessing America's Final Years in Vietnam* (Oxford University Press, 2017), 103–4.

14 For one description of the scope of Soviet aid to Vietnam see: Oleg Sarin and Lev Dvorestsky, *Alien Wars* (Presidio Press, 1996), 87–114.

15 Elisabeth Leake, *Afghan Crucible: The Soviet Invasion and the Making of Modern Afghanistan* (Oxford University Press, 2022), 178–9.

16 Mark Urban, *War in Afghanistan* (Macmillan, 1990), 120–21.

17 Alan J. Kuperman, 'The Stinger Missile and U.S. Intervention in Afghanistan', *Political Science Quarterly*, 114/2, (1999), 219–63, https://doi.org/10.2307/2657738.

18 'The United States and the Mujahideen', Lumen Learning, https://courses.lumenlearning.com/suny-hccc-worldhistory2/chapter/the-united-states-and-the-mujahideen/.

19 Kurt Lohbeck, *Holy War, Unholy Victory: Eyewitness to the CIA's Secret War in Afghanistan* (Regnery Gateway, 1993), 87–97.

20 The Editors of Encyclopaedia Britannica, 'Soviet invasion of Afghanistan', *Encyclopedia Britannica*, 20 December 2024, https://www.britannica.com/event/Soviet-invasion-of-Afghanistan.

21 Directorate of Intelligence, *The Costs of Soviet Involvement in Afghanistan*, https://www.cia.gov/readingroom/docs/DOC_0000499320.pdf.

22 'Russian Military Budget', FAS, WMD Resources, https://nuke.fas. org/guide/russia/agency/mo-budget.htm.

23 Ali, *US-China Cold War Collaboration*, 205.

24 Office of the Historian, 'The Gulf War, 1991', https://history.state.gov/ milestones/1989-1992/gulf-war.

25 Kate Bateman, 'In Afghanistan, Was a Loss Better than Peace?', US Institute of Peace, 3 November 2022, https://www.usip.org/publications/2022/11/afghanistan-was-loss-better-peace.

26 Ibid.

27 Bob Woodward, quoted in '"That son of a bitch": New Woodward book reveals candid behind-the-scenes conversations of Biden, Trump, Harris and Putin', CNN, 8 October 2024, https://edition.cnn.com/2024/10/08/politics/ bob-woodward-book-war-joe-biden-putin-netanyahu-trump/index.html.

Conclusion: War and Power in the Indo-Pacific

1 Stephen Peter Rosen, 'Military Effectiveness: Why Society Matters', *International Security*, 19/4 (1995), 5–31, https://doi.org/10.2307/2539118.

2 'Deputy Secretary of Defense Kathleen Hicks' Remarks: "Unpacking the Replicator Initiative" at the Defense News Conference (As Delivered)', Department of Defense, 6 September 2023, https://www.defense. gov/News/Speeches/Speech/Article/3517213/deputy-secretary-of-defense-kathleen-hicks-remarks-unpacking-the-replicator-ini/.

3 Mark F. Cancian, Matthew Cancian and Eric Heginbotham, 'The First Battle of the Next War: Wargaming a Chinese Invasion of Taiwan', Z Center for Strategic and International Studies, 9 January 2023, https://www.csis. org/analysis/first-battle-next-war-wargaming-chinese-invasion-taiwan.

4 https://www.statista.com/statistics/1064162/china-global-market-share-of-shipbuilding-industry/.

5 'China's Export Restrictions on Drone Parts Could Reshape Global Supply Chains', *Drone Life,* 10 December 2024, https://dronelife.com/ 2024/12/10/chinas-export-restrictions-on-drone-parts-could-reshape-global-supply-chains/.

6 'Australia has "absolutely not" committed to join US in event of war over Taiwan, Marles says', *Guardian*, 19 March 2023, https://www. theguardian.com/world/2023/mar/19/australia-has-absolutely-not-committed-to-join-us-in-event-of-war-over-taiwan-marles-says.

7 'No, Japan Will Not Defend Taiwan', *The Diplomat*, March 2024, https://thediplomat.com/2024/03/no-japan-will-not-defend-taiwan/; 'South Korea Will Stay Out of a Taiwan Strait War', *The Diplomat*, March 2023, https://thediplomat.com/2023/03/south-korea-will-stay-out-of-a-taiwan-strait-war/.

8 I talk about a number of these games in this piece: https://phillipsp-obrien.substack.com/p/war-games-and-nuclear-weapons-a-modest.

9 Woodward, *War*.

Index